Mexican-Americans Tomorrow

Mexican-Americans Tomorrow

Educational and Economic Perspectives

Gus Tyler, Editor

Published in Cooperation with
The Weatherhead Foundation

UNIVERSITY OF NEW MEXICO PRESS

Albuquerque

Contents

4.95

Foreword

The Founder of the Weatherhead Foundation, Albert J. Weatherhead, Jr., like his father before him, was fascinated by the Southwest. In the 1880s, the elder Weatherhead went from Cleveland, Ohio, where he lived, to New Mexico and southern Arizona in search of gold and other rich ores and was lucky enough to find mines that brought him modest rewards. Although he maintained his principal business and family activities in Ohio, for a time he owned mining property in Socorro, New Mexico ("Deadwood Mine"), which still produces ore and dividends. His son, although an inventor and manufacturer of automotive parts in midwest America, felt the same, and probably a stronger, lure of the Southwest and its people. In the late 1930s, he and his family made frequent visits to a dude ranch not far from Nogales, Arizona/Sonora, and in the early 1940s he purchased property in the same area and began building his own ranch. A good part of his life was shaped by his image of the cowboy and the rancher and his familiarity with the changing yet enduring landscape of the country.

When its founder died in 1966, it seemed appropriate for the Foundation to convert his personal liking for the Southwest into one of its main fields of endeavor. Not only would his particular interest be continued and expanded, but also the Foundation would be doing work in an important section of America. In the Southwest—defined for the Foundation's purposes as a core area of New Mexico, Arizona, Sonora and Chihuahua, and parts of Texas and California where there are significant populations of Mexican-Americans—the Foundation could develop and carry out socially useful projects in an instructive cultural and demographic laboratory of the United States.

In the Southwest there are three basic cultural identities: the Indian, the Mexican, and the Anglo-American. Over the past one hundred years or so, these groups have learned to adjust to one another in the rugged rural setting and more recently in the compact communities of the cities. The Southwest is a vast, imposing land where man is never entirely in control of the fell forces of nature—the desert, the mountains, the sudden heavy rains, the big scale of the land and its incredible beauty; all somehow work to return man to his elemental concerns of spirit and survival, even in this latter part of the twentieth century. In this region one can study the ways that cultural groups living side by side have developed for tolerating each other or one can study the improbable rise of such cities as Los Alamos and Phoenix. The Southwest, then, is an ethnic and ecological region unique in the United States, but sharing common characteristics with other parts of the world, as, for example, in the Middle East.

These were some of the reasons which led the Weatherhead Foundation to develop its Southwestern program. The activities in this program include the encouragement of new knowledge about the region, support of the traditional and contemporary arts, efforts to help relieve groups suffering from ill health or in need of greater educational opportunities, and a concern with the historic ecological balance in an era of "progress" and technology.

Since 1969, the Weatherhead Foundation has been sponsoring a program of philanthropic activities in and about the Southwest, with particular emphasis on Arizona, New Mexico, and west Texas. The Foundation's grants have been made to assist various regional organizations in their efforts to interpret the area's complex of cultures and to improve the urban and rural environments in which they exist and interact. Grants are usually modest in size and are approved only after visiting and consulting with the organizations involved. The Foundation has sponsored conferences every two to three years with the objective of encouraging research that will lead to a greater understanding across the nation of the special qualities of the Southwest.

Mexican-Americans Tomorrow is the result of a conference held in 1972. This paperback edition, published by arrangement with the University of New Mexico Press, will make this significant book available to a wide audience.

Richard W. Weatherhead
President
The Weatherhead Foundation

April 1975

Preface

In the summer of 1972, a conference of carefully selected experts on Mexican-American affairs was held at the Aspen Institute for Humanistic Studies in Colorado. The meeting revolved around several papers submitted by some of the conferees. The object was to convert these papers into a book—after each manuscript had been discussed, debated, and finally polished against this give-and-take. The present volume is the product of that conference.

The entire undertaking was sponsored by the Weatherhead Foundation as part of its continuing concern with America's Southwest. In 1972, the Foundation sponsored the publication of *Plural Society in the Southwest*, based on a conference held in Patagonia, Arizona. The Aspen consultation was the second in this series. A third conference on the impact of the Mexican–United States border was held in April 1975.

When the Weatherhead Foundation asked me to organize the conference on the educational and economic perspectives of the Mexican-Americans, my first concern was to find a small, select body of participants who—collectively—would compose a balanced group. I spent more than a year in the search. The first effort was to balance academics with activists because out of decades of personal experience I knew how separated those two worlds can become and how either sphere, in itself, tends to become isolated. Then I tried to arrive at some balance between "insiders" and "outsiders"; that is, between people who are themselves Mexican-Americans and others who, although not out of the Mexican-American community, have had a continuing interest and involvement in this area of concern. Then I tried to get a geographic balance with people from Texas, California, Colorado, Arizona, New Mexico, and other areas. This need for some such mix became increasingly desirable as I came to realize the "communities" within the Mexican-American community. Finally, I looked for people of authority in the assigned subject of their papers.

The conference was opened by Dr. Clark S. Knowlton, Director of the Center for the Study of Social Problems at the University of Utah. He offered an overview of the Mexican-American community—with its scope, diversity, history, and present plight. He spoke with the passion of a man who, for many years, has been in the thick of things: an academic activist.

This opener was followed by Dr. Julian Samora, Department of Sociology, University of Notre Dame, with a paper on Mexican immigration. Samora has been a prolific writer and produced many books, magazine articles, and conference papers on Mexican-Americans. A scrupulous scholar, a respected researcher and teacher, Samora is also a man of deep personal involvement in the movements of Mexican-Americans.

The current economic condition of the Mexican-American was presented in a paper from Fred Schmidt, former Senior Researcher at the Institute of Industrial Relations at the University of California in Los Angeles. To his writing, Schmidt brings the background of a man who was a top leader in Texas labor, an administrative assistant to a Mexican-American Congressman, and a trusted consultant to community activists in the Southwest. At the conference Schmidt's paper was presented by his assistant at the Institute, Kenneth Koford.

The "educational perspectives" of the Mexican-Americans were discussed by two men: one with an intense involvement at the elementary level in his capacity as a member of the Los Angeles Board of Education, Dr. Julian Nava; the other, Father Henry Casso, with a background in promoting higher education for Mexican-Americans in his work with the Mexican-American Legal Defense and Education Fund.

Finally, the story of what Mexican-Americans have been doing through their own organizations was related by Henry Santiestevan, then National Director of the National Council of La Raza.

Each of these contributors was the beneficiary of the information and insights imparted by his cocontributors. In addition, however, the conference had the benefit of active participation by Ray Marshall, Department of Economics, the University of Texas; Edward R. Lucero, President, Committee for Economic Development, Denver, Colo.; and Alfredo G. de los Santos, Jr., President, El Paso Community College.

The Foundation itself was more than a sponsor or onlooker. There was active participation by its officers: Dr. Richard W. Weatherhead, President of the Foundation; Professor John H. Parry, Gardiner Professor of Oceanic History and Affairs, Harvard

University; Stanley Salmen, former President, French and Polyclinic Medical School and Health Center (New York City); and Professor Richard Eells, Director, Program for Studies of the Modern Corporation, Columbia University.

Also participating as discussants were Robert Goldman, Ford Foundation; Robert Solomon, Educational Testing Service; Patricio Serna, Equal Employment Opportunity Commission; and James Wiley, Valley National Bank, Phoenix, Arizona.

An early point of discussion in the conference was the use of the word "Chicano." To some of the participants, the word was to be used interchangeably with "Mexican-American." Others felt that this was an improper and inadmissible translation since many Americans with Spanish surnames in the Southwest view "Chicano" as a term of opprobrium.

This difference about terminology was not resolved. In the essays that follow in this volume some authors use "Chicano" and "Mexican-American" synonymously while others make a deliberate distinction. In this way, some of the "flavor" of the gathering is preserved.

Likewise, there has been no effort to fit the papers into any patterns preconceived by the Foundation or myself. Several of the papers are clearly and caustically composed in the tone of the advocate. Other papers are more detached. Some analyze; others propose. Some are "third" person; others are "first" person. In all cases, we have tried to keep the mood, as well as the matter, of the authors intact.

G.T.

1

Introduction: A People on the Move

Gus Tyler

Gus Tyler, Director of Education and Politics for the International
Ladies' Garment Workers' Union, has spent almost half a century
personally involved in the economic and educational problems of
migrant and immigrant working people in the United States. Through his
union, he has been engaged in the organization of Mexican-American
workers in the Southwest. He represented garment workers in the
Mexico City conference for Latin American trade unionists and has
regularly lectured for the American Institute for Free Labor Development
(AIFLD). In his capacity as Administrator of the David Dubinsky Foundation, Mr. Tyler has worked with the Mexican-American Legal Defense
and Educational Fund (MALDEF), the American Association of Junior
Colleges (El Congreso Nacional de Asuntos Colegiales), and the Center
for Migration Studies. He has, over many years, been a close advisor to
the National Farm Workers' Union. As author of *The Labor Revolution* (Vi-
king), *The Political Imperative* (Macmillan), and *Labor in the Metropolis* (Charles E. Merrill), he has established himself as labor's foremost
authority in spotting and explaining trends among newly emerging
working-class elements. He has written extensively on subjects of
education for *Change Magazine*, the Office of Education, and the
National Institute for Education, with a continuing focus on the need to
open academia to ethnic and economic groups that, up to now, were
largely absent from the campus. He served as a member of the
Governor's Committee to Review New York Laws and Procedures in the
Area of Human Rights and is presently serving on New York State's Task
Force on Aid to Education.

As a perennial moderator for the Aspen Institute for Humanistic
Studies (where the conference on economic and educational perspectives of the Mexican-American was held), Mr. Tyler has a continuing
interest in the development of the Southwest and its peoples. To the
subject of his special interest in this volume, he brings a wide background of social insight and involvement that he expresses thrice weekly
in a nationally syndicated column for the United Feature Syndicate.

"1970—the year of the Chicano . . . the new shibboleth heard in
Mexican-American communities throughout the country," proclaimed the official publication of the Inter-Agency Committee
on Mexican-American Affairs.[1] "It is the rallying cry that symbol-

izes the crystallization of the Mexican-American movement as it moves into a new decade. In a different sense, 1970 is indeed the year of the Chicano and all other Spanish-speaking people in the nation. It is of paramount importance that all Spanish-surnamed residents stand up and be counted for it marks the taking of the U.S. Census."

The obvious excitement did not derive from the simple fact that this was just another enumeration, like those in 1960 and 1950. This was a landmark census. "For the first time in history, the census will enumerate Spanish 'origin or descent' distinguishing the specific population distribution and ethnic characteristics of Mexican-Americans, Puerto Ricans, and Cubans." In addition, there were separate categories for Central and South Americans and "other Spanish."

To Mexican-American leaders, it was very important to "stand up," because to be counted, counted: The census would provide "the information necessary for reapportionment of the Congress and state legislatures . . . and determine the apportionment of federal and state funds in areas where needs are greatest." Because it was felt that the more Mexican-Americans there were, the greater influence they would have, the census became a weapon of social struggle.

The date—1970—is revealing. It was during the 1960s that the "Black Revolution" shook the nation with its demands, marches, riots, sit-ins, pray-ins, petitions, and picketing. America's largest racial minority made its presence known in a demonstration of black power. How long before America's other large minority—the Mexican-Americans—would follow a like course?

There is much that the two movements have in common. In both cases, there is a racial element. Although Mexican-Americans are counted in the census as white, many are a mixture of Caucasian and American Indian. In both cases, past generations have experienced outright oppression followed by segregation and discrimination. Economically, poverty runs high—with attendant dependency, delinquency, and disease. Educationally, both communities are deprived subcultures of the society.

In the post–World War II years, both these minorities have been striving towards a new future. First the blacks and then the "browns." In the 1960s their most noted leaders were highly charismatic: Martin Luther King and César Chávez. Characteristically, the first was nurtured in the ministry and the other was the son of migrant workers. Both groups have—in their more militant mood—sought a new name for themselves: the Negroes who now want to be called blacks, and the Mexican-Americans who want to be called Chicanos. Activists of both minorities sought majority coalitions in alliances with unions and liberal politicians—in particular with the Kennedys. Both organized political movements to turn out the vote for the candidates of their choice.

They have now come alive in the same post-war generation and for the same reasons. The war itself was a liberating factor. Millions of black and Mexican-American youths volunteered or were drafted into military service; they were scattered around the country to different training camps and then shipped overseas. In the process, they discovered the world and—more importantly—themselves.

The post-war GI Bill of Rights offered further opportunities. A black or Chicano veteran could now think seriously about a high school equivalency and a college career—paid for by the government. He could buy a new house on easy terms. He could open up a business with a low-interest loan. He was free to move beyond the early expectations of his ghetto or barrio.

World War II also created models for "nation building" among former colonial peoples. Asia belonged to the Asians and Communist China was displacing Soviet Russia as the revolutionary spokesman of the oppressed peoples of the earth. Africa gave birth to a brood of new nations. The notion of a "Third World" became a religion for some. To racial and ethnic minorities in the U.S.—specifically the blacks and the Chicanos—the new world in the making was one in which they would be heard.

In both communities there was a high percentage of teenagers in the 1960s and into the 1970s. They were part of the post-war baby boom. These young people displayed the restlessness common to the youth of all times but particularly characteristic of that numerous generation in the decades immediately following the war. In one respect, however, the militant young folk of the black and Chicano communities differed from those in the nation as a whole. The "minority" youngsters personally identified with a subculture fighting to establish itself before the societal parent.

The 1960s and 1970s are also a period when the unorthodox felt free to speak out against inherited concepts. The old order had been shaken by the war. Established empires were shattered. Old idols were destroyed. New ideas, nations, and peoples were in the making. Accepted authorities—with their systems and structures and rigidified relationships—were open to challenge.

In a way, the "uprisings" of blacks and Chicanos were and are part of a larger world phenomenon issuing from the almost universal presence of factors similar to those underlying the minority push in America. In Canada, there are French-Canadians. In Belgium, Flemings and Walloons. In Northern Ireland, the Catholic minority. These—like their American counterparts—are people and episodes in the "retribalization" of mankind that has marked the post-war decades.

But in each country and for each group there are special reasons underlying their new found self-image. While the 1960s and 1970s provided the atmosphere for the emerging minorities, each of the minorities had its own grievances and agenda.

In this respect, the Mexican-Americans are quite unlike the Negroes. Historically, the Mexican-American was not brought to this land in a state of captivity to labor as a slave under an alien master. The Mexican-American can properly claim that he was here before the "Anglos" grabbed the land, that he is "white," and that he was always "free." Linguistically, the Mexican-Americans were—and many still are—a Spanish-speaking people, associated with a Latin culture.

Paradoxically, the Mexican-Americans who were here *before* the Negroes (especially if the Indian strain is included) are also a people who came here *after* the Negroes. The paradox arises from the fact that while Negro immigration came to a halt many generations ago, immigration from Mexico has continued over the years. Indeed, in the post-war years that wave from the other side of the border assumed ever-increasing proportions.

Because Mexican-Americans are among the earliest settlers and also the latest immigrants, they are a paradox: native aliens. This apparent incongruity has made it difficult for most Americans to understand either the past or the present of Mexican-American life.

The popular notion is that the Chicano is a simple man of the soil whose ancestors occupied the same bit of land since time immemorial. Over the centuries, this peasant has not moved, has not complained, and has not changed. Like the petrified forest, he is part of the eternal scenery.

This image of the Mexican-American can be most mischievous. For the nation's policy makers, the Chicano becomes a matter of little concern: he is as he was and as he will be. For good or evil, that's the way it is fated. This failure to sense the drive and dynamism within the Mexican-American community leaves regional and national leadership unprepared to cope with or anticipate emerging and potentially explosive developments.

One such situation is the revolutionary use of the accepted notion that the Mexican-American of today is the direct descendant of the original settlers. To a militant Chicano youth, this piece of historical data is justification to claim the Southwest as the property of its first dwellers. From this inspiration has arisen the concept of Aztlan.

While there is truth to the belief that the Chicano is an ancient inhabitant of America's Southwest, this credo is only a half truth. An unusually high percentage of Mexican-Americans (about half in 1960) are immigrants or persons at least one of whose parents was born in Mexico.

Not only are they immigrants but they are immigrants of recent origin who "constitute the largest foreign language speaking element in the U.S."[2] This enigma of the "first families" turning out to be our biggest body of "aliens"—born elsewhere and speaking a stranger's tongue—comes from the unusual circumstance of the Mexican-Americans as an immigrant people in the United States. Whereas in almost every other case the flow of immigration has slowed down to a trickle in the last century, in the case of the Mexican-Americans just the opposite has happened. At the time the United States converted the Mexican Northwest into our Southwest, the land was sparsely settled: we took over one-half the total land area from Mexico but only one percent of the population—about eighty thousand souls. From then to the present, several waves of immigration have swollen the size of the Mexican-American population. In the last fifty years, a trickle turned to a flow and, in the last twenty-five years, the flow to a flood.

As a racial minority, the Mexican-Americans have much in common with the blacks, but as an ethnic minority, they have even more in common with the European and Asian immigrants. Indeed, immigration from Mexico has been closely intertwined with immigration from across the Atlantic and the Pacific. When the immigration of Orientals was halted in the late nineteenth century, the great railroad companies turned to Mexico for a cheap source of labor. When, after World War I, restrictive immigration policies turned down the tap on European labor, employers once again turned south of the border. Whenever this country began to run out of cheap labor, there was always the overflowing Mexican reservoir.

In their own unique way, Mexican-Americans have been reliving the immigrant experience in the United States. They come out of distress; they speak an alien tongue; they suffer the uncertainties of the newcomer; they are exploited by their own countrymen who contract their labor and are then exploited again by the employer to whom they are peddled; they are the underclass on whom others look down; they are disproportionally underpaid, uneducated, unacculturated, and unwanted. They—like the Irish, Poles, Jews, Italians, and Slavs of other times—are the un-people.

In retrospect, each of these other groups is recognized—sometimes celebrated in song, story, and cinema—for its considerable contribution to the material growth and intellectual development of this country. But only in retrospect. For each in its own time has been denied, denigrated, and despised. And out of such tensions arose conflict—personal and collective, crime and gang warfare, riot and rebellion. Only after much turmoil, travail, and time did the stranger become a neighbor.

While the Mexican-American, in this respect, reenacts the epic of immigration to America, there are ways in which he is different—for better or worse. This stranger—unlike the European, Asian, or even African—has been a next-door neighbor. This factor—proximity—has made Mexican immigration a problem of far greater complexity than that of other ethnic elements.

Because Mexico is so close, it is easy and natural for people to migrate from one country to the other. Because the border is so long and the Rio Grande so narrow, it is virtually impossible to control the frontier—just a few yards to wade. Consequently, to the inflow of legal immigrants are annually and decennially added millions of illegal border crossers. Because the points of entry are fixed by geography—namely, the Southwest—that part of the country where by official count about 85 percent of the Mexican-Americans live is constantly inundated by a desperate, depressed, and depressing flood of cheap labor. As a result, the Mexican immigrant finds it far more difficult than other newcomers to get a firm footing in the new land as the ground is constantly being washed away from under him by the steady inpouring of his compatriots.

The magnitude of illegal migration may be measured by a few random samplings from current news items. "In the Chula Vista area last year," reported the *New York Times* on July 13, 1973, "128,889 persons were apprehended while trying to cross the border illegally." On September 5 of the same year, the United Press reported that "a record total of 11,176 Mexican aliens had been picked up in August in the El Paso area." To cope with the problem—two thousand miles of border with hundreds of thousands of illegal crossings every year—the Border Patrol has been implanting a complex series of electronic devices.

The border makes the Mexican immigrant different from any other immigrant group in the nation's history. The count on how many Mexican aliens are in the United States is consistently inaccurate since hundreds of thousands—perhaps millions—hide from the tally. (They certainly don't respond to a mail count.) Average employment, earnings, schooling are consistently overstated for Mexican-Americans because the "illegals"—with their low standing—are not included.

A number of the essays in this volume explore the impact of the border on the Mexican-American: the resultant ignorance about the true status of Mexican-Americans on our soil and their consequent geographic instability and economic indigence.

In still another respect, the Mexican-Americans have been a specifically disfavored minority. In two brief wars and a series of conflicts that fell just short of being "official" wars, they were the "enemy." The first was the war for Texan independence in 1835 and the second was the Mexican War of 1846. In the twentieth century, during the Mexican Revolution of 1910–20, hostility between the two countries culminated in the occupation of Veracruz by U.S. forces in 1914, and the famous "Punitive Expedition" into Chihuahua led by Pershing in search of Pancho Villa after the latter's raid on Columbus, New Mexico. Because the Mexican was the foe, Mexican-Americans suffered indignities as did some German-Americans during World War I, and as almost all Japanese-Americans during World War II. But in the case of the Mexican-American, the stereotype of the "greaser" as a cruel and cowardly alien continued for generations, embedded in popular passions and in academic texts. In a 1973 examination of American history texts, it was found that Mexican "brutality in victory and cowardice in defeat during the War for Texas Independence is contrasted with American heroism."[3]

Although Mexican-Americans can be considered a racial minority because of their generally darker skins and classified alongside white ethnics because of their immigrant origin, they are not perceived as either. When racial problems are confronted in the U.S., they are seen in "black and white." When "white ethnic" problems are discussed, the references are to Poles, Italians, Hungarians, or Irish—but not to Mexican-Americans. Consequently, they feel they have good reason to complain that they are truly the forgotten people. Mexican-Americans are the invisibles at a time when every other community is establishing its visibility.

In *The Mexican-American People—The Nation's Second Largest Minority*,[4] the authors point out the woeful insufficiency of hard data on which to base social policies. "The Federal government has been slow to recognize Mexican Americans as a nationally significant minority," says the study in its opening pages. "The U.S. Census in both 1950 and 1960 provided valuable data on Spanish-surname people living in the five Southwest states—a statistical classification closely approximating the Mexican Americans in the region. But 'white-nonwhite' has remained the standard classification in the vast array of other government statistics and official studies which often are the foundation for social action. Much less attention is given to people of Mexican descent. Characteristically, an unofficial resumé of a five-volume report of the U.S. Commission on Civil Rights, published in 1962, deals only with Negroes and Puerto Ricans—reflecting the focus of the report itself. When the Federal Equal Employment Opportunity Committee in late 1963 held its first regional meeting in Los Angeles, it was clear that many Washington officials in policy-making positions had their first real encounter with the problems of Mexican Americans."

For that reason the Census of 1970 was hailed as a revolutionary event. It would, for the first time, officially establish the presence of the hitherto invisible.

The census—followed by sample surveys conducted by the U.S. Department of Commerce Bureau of the Census—reveals that Mexican-Americans are a sizable and significant portion of the American people.

A March 1972 count showed 9,178,000 persons of "Spanish origin" in the U.S., of whom 5,254,000 were listed as "Mexican."[5] A March 1974 count showed about 11 million of "Spanish origin" and about 6.5 million of "Mexican origin."[6]

The numbers become more significant when measured against past ratios. Since there was no formal count of Mexican-Americans as such in 1960, the best base is the estimate in *The Mexican-American People*, where the total number of Mexican-Americans is set at 3,842,100 (see Appendix, p. 606). On this basis, the Chicano population grew in the U.S. by 36.75 percent between 1960 and 1972. This contrasts dramatically with the general growth of the overall population in the U.S. in the same period by a relatively small 14 percent (179 to 204 million). This means that the percentage of Mexican-Americans in the U.S. is growing. Indeed, it is growing more rapidly than the figures suggest because the official count—as noted—invariably omits most, if not all, illegals.

In the five states of the Southwest where the Mexican-American population is concentrated—California, Texas, Arizona, New Mexico, and Colorado—it grew at 36 percent—just a fraction under the national rate. The most rapid expansion of Mexican-American population took place *outside* the Southwest from 497,000 in 1960 to 705,000 in 1972, a growth of 62.3 percent. (Again, an allowance must be made for the illegals.) There are, for instance, more Mexican-Americans today in Illinois than in Arizona or Colorado.

This increase in the number of Mexican-Americans outside the Southwest is viewed as the precursor to a significant change in their national role. They are no longer just a backdrop to the Southwestern scene. As their numbers move toward the million mark in the rest of the country—counting illegals that point has probably been reached—the Chicano becomes a national presence. In this respect, the "brown" and "black" problems are akin: what were once considered regional difficulties become a nationwide concern.

Mexican-American growth—especially as contrasted with the general growth of U.S. population—is due to a double factor. First, the increase arising from immigration. The second is the rate of reproduction of Mexican families. Whereas only 1.6 percent of American families had six or more children aged eighteen or under, among Mexican-Americans nearly 6 percent had such large families. On the average, the Mexican-American family had about twice as many children under eighteen as the average family in the overall population.

**Mexican-American Population Increase
from 1960 to 1972 (in thousands)**

	1960	1972	% change
Total U.S. Population	179,323	204,840	14
Total Mexican-American Population for U.S.	3,842	5,254	36.7
Mexican-Americans in Southwest	3,344	4,549	36
Mexican-Americans outside Southwest	497	705	62

The distress within this growing sector of the U.S. is immediately apparent from 1970 census figures on the number and percentage of "persons below the low income level." For that year, there were 1,407,000 under the poverty level: making up 28.3 percent of the Mexican-Americans in the country. That contrasted with the overall figure of 12.6 percent for "all persons" in the nation. Plainly, poverty is more than twice as prevalent among Mexican-Americans as in the nation as a whole. In the Southwest, matters are worse: 29.4 percent of the Mexican-Americans were "below the low income level."

Widespread as poverty is among Mexican-Americans, however, there is apparent movement toward a modicum of improvement. In 1960, 34.8 percent of the "Spanish surnamed" in the Southwest were below the poverty level (as contrasted with 29.4 percent in 1972).

A similar pattern prevails for average (median) family incomes, showing the Mexican-Americans lagging well behind despite gains in the last decade. In 1970, the median family income for Mexican-Americans was $7,117 as contrasted with $10,236 for whites. A measure of the change over the decade is suggested in the figures from 1959: $4,164 for Mexican-Americans and $6,448 for whites.°

The paradox about these figures is that while they show a 75 percent gain for Mexican-Americans over the decade and only a 66 percent gain for whites, the dollar gap gets greater: from $2,284 in 1959 to $2,902 in 1970. While some will read the trend as moving up others will read it as falling behind. In either case, it is clear that family income among Chicanos is generally distressingly

---

°Although the 1959 figures are based on the Southwest, rather than the country as a whole, they are offered as an approximation of the national situation.

inadequate. (This is doubly so in view of the size of the Mexican-American family where fewer dollars have to feed more mouths.)

Mexican-American income is better outside the Southwest. In large measure the relatively lower level in the Southwest is due to its proximity to the border and to the greater number of recently arrived immigrants, both legal and illegal.

The unemployment rate in the Mexican-American community runs much higher than in the population at large and at almost twice the rate in the Anglo community. In March 1971, for instance, when the general rate of unemployment stood at 6 percent for the nation and at 5.6 percent for whites, the Mexican-Americans experienced a rate of 10.1 percent. These figures that refer to male employees are repeated among females, though not as severely. When the female jobless rate ran at 7 percent for the total population and at 6.5 percent for whites, it was 10.1 percent among Mexican-American women.[7]

Mexican-Americans also receive less schooling. In March 1972 a huge 26.7 percent of the Mexican-American population—aged 25 and over—had completed less than five years of schooling. This contrasts with the relative low figure of 4.6 percent for the population as a whole. At the other end of the educational spectrum, only 25 percent of the Mexican-Americans completed four years of high school or more while the figure for the total population was 58 percent.

Just as the economic plight of the Mexican-American is deepened by the impact of the border, so too is the educational difficulty of the Chicano child bedeviled by proximity to Mexico and the reluctance of schools to institute bilingual programs. The constant inpouring across the border reinforces the presence and power of the Spanish language. For many years, this was the dominant tongue of the Southwest. When Mexican-Americans became outnumbered by the English-speaking, Spanish continued as the language of the barrios and colonies. In the last generation, the Mexican immigrant has revitalized the use of the traditional vernacular.

Spanish—like any language—is more than a means of communication; it is the embodiment of a culture. As such it offers a measure of cohesion, a reason for cooperation, a sense of security, even a point of pride to a people who might otherwise be atomized by the grinding anticulture of physical deprivation. Understandably, the Mexican-American clings to his Spanish.

But, in the schools, the child raised in the Spanish-speaking home is at a disadvantage if the school is geared to teach only in English by monolingual English-speaking teachers. While the problem is not exclusively Mexican-American (Puerto Ricans in the East, French-Canadians in the Northeast, Cubans in Florida), the situation in the Southwest is greater in numbers and different in dynamic because of the border.

Two essays in this volume, written by men who have been involved with Mexican-American education at both the elementary and university level, address themselves with some passion to the question of schooling the Chicano child.

Despite the dimensions of the Mexican-American problems, the national consciousness was almost without any awareness of them until recent years. And then, quite ironically, when awareness came, a totally distorted notion of the Chicano appeared. Because of the dramatic uprising of the farm workers under the leadership of the Gandhi-like César Chávez, millions of Americans concluded that Chicanos are an agricultural people. This notion was reinforced by the militant march of Reies López Tijerina in New Mexico with its demand for a return of the land to its "original" owners.

While both these movements are significant because there are hundreds of thousands of Mexican-American rural hands, whose numbers are annually swollen by the border-crossers, and because there are entire Mexican-American communities in deep poverty because they have been deprived of their land, nevertheless, these vital—and symbolically stirring—struggles are directly relevant to only a small minority of the Mexican-Americans in the nation, most of whom are city dwellers. These once rural people are today overwhelmingly urban.

In 1966 a report on Mexican-Americans noted: "In California, the Mexican-American male labor force is over 80% urban; in Texas, over 75%; in Colorado, New Mexico and Arizona, between 55 and 70%." The projection was for an ever-rising percentage of Chicanos going urban. This trend was heavily toward the big city areas, the great metropolises of the Southwest—with "more than one third of the Spanish-speaking population of the Southwest living in the metropolitan compass of 16 cities, including Los Angeles, San Antonio, San Francisco and El Paso."[8]

The urbanization of the Mexican-American puts him at the very vortex of one of the United States' most pressing domestic problems: the decay of the inner city. The symptoms are poverty and hunger, unemployment and vagrancy, dependence and delinquency, corruption and crime, functional illiteracy and dysfunctional authority.

Increasingly, those concerned with the survival of urban America conclude that the cities have been traumatized, hit by a tidal wave of rural poor who are unfit and unprepared for city life. These people came in great numbers: about a million a year during the twenty years following the Second World War. They did not come to the cities because they wanted to. They were dispossessed from the soil—by the miracles of productivity on the land and by the manipulation of production in the hands of agro-business. They trudged into the already crowded, overburdened, decaying slums carrying with them all the problems of the uprooted. They were reenacting an ancient British tragedy: the dispossession of the English yeoman by enclosure of the land, his drift into the cities, the consequent economic distress and social disorder.

The rural-push urban-pull of the post-war decades is generally depicted in terms of movements *within* the U.S. from soil to city. In the case of the Mexican-Americans there is an *international* dimension to be added to the intra-American population migrations.

Although Mexico's economy has been expanding rapidly since the 1950s, the country is still burdened by a high birth rate and the grinding poverty of millions who have not been able to share in the prosperity of their countrymen. Each year, added thousands face disaster: big families with tiny or no income. Quite naturally, they flee their fate.

In the first instance this means a massive movement into the northern tiers of Mexico. American employers, with the encouragement of the Mexican government, locate plants there to take advantage of the cheap labor. Daily, a legion crosses back and forth to the American side to work and shop. "In 1965 nearly 65,500,000 individual crossings of Mexican citizens under day permits were recorded . . . This figure does not include the many thousands of men and women who cross illegally to work on the American side."[9] For many the northern border states are the jumping-off sites for permanent entry into the U.S.

The crowding of the Mexican border cities puts pressure on

the towns on the American side of the Rio Grande. To escape the plight, many Mexican immigrants move on—to California or the Midwest.

In the process, the Mexican-American community undergoes an occupational change. The "peasant" becomes a proletarian; the rural hand becomes a factory operative; the man of the soil becomes a man of the city.

But even in the city, the Mexican-American may not long rest his weary head. His "home"—the decaying slum that is now called the barrio—is imperiled by the bulldozer: for urban renewal, highways, malls, art centers, or corporate headquarters skyscrapers. Consequently, the Mexican-American—one of the dispossessed of the land—is again facing dispossession.

The Mexican-American of the 1970s—geographically, economically, culturally, and politically mobile—has little in common with the prevailing image of the immobile peasant rooted to the soil. The Mexican-American of today is on the move.

While the Chicano—when he uses the appellation with public pride—is a symbol of the "new" Mexican-American, it would be a great error to assume that prior to the 1960s there was no dynamic among the Spanish-surnamed of the Southwest. There was constant *movement* in both senses of the word: demographic shifts of populations and organizations for social action.

The movements from Mexico northward and the countercurrents southward and the migrant stream within the U.S. are recounted in several essays in this volume. From this long story of a wandering people, it is apparent that the "natives" of the lands north and south of the Rio Grande have never been static. They have moved from place to place almost incessantly in response to changing economic and political circumstances.

Over these many generations, too, there have been "movements" expressed in rebellion and revolution, agitation and organization, talk and violence.

At a time when the future United States was still unsettled by the people of northern Europe, there was a widespread and momentarily successful revolt of Indians in the years 1541–42 in Mexico. This Mixton uprising was but one—although the most overwhelming—of dozens of rebellions over a couple of centuries. In *The Chicanos, A History of Mexican Americans,* the authors record the turmoil:

The seventeenth century was marked by numerous Indian rebellions motivated largely by hunger. . . . The most notable of these revolts took place in 1624, when Indians . . . burned the government headquarters in Mexico City. In 1692 another significant attack against the Spaniards led to the burning of the viceroyal palace by Indians who shouted, "Death to the Spaniards who are eating our corn."

Hunger and exploitation by the Spaniards caused the Indians of Nuevo León to try to expel the hated gachupines from their lands early in the eighteenth century. After a long four-year campaign the revolt was finally suppressed, only to break out anew a few years later.[10]

The running resistance of the Indians over some three centuries is attributable in part to the fact that "contrary to what happened elsewhere, the native Mexican tribes were not annihilated. They were, rather, kept in a servitude whose economic molds were well known, such as the encomienda, the hacienda and the mita. The native economic systems did not totally disappear." The number of white men who came from the Iberian peninsula to New Spain over these several centuries was less than a million. Consequently, "the indigenous Mexican survived and multiplied until he put his genetic and cultural stamp on the mixed society that emerged."[11]

Within the "mixed society" social conflict did not end, however. As the racial conflict between Indian and white diminished, a new clash developed between mestizos and creoles (whites of Spanish ancestry). While there were racial undertones, the principal causes of friction were economic and political: lower classes versus upper, democracy versus oligarchy, egalitarianism versus aristocracy.

In a succession of revolts, starting in 1810, two local priests played a central role. In September of that year, Father Miguel Hidalgo led some fifty thousand Indians and mestizos in a *jacquerie* against Spaniards and creoles. When Hidalgo was captured and executed, his place was taken by Father José María Morelos—himself a mestizo. He held a convention, declared independence, wrote an egalitarian constitution, and held out until 1815 when he was captured and executed. In subsequent years, priests played a significant role in the political and social movements of the Mexican-Americans.

The assumption that the Chicano can be counted upon to be

uncomplaining and inactive because of the restraining presence and influence of the Catholic Church misreads the history of these people. Religious devotion has not meant political passivity. Indeed, there is some evidence that the Church—or at least some of its priests—has been among the prime movers of popular action. This tradition of the "actionist" priest has continued right down to the present, as exemplified by the involvement of Monsignor George S. Higgins of the National Conference of Catholic Bishops in the crusades of the United Farm Workers.

In the years following Mexican independence from Spain in 1821, the northern areas of the new nation (America's present Southwest) were centers of unrest. Santa Anna tried to impose a centralism on the country that made the outer reaches of the north uneasy. In several cases, tensions led to armed conflict.

After the acquisition of the Southwest by the U.S., the new states became a battleground for the conflict of cultures. Typical of Mexican-American resistance was an undeclared guerrilla war-fare—seen by Chicanos as a natural human response, and by Anglos as acts of banditry. "Joaquin Murieta is perhaps the best known (if partly legendary) californio bandit-hero."[12] There were others, like Juan Flores and Three-Fingered Jack García. In the mixed judgment of history these outlaws are seen as Robin Hoods—one of the almost inevitable by-products of prolonged, bitter, and unresolved social strife.

Labor union action appears early in the Mexican-American communities. As far back as 1904, several men who had fled oppression in Mexico set up a labor newspaper, *Regeneración*, in San Antonio. The publishers were the Flores Magón brothers (Ricardo and Enrique), Antonio Villareal, and Juan Sarabia. In southwestern Arizona, during the same years, a union of Mexican-Americans was organized among the copper miners: the Obreros Libres, headed by Praxedis Guerrero. At the border town of Douglas, Enríquez Bermúdez published his agitational paper *El Centenario*.

For Mexican revolutionaries, the American Southwest became a base from which to foment rebellion against the regime of Porfirio Díaz. They made their modest contribution to ousting that incumbent and to aiding the revolutionary movements of Francisco Madero and Venustiano Carranza.

There is enough evidence about Mexican-American movements in the Southwest to conclude that they have never been a submissive people. But whatever evidence we have is but the tip of the volcano: the deep seething over centuries is still obscured. Great chapters in the history of the Mexican-American are missing.

Two essays in this volume deal with Chicano movements. One of these sketches areas of necessary investigation about the past. The other focuses on the living movements of recent past and the present.

During the 1970s, Mexican-Americans have become aware of themselves as a people. This sense of collective presence adds to the potential and power of America's second largest minority. But this same sense of oneness can confuse the true state of Mexican-American affairs in the United States because within the larger community there are many different smaller communities.

Awareness of differentiation is important in more than an academic way. To know the various subcommunities is indispensable to intelligent social planning and action. What is a reasonable way to grapple with a Chicano problem in Los Angeles may make absolutely no sense at all in northern New Mexico. The circumstances of a Chicano union leader in a Gary steel plant is totally unlike the situation of a union leader in the lettuce fields of California. A barrio made up of people who are 90 percent "immigrants" has little in common with a colonia of "first families" of Arizona.

In the discussions of the Mexican-American in this volume there are repeated references to these distinctions. They reflect more than a pursuit of cultural curios. They are attempts to get to the discoverable truths about the Mexican-Americans on the general faith that the truth can still set people free.

NOTES

1. Inter-Agency Committee on Mexican American Affairs, *Mexican-American* 2 (newsletter), No. 1 (Washington, D.C., January 1970).

2. John S. Gaines, "Treatment of Mexican American History in High School Textbooks," *Civil Rights Digest* (October 1972).

3. Ibid.

4. Leo Grebler, Joan W. Moore, Ralph C. Guzman et al., *The Mexican-American People: The Nation's Second Largest Minority* (New York: The Free Press, 1970), p. 7.

5. *Population Characteristics*, Bureau of the Census (July 1972), Series P-20, No. 238.

6. *Population Characteristics*, U.S. Department of Commerce (July 1974), p. 1.

7. Ibid., p. 10.

8. Ernesto Galarza, Julian Samora et al., *Mexican-Americans in the Southwest* (Santa Barbara, Calif.: McNally and Loftin, 1970), p. 21.

9. Ibid., p. 13.

10. Matt S. Meier and Feliciano Rivera, *The Chicanos: A History of the Mexican-Americans* (New York: Hill and Wang, 1972), p. 24.

11. Ernesto Galarza, "Mexicans in the Southwest," in Edward H. Spicer and Raymond H. Thompson, eds., *Plural Society in the Southwest* (New York: Interbook, Inc., 1972; paperback ed., University of New Mexico Press, 1975), pp. 274–75.

12. Meier and Rivera, *The Chicanos*, p. 81.

2

The Neglected Chapters
In Mexican-American History

CLARK S. KNOWLTON

Dr. Knowlton is Director of Social Research and Development at the American West Center, University of Utah. He has written extensively on the Spanish-speaking peoples of the Southwest.

Mexican-Americans—for many generations an invisible minority —have recently begun to be noticed. Individual leaders, movements, and events have stirred interest: César Chávez and Reies López Tijerina; student strikes; Mexican-American political parties such as La Raza Unida in Texas, Colorado, and California; riots in East Los Angeles. The new "brown" presence has caught the uneasy attention of state and federal governments, of national foundations, and of publishers who scent a new item for the market.

As of yet, however, this emerging people has not caught the eye of the somewhat incestuous "intellectual families" gathered around major national "think" journals. Although many of these have been preoccupied with racial and ethnic problems, they are just so many blank pages so far as references to "Chicanos" go. In this respect, this intelligentsia is not unlike the general liberal community that has been far more involved with activism to influence foreign policy than with concern about Mexican-Americans who live in poverty and segregation under the very shadows of the universities, offices, and dwellings of the Anglo-liberal.

Mexican-Americans have also been neglected by Anglo-American historians whose interest in western history has focused more on the romantic periods of Spanish exploration, conquest, settlement, and on Indian-Spanish relationships or Spanish colonial institutions, than on the somewhat humdrum economic, social, and cultural story of Mexican-American inhabitants of the Southwest.

Historians have also preferred to dwell upon the westward movement of Anglo-American frontiersmen rather than upon the problems of Mexican-Americans in adjusting to strange political, economic, legal, and social systems imposed upon them by superior Anglo-American conquering forces. Chroniclers have recorded all sorts of insignificant doings of obscure Anglo-American mountain men, trappers, or criminals while overlooking Mexican-American political leaders, military men, explorers, frontiersmen, ranchers, and businessmen who played important roles in the history of the Southwest.

This scholarly neglect has left us without a single comprehensive history of the Mexican-American people or of any major subgrouping, except for the early Mexican-American inhabitants of California.[1] Almost none of the many important Mexican-American leaders from the time of the American conquest until the present has found a biographer. Mexican-American history is shrouded in darkness.

The historians are not alone in their apparent lack of interest. They are joined by the sociologists, anthropologists, and other social scientists.[2] Only recently have Mexican-Americans become an acceptable topic of social science research, even in the Southwest. Because of past neglect, only a few sporadic studies of various aspects of Mexican-American life in rural villages or urban neighborhoods exist, and even these are badly dated. Mexican-American communities remain a *terra incognita*. Fortunately, the number of interested social scientists is increasing—including a few who are Mexican-Americans. These latter are often torn by the conflicting demands of the canons of social science research, by the need to assert a militant identity, and by the desire to refute half-truths and misinterpretations by Anglo-Americans.[3]

Scholarly neglect of Mexican-Americans has serious negative implications for both Anglo- and Mexican-Americans. At a time when government and foundations seek to reduce poverty, discrimination, and cultural isolation among Mexican-Americans, they find that their programming lacks basic data. Millions of dollars are consequently wasted in programs that fail and will continue to fail because we do not have needed input: about local Mexican-American cultural values and social systems; about the hierarchy of felt needs; and about leadership patterns among Mexican-Americans.[4]

Myths about Mexican-Americans

Many stereotypes and half-truths handicap understanding and communication between Mexican- and Anglo-Americans. For one, a variety of myths obscure a significant cultural diversity among Mexican-Americans. Programs derived from one Mexican-American community are consequently transported to other areas where they are inappropriate. To lay a realistic basis for future planning it is vital to delineate the varied Mexican-American subgroupings and to study the rapidly changing life patterns of diverse Mexican-American rural and urban communities and neighborhoods throughout the United States.

Examples of negative stereotypes, nurtured by lack of research in Mexican-American history, are the following:

(1) The assumption that, since illiteracy was prevalent among Mexican-Americans in the late nineteenth and early twentieth centuries, literature could not have flourished among them and there is therefore little written Mexican-American literature.[5] This assumption ignores the many and varied Spanish-language newspapers and magazines that flourished in the Southwest from the 1870s to the 1930s. These newspapers and journals published poetry, essays, commentaries, letters to the editor, and fiction written by Mexican-Americans. The very existence of these journals has been ignored by Anglo-Americans and, unfortunately, by many Mexican-Americans working in the English language. The revealing literature of a people, embedded in these pages, remains to be recovered and analyzed.

(2) Another stereotype is the belief that voluntary associations are not common among the Mexican-American people.[6] This stereotype, handed down from one scholar to another, ignores the many Mexican-American protest organizations that have flourished in the Southwest from the 1840s to the present time as well as labor unions and religious, social, cultural, and recreational associations common to middle-class Mexican-Americans.[*] The myth is fostered by the neglect of such middle-class phenomena by scholars who

---

[*]A perusal of Southwestern newspapers from the 1870s to the 1950s reveals the existence of numerous relatively unknown Mexican-American organizations throughout the Southwest that ranged from militant protest groupings and political organizations to social clubs. The whole history of ethnic organizations among Mexican-Americans is an unexplored area that promises rich dividends to the scholar who mines it.

focus on lower income, isolated, rural villages, or poor urban neighborhoods where voluntary associations are not common even among Anglo-Americans.

These and other stereotypes—held by the man in the street—have unfortunately crept into scholarly literature. It is curious, for example, how many Anglo-American students of Mexican-Americans tend to assume that the Spanish-speaking people of the Southwest have lived in a sort of timeless vacuum, apparently isolated from the impact of social forces in the United States.[7] Although cultural isolation, geographic distance, and poor means of communication and transportation may have delayed the impact of outside forces, they have never blocked them. The Mexican-Americans have been influenced in one form or another by the various dynamics in our society since the Southwest became part of the United States. They have also been influenced by the dynamics of Mexico. The impact of these trends has seldom been the subject of scholarly endeavors.

Now that the Southwest is becoming ever more firmly articulated into the United States, even the partial physical and cultural isolation that marked the lives of some, but not all, Mexican-American groups is coming to an end. Mexican-Americans are reacting to the same cultural and economic forces that are reshaping the contours of modern American society. While some responses will be the same as those of other elements, certain patterns of adjustment will be uniquely different, even varying distinctively from one Mexican-American subgrouping to another.

In this presentation, an effort will be made to delineate certain historical events in the American Southwest that have determined the character and role of the Mexican-Americans—with an emphasis on those facets that have been least investigated or evaluated.

Mexican-American Diversity

Although each of the larger minority groups in the United States tends to be more culturally differentiated than most Americans realize, Mexican-Americans may well possess a greater variety of culturally differentiated subgroupings than other large minorities. Even though the numerous Mexican-American subgroupings are related by a complex of subtle core values and social systems, they do differ from each other in many ways: length of residence in the United States, racial composition, history, use of Spanish or English as the language of the home, dialect, degree of acculturation, integration, and participation in Anglo-American society, class structure, occupational distribution, rural or urban residence, types of experienced discrimination or segregation, and levels of living. With a few exceptions[8] little effort has been made to delineate or to compare the socioeconomic and cultural characteristics of these subgroupings. Among some of the fundamental factors responsible for the proliferation of Mexican-American subgroupings are: (1) the physical geography of the Southwest that partially isolated one Mexican-American group from another; (2) Spanish colonial policy that frowned upon direct trade or intimate contacts between one colony and another; (3) different cultural characteristics of local Indian tribes; (4) the differential impact of Anglo-American conquest upon the Mexican-American inhabitants of the Southwest; (5) the slightly different values and changing culture of each generation of Mexican immigrants to the United States; and (6) the varying exposure and types of response to Anglo-American political, demographic, economic, and cultural pressures.[9]

During the Spanish and Mexican periods, the Southwest was a sparsely populated frontier region far from the major centers of colonial and national life in Mexico. Spanish settlements in New Mexico, California, and south Texas were not only formed to Christianize the Indians and to develop whatever natural resources might be present, but also to serve as buffers to protect the major approaches to Mexico from foreign infiltration and aggression. Each of the three major areas of Spanish settlement had little communication with each other and differed climatically and geographically. Cool, forested, mountainous northern New Mexico, rising high over the neighboring semiarid deserts, plains, and smaller desert mountains of the Southwest; the brushy rolling plains, plateaus, and hills of southern Texas; the semiarid plains, low coastal ranges, and hot interior valleys of California—all provided diverse environments for Spanish settlement.[10]

The Pueblo Indians of northern New Mexico, resistant to Spanish and Mexican control, insisting upon their local autonomy and traditional ways of life, successfully opposed Spanish attempts to gather them into missions or genuinely to Hispanize and Christianize them.[11] The populous, peaceful California Indians, possessing a simpler socioeconomic way of life, offered little resistance to Spanish endeavors to concentrate them into missions. The fragments of tribes in the lower Rio Grande Valley that disappeared through disease and miscegenation, posed no threat to the Spanish. There were also the powerful, nomadic Ute, Comanche, and Apache tribes that ringed northern New Mexico and sharply limited Spanish and Mexican settlement of the Southern Plains.[12] These varying interrelations all deeply influenced the Spanish and Mexican settlement patterns as well as local social systems and land use patterns.

New Mexico

In all the Spanish and Mexican Southwest, it was only in northern New Mexico that a genuine peasant class of small farmers came into existence.[13] The Spanish-speaking people of northern New Mexico, known as "Spanish-Americans," have been, since the initial thrust of settlement in the late sixteenth and early seventeenth centuries, a cultural island separated from other Spanish settlements by hard-fighting Indian tribes, deserts, and mountains. Very few new immigrants, after the initial surge of settlement, ever came up the long, hard, dangerous trail from Mexico. As population increased and Indian presence allowed, migrant streams moved north and south from the initial settlements in the upper Rio Grande Valley: from Taos in the north to Belén in the south, trickling into valleys of the Sangre de Cristo Mountains, and finally flowing down the rivers running south and east from the mountains.[14] During the American period, the Spanish-Americans formed a regular eastward-moving frontier that, as Indian dangers diminished, moved out into the plains in western Texas and eastern New Mexico. This eastward-moving Spanish-American frontier collided with the westward-moving Texan frontier and was rolled back in a sequence of violence that is still largely unknown.[15] Spanish-Americans are still in retreat before the advance of the Texans and other Anglo-American ranchers in eastern and central New Mexico.[16]

Northern New Mexico was dominated by powerful landowning families during the Spanish and Mexican periods, operating sheep and cattle ranches under a feudal system encompassing impoverished laborers and Indian slaves. The former—the peons—were in debt to their employers and could not leave their employment so long as they were in debt: they had to buy their necessities from the rancher; and their children inherited the debts of their fathers. The majority of the people, however, were free, living in multitudinous rural farm villages that still dot northern New Mexico. Each of the villages was founded for the most part on community land grants granted to heads of village families. Each family owned its own house site and its farmlands.[17] The village, as a cooperative unit, developed and operated its own irrigation system. The rest of the land grant, usually the largest portion—the *ejido*—communally belonged to the village. Every village family had the right to use the ejido. By tradition, the village community included the village site, its farmlands, its irrigation system, and its ejido. Each village became a self-contained, subsistence farming unit, frequently isolated for long periods from contact with other villages by poor communications. The inhabitants were reluctant to leave the village and mistrusted all outsiders.[18] Three major types of village communities came into existence—those in the mountains, the river valleys, and the plains—each differing somewhat in societal contours. Vital as these variations are for social programming, they go almost unnoted in the existing literature.

The farm villages predominated in the mountain valleys and smaller river valleys north of Albuquerque. The large ranches, although found in every part of the region, tended to cluster in the larger river valleys and grasslands east and south of Albuquerque.[19] The Hispanic village people were most resistant to acculturation into and control by Anglo-American society. They rose in revolt toward the end of the war between Mexico and the United States and killed the first American governor, Charles Bent. Other Americans were killed in Mora and elsewhere. The revolution was harshly put down with several villages, such as Mora, being destroyed. Guerrilla activities were carried on for several years against American occupation. The hostility of the local village people caused chronic apprehension among Anglo-Americans of New Mexico for several generations. This hostility has never really died out.[20]

The wealthy landowning Spanish-American families of New Mexico had become rather familiar with Anglo-Americans—their customs and life styles—during the Mexican period. They were hospitable and friendly toward the Anglo-American and French-Canadian merchants, trappers, and traders who entered New Mexico during the Santa Fe Trail era. Many of these immigrants married Spanish-American girls and settled down in New Mexico. Spanish-American merchants, wagon masters, hunters, teamsters, and guides played an important role in the Santa Fe trade (another facet of the Southwest that has escaped the notice of most historians of the Trail). Quite a few of them lived for varying periods of time in American cities at the eastern end of the Trail. Some of the wealthier New Mexican families sent their sons to be educated in American universities and colleges. Upon their return, these young men, favorably inclined toward the United States, facilitated the adjustment of the upper-class Spanish-American landowners to American dominance.

Because of physical isolation, the persistence of Indian troubles until the 1880s, and the lack of a favorable national image, New Mexico was slow to attract immigrants. Although Anglo-Americans came to predominate in southeastern New Mexico by the 1900s, it was not until the 1940s that Anglo-Americans came to outnumber Spanish-Americans in the entire state. Most of the Anglo-American immigrants were merchants, lawyers, government employees, ranchers, and various types of white-collar, professional, and skilled workers. Very few unskilled or semiskilled Anglo-American workers, white or black, entered New Mexico until World War II. As Anglo-American merchants, professional men, and politicians could not afford to alienate their clients and voters, discriminatory practices seldom developed in northern New Mexico.

Anglo-Americans entering New Mexico found that commerce and access to the natural resources of the land were the important roads to power and wealth. Within a few years after the American conquest, Anglo- and Spanish-American merchants were found in virtually all of the larger Spanish-American villages. Although a few Spanish-American merchants survived, the Anglo-Americans, through access to credit and wholesale markets and knowledge of business techniques, were able to eliminate much of their Spanish-American competition. These Anglo merchants, selling goods on credit, buying village products at prices set by themselves, providing credit at their own rates, and knowing the state of village accounts, came to control the economic activities of many Spanish-

American villages. The merchants were also able to build up large landholdings through foreclosure.[21]

A few shrewd Anglo-American lawyers, politicians, territorial government appointees, ranchers, and merchants, with Spanish-American allies, put together a political machine—the Santa Fe Ring—that dominated the political and economic life of New Mexico from the late 1870s to the 1900s. Often working through Spanish-American lieutenants, the members of the Santa Fe Ring, using violence, manipulation of the land tax, and political chicanery, were able to wrest control of most of the land grants from the village people by the 1900s.[22] The village people had been struggling without assistance from any source to maintain their independence and to carry on their traditional ways of life. The erosion of their landholdings, plus the depression and the drought of the 1930s, brought these rear-guard efforts to an end. To avoid actual starvation, large numbers had to fall back upon the welfare and employment programs of the New Deal.[23] Not only did they lose their land and independence, but they also lost pride and self-confidence. The impact of land loss and poverty upon the village people is only just now coming under scholarly scrutiny. The operations of the Santa Fe Ring still remain shrouded in darkness, as another one of the many little-studied subjects of New Mexican history.[24]

Although Spanish-Americans have suffered severely under Anglo-American dominance in New Mexico, they have still managed to preserve a stronger economic and political position in New Mexico than have Mexican-American subgroupings in Arizona, California, Colorado, or Texas. From the late 1840s on, Anglo-Americans have been forced to share political and economic power with wealthy, landed, Spanish-American dynasties. The success of Spanish-Americans in maintaining political power is illustrated by the large number of Spanish-American judges, county commissioners, mayors, powerful members in the state legislature, heads of local, federal, and state public agencies, senators and congressmen. For long periods of time, Spanish-Americans from New Mexico were the only Spanish-speaking representatives in Congress. A leitmotif of New Mexico history is the constant effort to structure political relationships between Spanish-Americans and Anglo-Americans in such a way as to maintain Anglo-American dominance and yet provide powerful Spanish-American political leaders with the prerequisites of political office that their influence requires.

Because Spanish-Americans in New Mexico were protected against rapid Anglo immigration by relative isolation and lack of easily exploitable natural resources, they were able to generate a better-educated middle class, partially acculturated into Anglo-American society, composed of white collar, professional, small business, public employees, and skilled workers. This socio-economic element—facing little Anglo-American competition—has steadily improved its position in New Mexico. The most successful of these, together with those older, upper-class Spanish-American families, have played important roles in the creation of banks and large scale business establishments in New Mexico. Undoubtedly, the power of this group will steadily increase in New Mexico, reshuffling established patterns of power relations.

Unfortunately, the majority of the rural Spanish-Americans in northern New Mexico have not shared in the progress of the Spanish-American urban middle class. Many of the rural people, forced to migrate from their native sites because of the collapse of village economics, end up in urban slums. Those who remain struggle to survive under ever more difficult economic conditions. These villagers have been the prime victims of Anglo-American "colonialism" in New Mexico.

Without being aware of it, the Anglo-American establishment of New Mexico has been paying a high price for the tragic plight in which the village people are forced to live. These Mexican-Americans are profoundly cynical about the claims of American democracy and about the moral foundations of Anglo civilization. Very few ethnic or racial groups in the United States are as deeply alienated from American society as are the village people of northern New Mexico. As a recent governor of New Mexico said, "The Spanish Americans regard the government as their enemy."[25] Unrest is chronic in the mountains of northern New Mexico; the threat of violence is always present.

Northern New Mexico need not be poor. In topography, climate, and natural resources it is much like Switzerland, Norway, and Austria—mountainous countries that are among the more thriving in Europe. In contrast, Spanish-American northern New Mexico is one of the poorest rural areas of the United States. Its major source of income is welfare and unemployment compensation; it is plagued by malnutrition and extremely high disease and mortality rates. Alcoholism, vandalism, and juvenile delinquency are on the rise. Water is unsafe and sewage facilities scarcely exist. Roads are extremely bad. A majority of students drop out before they finish high school. The educational, political, and legal systems are almost nonfunctioning.

This distress in northern New Mexico is not due to any genetic or cultural characteristic of the local Spanish-American inhabitants; it is due to the Spanish-American's loss of ownership or access to the natural resources of the region that have passed into Anglo-American or government hands.[26] Thus, the end result of more than a century of American occupation has been a poverty culture whose characteristics more closely resemble some poor areas of Latin America than the rest of the United States. Most government programs designed to reduce poverty in the region have failed, in part, because of cultural and linguistic conflicts. More basically, they have failed because they have struggled with the symptoms rather than with the fundamental cause of poverty, namely, the alienation of the land from the Spanish-American people of northern New Mexico.[27]

Texas

The Mexican-American inhabitants of Texas suffered harsher treatment at the hands of Anglo-Americans than did the Spanish-Americans of northern New Mexico.[28] The socioeconomic and political positions of the Mexican-Americans in Texan society varied from one county to another depending upon: (1) The proportionate numbers of Mexican-Americans in the population: the larger the percentage of Mexican-Americans in a county, the better they were treated. (2) The complexity of the Mexican-American class structure: Mexican-Americans did better in counties where there was a higher rate of literacy, a larger number of Mexican and Mexican-American priests, and where there existed many Mexican-American business and professional men and skilled artisans as well as wealthy, influential, Mexican-American land-owning families and men with military experience. (3) Nearness to the Mexican border.

Population, goods, and ideas flow freely across the border,

whatever the Texan, American, or Mexican government think about the situation. The border regions in Texas have always been predominantly Mexican-American in population. Anglo-Americans in the border area until well into the twentieth century were dependent upon Mexican-American labor, patronage, and votes. Many of these Anglo families intermarried freely with high-status Mexican-American families. Some of these Anglo-Americans filled the role of economic and political *patrones*, often providing protection against Anglo mistreatment of the Mexican-Americans.

The border regions were chronically troubled by Anglo-American and Mexican outlaws and border raiders seeking revenge for actual or imagined injuries and looking to enrich themselves at the expense of the inhabitants of the opposite side. Indians also raided both sides of the border impartially. The Mexican-Americans caught between Anglo-American and Mexican raiders were seldom trusted by either side and were frequently victimized by both. They, of course, raided at times on their own. Many Mexican and Mexican-American border fighters became folk heroes and were glorified in songs and stories still heard along the border. It should be noted, however, that no section of Texas was completely free of Anglo-American lands, fear of Mexican-American and Mexican uprisings, and the chronic need to maintain Anglo-American political and economic dominance.

The total dynamic of the Texas development is still another unwritten chapter of Mexican-American history, including the varying patterns of superordinate-subordinate accommodation between Anglo-Americans and Mexican-Americans in Texas; the institutionalized use of violence by Texas Rangers against Mexican-Americans; land alienation; the complex patterns of land use; the flow of Mexicans in search of employment across the border; the steady erosion of Mexican-American landholdings; the socioeconomic factors responsible for the chronic violence in Texan border regions; the flow of ideas as well as population and goods across the border; and the influence of Mexican-American and Mexican life styles upon English-speaking Texans.

A knowledge of the Texas war of independence is fundamental to an understanding of Anglo-Texan hostility toward the Spanish-speaking population of the area. To accelerate settlement of Texas, the Mexican government offered American entrepreneurs large land grants on condition that grantees populate the holdings with settlers from the United States or from Mexico. Large numbers of Americans were attracted, primarily from the South, to Texas.[29] Inevitably the weak Mexican government, distraught with civil, political, and economic problems, was unable to cope with the stresses and strains resulting from conflicts between Mexicans and Anglo-Americans in the distant northern frontier.[30]

The Texas rebellion against Mexico seems to have passed through two stages. In the first, Americans and Mexicans jointly rose in rebellion against the dictatorial Santa Anna, calling upon him to respect the provisions of the Mexican Constitution of 1824 which they felt had been violated.[31] It was not until Mexican troops summarily shot Texans defeated (among whom were Mexicans) at Goliad and took no prisoners at the Alamo, that the revolution entered its second phase, a clear-cut fight for independence under Anglo-American dominance.[32]

The events at Goliad and the Alamo unleashed murderous currents of Anglo hostility against the Texas Mexicans (including those who had fought with the Anglo-Americans) who were treated as a conquered people without any rights. "Killing a Mexican was like killing an enemy in the independence war that apparently each Texan waged and since it was a conflict with historic scores to settle (Goliad and El Alamo) the killing carried a sort of immunity with it."[33] As Texan cattlemen migrated into other sections of the West, they infected other Anglos with their attitudes. Thus an Anglo-American rancher in eastern New Mexico around the turn of the century stated:

> For the Texan of those days—it is true even of the present generation—the memory of that spot [the Alamo], with its record of Mexican savagery kept alive a never failing flame of hatred and contempt for everything Mexican. As a consequence, the range men of those times [speaking of the last half of the nineteenth century] treated the entire Spanish-American people as if they had no rights at all, refused to have any social relations with them, although some were of proud Spanish blood, killed them, dispossessed them of their lands, scattered their sheep and drove off their cattle.[34]

Claiming the Rio Grande as their destined western boundary, the Texans tried to annex all of New Mexico east of the Rio Grande shortly after the Mexican war. No matter how much the Spanish-speaking New Mexicans may have disliked the Americans in New Mexico, they hated Texans even more. The Texan claim was extinguished by the federal government's paying Texas for territory that had never belonged to or been occupied by Texans.[35] New Mexicans demonstrated their attitudes toward Anglo-Texans by raising three thousand volunteers in three regiments with their own Spanish-speaking officers to help defeat the Texan invasion of New Mexico during the American Civil War.[36] The role played by the Spanish-Americans in the conduct of the Civil War in New Mexico and the economic and political impact of the war upon them are other neglected chapters of Southwest history.

As a result of the American victory in the Mexican-American war, Texas acquired the solidly Mexican area of southern Texas located, for the most part, between the Rio Grande and the Nueces River. Located on the Mexican-American border, south Texas has experienced a bloody, violent history as Indians, Mexicans, and Americans fought and raided each other. Victims of raids[37] and of Anglo-American efforts to seize their landholdings, some Mexican-Americans turned to banditry and guerrilla warfare.[38] The names and exploits of the Mexican-American and Mexican guerrilla and bandit leaders may have been forgotten by many Anglo residents of south Texas but they are still commemorated in Mexican and American folk stories and ballads.[39] Even as late as World War I, a small clique of Mexican revolutionaries and Mexican-Americans, with German backing, plotted to retake Texas and the Southwestern states for eventual annexation to Mexico.[40]

Effective American rule was not established in the region until the 1900s. Railroads and highways were built crisscrossing the region, ending its partial physical and cultural isolation from the rest of Texas. Rising land values—spurred by irrigation projects—attracted American speculators and land companies who dispossessed local Mexican-American landowners through fraud and violence. Speculators and companies cleared large extensions of land, which were subdivided into farming units and, through high-pressure merchandising, were sold at a good profit to Anglo-American farmers.[41] South Texas thus rapidly became a major winter vegetable, citrus fruit, and cotton-producing area.

Dispossessed Mexican-Americans were forced to move to the numerous new towns springing up along the highways and railroads. Here they were joined by enormous numbers of legal and illegal Mexican immigrants drawn across the border by employment opportunities in agriculture.[42] The abundant supply of labor depressed wages to subsistence level—or below. A flood of Mexican-Americans moved from south Texas in the early spring into the harvest fields of the Middle West, Southwest, Great Plains, Rocky Mountains, Pacific Coast, and the Northwest—flowing back to Texas in the late fall. Traditional Mexican-American political organizations were destroyed in the region and replaced by a precarious Anglo-American establishment that is now being challenged.[43]

Although several histories of south Texas exist, none has focused upon the complex patterns of accommodation and interaction between Mexican-Americans and Anglo-Americans, or upon the socioeconomic characteristics of Mexican-American resistance to Anglo-American encroachments, nor upon the persistent outbreaks of what Anglo-Americans call banditry, but that Mexican-Americans look upon as armed resistance movements. The raw material for such a revealing chapter awaits the hand of the scholar.

The American conquest of the Southwest was formally sealed by a treaty intended to protect the rights of Mexicans who became U.S. citizens by fiat rather than by choice. The Treaty of Guadalupe-Hidalgo guaranteed the property, civic, and personal rights of the conquered people.[44] Very little scholarship has been devoted to this formative half century of American occupation and Mexican-American adjustment from the 1850s to the 1900s. The open questions about this period are:

(1) Did the United States make any effort to enforce the protective provisions of the Treaty of Guadalupe-Hidalgo; (2) what were the political and economic factors that controlled either the enforcement or nonenforcement of the treaty; (3) what were the socioeconomic characteristics of Mexican society in the Southwest upon the eve of American conquest; (4) what elements among Mexicans of the area favored American annexation and what elements opposed it; (5) what impact did growing Anglo-American movement and dominance have upon the diverse elements among Mexican-Americans; (6) what were the variables responsible for the widespread rise of Mexican-American guerrilla and/or bandit operations in the Southwest during this period, and from what occupational and social class strata did the guerrilla bands originate; (7) what were the social origin, composition, and chang-

ing goals of Mexican-American political and protest associations formed during this era; (8) what effect did the American-Mexican border and the ideas, commerce, and men flowing across it have upon the history of the Southwest?

The United States-Mexican Border

Knowledge of the complex interplay of forces along the American-Mexican border from the 1850s to the present is essential to understanding many of the trends on both sides of the border. Events on each side of the border have influenced the other side. The border, in many ways only an artificial line on the map, has been a passageway for ideas, goods, and people, flowing from north to south rather than east to west as do the major highway and railroad systems in the American Southwest.

From the Pacific Ocean to the Gulf of Mexico, the border runs through a sparsely populated, semiarid terrain. The length of the line, the difficult nature of the mountainous and desert terrain, and the sparse population have made it difficult for either the Mexican or the American government effectively to control this frontier. Along this long strip, the majority of inhabitants are concentrated in border communities, each with a counterpart on the other side. In some sections, the Mexican community is larger; in other areas it is the American town or city. The paired settlement—Mexican and American—are halves of urban oases, dependent upon each other, and isolated from other oases in either the United States or Mexico by long stretches of desert and mountains.

Although Mexicans and Mexican-Americans are most numerous in this area, the towns are marked by vast ethnic diversity. Indian tribes are still important; a few—the Yaqui, Pima, and the Papago—have villages on both sides of the frontier line.[45] While the majority of tribes in the border region are located clearly on one side or the other, sporadic communication and trade are still carried on between Mexican and American Indian groups without the knowledge or the permission of their respective governments.

Mormon villages—numerous in both Arizona and New Mexico—are also found in the eastern flanks of the Sierra Madre Mountains in the Mexican state of Chihuahua.[46] From these villages, Mormons have moved to nearby urban centers in both countries. The Mormons, many of whom are bilingual and own land on both sides of the border, often move freely across the line without requesting anyone's permission. South of the Mormon villages in Chihuahua are large colonies of German-speaking Mennonites from Canada.[47] A few Mennonites are also found in New Mexico. Immigrants of many nationalities—Syrians, Lebanese, Jews, and Chinese—are active in commerce in northern Mexico and the American Southwest. Families of Anglo-American origin, now partially acculturated into Mexican society, own ranches and businesses throughout northern Mexico, and a number of Mexican landowning and business families have similar interests in the American Southwest.

The history of the border regions has been stained with violence. Spanish, Indians, French, Mexicans, Mexican-Americans, and Anglo-Americans have fought each other over power and possession of the natural resources. Anglo-Americans crossed the border freely to seize additional Mexican territory, to rustle livestock, or to seek revenge for the Alamo. Mexicans, in turn, raided the American Southwest, seeking revenge for the loss of Mexican territory, to secure supplies for revolutionary activities, or to pick up what livestock and booty they could find. Mexican-American freebooters, not fully trusted by either side, also raided the American side of the border.[48] Indian tribes in northern Mexico went on raids in the American Southwest and deep into northern Mexico. Mexicans, Mexican-Americans, and Anglo-Americans crossed and recrossed the border to enlist in revolutionary Mexican armies, to escape the bloodshed of Mexican revolutions, and in search of wealth and adventure. Even as late as the 1930s guns crackled along the border as Americans, Mexicans, and Mexican-Americans, smuggling liquor from Mexico, fought it out with American prohibition agents. Even today, guns still flare in the night as the police of both countries continue to battle smugglers and illegal border crossers.

Although bandit and guerrilla groups no longer are active in the border areas, criminal elements still flourish. American and Mexican smuggling rings with widespread connections use cars, trucks, motorcycles, ships, and planes to smuggle arms and ammunition, autos, trucks, new and used industrial and farm machinery, cigarettes, and even eggs into Mexico; and drugs, ores, silver, gems, foreign-made goods, and people into the United States. Car-theft

gangs steal cars and trucks in the Southwest and smuggle them into
Mexico to be sold there. Professional burglars, operating from one
side of the border, are active on the other. American deserters from
the military, criminals, and men sought by the American police
seek refuge and business opportunities in Mexico, while Mexican
criminals hide out on the American side. Criminal gangs often hire
out-of-country killers to eliminate enemies and competitors. While
central government law enforcement agencies work fairly smoothly
together, cooperation between local law enforcement agencies is
stymied by corruption, personality conflicts, and politics.

The border regions, in the twentieth century, continue to draw
population from the interior of both countries. Retired Americans
flock to the border in search of a warm climate and low-cost living.
As the price levels have risen in the American Southwest, many
senior American citizens are now moving into the semitropical
states of Mexico. Large numbers of Anglo-American workers,
businessmen, and professionals have migrated into the American
Southwest since the 1940s to work in defense and military
installations, and in the growing industries and businesses. Among
them are many blacks who are introducing still another racial
element. Affluent Americans have turned many sections of the
borderland into playgrounds.

As the Southwest has always been part of the known world of the
Mexican people, long before it became part of the United States,
many generations of Mexicans have crossed the border in search of
employment and adventure. Large numbers of Mexican citizens
are intimately acquainted with the Southwest, even though they
know little of Mexico except their home community and the routes
of migration. While the population of Mexico rises rapidly, her
people find it hard to survive as good farmland disappears, as mines
close, as drought sets in. There is not enough urban employment to
absorb these plagued people. Hence, Mexicans move north and
over the border into the U.S. Legally and illegally, they come—no
matter what American immigration officials do.

This abundance of cheap labor accelerated the economic
development of the Southwest. The railroads that crisscross the
region were laid by Mexican and Mexican-American labor. They
mined the ore and worked the smelters. They cleared the land,
dug the irrigation canals, built the dams, and harvested the crops
that have made the Southwest a flourishing agricultural region.

They staffed defense plants and industries established during and after World War II. They built the expanding cities. The rich economy of the Southwest was lifted to its present heights on the sweated backs of "Mexican" labor.

The flow of Mexican labor into the Southwest still continues heavily. Immigrants cross the border in several categories. There are those who secure buying permits to shop in American stores. These purchases add to the prosperity of American border towns. Using these permits, Mexicans cross the border illegally every day to work in domestic service, agriculture, industry, white-collar posts, and even in professions.

Even greater numbers cross the border in the spring as illegals or "wetbacks" to roam the Far West and Midwest for employment. While the majority return to Mexico within a few years, increasing numbers settle permanently out of the migrant stream. Fearful, exploited, and persecuted by American law enforcement agencies, they struggle to earn a living and to conceal their illegal status in the United States.

The "green carders"—still another category—are Mexican workers who have secured a permanent immigration visa (once green in color) entitling them to live in the United States. Many choose to live in Mexico where the cost of living is lower and to work in the United States where the wages are higher.

Finally, there are legal Mexican immigrants who cross the border with their papers in good order to join members of their families in the United States, to work for employers who testify that they have skills in scarce supply in the Southwest, or to study in American schools and colleges. Each generation crossing the border has its special characteristics—values, skills, education.

Commerce and capital also flow back and forth across the border. Mexican consumers, crossing the border in great numbers, purchase enormous amounts of American products retailed in American stores. American consumers, in return, buy large amounts of Mexican manufactured goods retailed in Mexican border communities as well as dental, medical, and other services that are cheaper on the Mexican side. Each American or Mexican border community is, to a surprising degree, dependent upon consumers from the other side.

Mexican and American tourists visit each other's border regions. American industrialists are now opening shops on the Mexican side of the border to fabricate industrial components utilizing low-cost Mexican labor and often Mexican raw materials to be assembled with better-skilled, more expensive American labor on the American side—or vice versa. Mexican fruits, liquor, livestock, and vegetables flow from northern Mexico to markets in the United States.

Economic forces are thus integrating northern Mexico and the American Southwest into a single economic system dependent upon American capital and technology, Mexican raw materials and labor, and upon the purchasing power of the Mexican and American border regions. The interdependence is steadily increasing even though local, state, and federal governments formulate policies that try to interrupt the free flow of capital, agricultural and mineral commodities, manufactured products, and labor across the border. So far, such restrictions have resulted in a flow of labor, capital, and goods through illegal channels.

The growing interdependence of northern Mexico and the American Southwest is creating new opportunities for Mexican-Americans. As few Anglo-Americans are familiar with the Spanish language or with Mexican culture, values, or procedures, Americans are increasingly forced to rely upon bilingual individuals with a feel for Mexican attitudes. Thus, some Mexican-Americans are increasingly the mediators between Anglo-Americans and Mexicans, a development of considerable future potential.

The Depression Years

Few scholars have studied the special impact of the depression of the 1930s on Mexican-Americans, an event whose traumatic effect was especially severe in northern New Mexico. Because of urban unemployment, Spanish-Americans were forced to return to their native villages in northern New Mexico to secure economic assistance from their extended families. The pressure upon the village land resources intensified precisely at a time when most of the villages had lost the larger part of their landholdings to the Anglo-Americans. Even the limited ability of village land to support the swollen population was destroyed by drought and crop failure. Under the blows of land depreciation, depression, and drought, the local village economies were shattered. At long last, the agonizing efforts of the Spanish-Americans to maintain their way of life was brought to an ugly end. They turned to the government for assistance. They have been a dependent people ever since—suffering from unemployment, malnutrition, disease, and a high death rate. They seek escape in out-migration.

Elsewhere in the Southwest, during the Depression, Mexican-Americans faced the same tragedies as others—with one big difference. With the encouragement of local political leaders and welfare organizations, law enforcement agencies repatriated large numbers of Hispanics to Mexico, including many who were here legally and married to American citizens. This exile of the "stranger," and a similar roundup in the 1950s sowed permanent seeds of distrust and dislike among Mexican-Americans toward American agencies. Some of these seeds are still bearing bitter fruit.

The sad story of the repatriation has never been told fully. Yet it is a moment out of the past that can profoundly affect our future.

World War II

The coming of World War II, following the Depression, brought about fundamental changes in almost all of the Mexican-American communities of the Southwest. During the war, thousands of Mexican-American volunteers and draftees from isolated rural villages and ranches, from urban slums and barrios, and from almost every part of the country, intermingled in military training camps and bases. Out of this arose a strong sense of self-identity as Mexican-Americans overcame cultural isolation and differences in dialects and subcultures. Mexican-Americans serving in the military, perhaps to their surprise, encountered little prejudice in the military service or outside the Southwest. They tested their manhood on the field of battle and won the respect of fellow servicemen by their fine combat record. The family allowances sent home brought the first ray of modest financial prosperity to thousands of poor Mexican-American homes.

These veterans came out of World War II not only stronger in their identity as Mexican-Americans, but also as American citizens. Military service brought into being the first Mexican-American generation to acquire a proud identification as a patriotic American, worthy of all the rights that presumably such citizenship should confer. This "new American" was also now willing to fight for those rights.

After World War II, Mexican-Americans began to give up the dream of a future outside the United States. For better or worse, they had come to accept their destiny as Americans. The remembrance of past injustices was beginning to fade among Mexican-Americans, just as the call to "remember the Alamo" was losing its urgency for Anglo-Texans.

The Mexican-American veteran, whose inability to speak English or to comprehend Anglo-American values were problems for him in the service, came home convinced that his community had to acquire a knowledge of English and of American values to improve its circumstances. They were also tempted by glimpses of life outside the Southwest and were naturally inclined to move into the American cultural mainstream.

The returning veterans filled the ranks of existing community organizations such as the League of United Latin-American Citizens (LULAC) which is probably still the most important middle-class Mexican-American organization in the country. Strongest in Texas but with chapters in many other states, LULAC has become the Mexican-American equivalent of both Rotary and Kiwanis clubs, with membership a cachet of and acceptance by the middle-class Mexican-American. The organization focuses on patriotic, social, and charitable programs designed to accelerate and to smooth Mexican-American social mobility into the American mainstream. More militant in its younger years, LULAC did, in the 1940s and early 1950s, carry out considerable litigation successfully to end the segregation of Mexican-American school children in the Southwest. In recent years, LULAC has passed resolutions supporting Mexican-American causes but has seldom become actively involved in social action.

Although the majority of Mexican-American veterans joined the American Legion and Veterans of Foreign Wars, organizations that provided sociability, a group of Mexican-American veterans formed the G.I. Forum. Strongest in Texas, the G.I. Forum has organized public demonstrations to support Mexican-American demands for greater opportunities.

Other recently founded organizations are the Mexican-American Political Association in California (MAPA) and the Political

Association of Spanish-Speaking Organizations (PASO) in Texas. These groups encourage Mexican-Americans to run for political office and conduct registration and get-out-the-vote drives. Purely pragmatic, these organizations operate on the principle of "reward your friends and punish your enemies." Although they have defeated few enemies, they have increased the number of Mexican-American voters and candidates since the 1950s. Their political successes, modest as they have been, have still had the effect of influencing Anglo political leaders to take the Mexican-American vote more seriously.

During the war, Mexican-Americans were recruited and trained by government agencies as defense workers, and they, with their families, were shipped to plants all over the Midwest and West. As skilled and semiskilled workers, they began to earn far more than ever before. Upon settling down, they sent for relatives and friends. Mexican-Americans began to move from New Mexico, Texas, Arizona, and rural California to the booming industrial centers west of the Mississippi River. As the labor shortage relaxed many discriminatory practices, Mexican-Americans began to move up the occupational ladder. A class of skilled and semiskilled industrial workers emerged. Their sons and daughters entered public schools and, upon graduation from high school, found employment as white collar and professional workers. Simultaneously, as restrictions against movement of Mexican workers into a labor-starved America was relaxed, thousands crossed the border into the United States, with the majority remaining. These latest immigrants filled the rural jobs of Mexican-Americans who were moving from the rural Southwest to urban communities within the region and to such neighboring regions as the Midwest, the Great Plains, the Rocky Mountains, and the Pacific Coast. The only large Spanish-speaking area in the Southwest to lose population sharply during this period was northern New Mexico.[49]

The G.I. Bill, providing education, skill training, and housing benefits to World War II veterans, accelerated the growth of professional, white collar, small business, and skilled labor elements among Mexican-Americans. Thousands of veterans enrolled in universities and colleges. Majoring for the most part in education, social work, business administration, and law, they became a cadre of partially acculturated professionals equipped to play a significant role in the evolving status of their people. An even larger number of veterans took on-the-job training courses under the G.I. Bill and emerged as skilled workers, repairmen, and small businessmen. By utilizing the housing provisions of the bill, Mexican-American veterans moved out of the segregated barrios, across the tracks, and into open Anglo neighborhoods; or into neighborhoods now being evacuated by Anglo-Americans moving to the suburbs. Residential segregation began to erode. Also a few Mexican-American landowners and businessmen quietly became wealthy through wartime opportunities. As a result of World War II and the G.I. Bill, the socioeconomic structure of Mexican-Americans was decisively altered as they began to penetrate Anglo-American society. The old barriers of cultural isolation and partial segregation were falling.

Post-War Changes

Acculturation and assimilation among middle-class Mexican-Americans were accelerated by the events mentioned above. The rapidly expanding Mexican-American middle class, eager to move out of poverty and into the mainstream of American life, soon sensed that acceptance depended upon an ability to speak English well, to secure a university or high school degree, to belong to the proper civic clubs, to live in a house in middle- or upper-class neighborhoods, and to maintain Anglo-American life styles. For many such the attempt to reconcile traditional ties with present pressures led to severe emotional and personal conflicts. Alcoholism and mental illness rose among middle-class Mexican-Americans.[50]

Generally, Mexican-Americans struggling to achieve middle-class status refused to let their children learn Spanish. They urged schools to focus on English and to punish students who persisted in speaking Spanish. For the first time since the American conquest of the Southwest, Spanish began to retreat before English, as Mexican-American traditions weakened. The areas where Spanish, as a spoken language, has held its own are along the border, among rural Mexican-Americans, and among poor Mexican-Americans in urban barrios. Outside the Southwest, the younger generations of Mexican-Americans are increasingly English-speaking. However, the constant flow of non-English-speaking Mexicans into the United States means that the number of Spanish-speaking entering the public schools will not diminish appreciably in the Southwest. This entire subject of language use—especially in the schools—is a challenge for social scientists.

Even though the new middle class of Mexican-Americans began to upset established patterns of ethnic relations, the dominant Anglo elites were flexible enough to modify these patterns to absorb socially mobile middle-class Mexican-Americans within the status quo. Mexican-Americans were allowed to move freely into lower echelon white-collar jobs. Mexican-American teachers were assigned to schools with predominant Mexican-American student bodies. Many professionals opened their own offices for a predominantly Mexican-American clientele. Anglo-American corporations hired Mexican-Americans for low level white-collar and professional positions.

When Mexican-American employees, over the years, realized that they were not going to move very far, many quit in disgust to form their own companies. Others resigned themselves to the situation, finding consolation in dreams about their children's futures and in measuring the distance that they themselves had traveled from the poverty of the barrio.

A major exception to this limited advance of the new middle class was along the border where bilingual Mexican-Americans received posts of considerable responsibility. The second exception was New Mexico where a fairly strong professional white-collar and business class had come into existence before the middle of the twentieth century. Many of these people had developed their own businesses; others were partners with prominent Anglo-American businessmen. Here, despite ethnic prejudice, this Spanish-speaking elite enjoyed a relatively high degree of mobility.[51]

Many Mexican-American lawyers and other professionals entered politics to advance their careers. Anglo politicians had an eye out for Mexican-Americans with a power base and awarded them positions in state and local government that kept them in the public eye, defined them as approved Mexican-American leaders, allowed them to award patronage, and to build up their fortunes, but denied them power to alter the local power structure. For example, on city councils they were placed in charge of parks and recreation but not finances or police. Even these secondary posts were allowed them so long as they did not challenge the status quo. Those who did were bought off, forced out of politics by the destruction of their political base, and replaced with more compliant Mexican-Americans; or, if they proved dangerously threatening, they would be forced to migrate.

Because of the strong pull toward acculturation and assimilation of minority groups in the Southwest after World War II, a cultural "tortilla curtain" fell over Hispanic culture. Mexican-Americans were increasingly withdrawn from the Latin world south of the Rio Grande. The Anglos in the Southwest had little desire to know anything about Mexican civilization. Many resented hearing Spanish in the streets; Mexican-Americans speaking Spanish on the job were often fired, even in northern New Mexico. The former bilingualism, once so prevalent among upper-class Mexican-American and Anglo-American families, began to vanish. Radio and television stations, except for a few along the border, banished the use of Spanish unless the programs were devoted to Mexican or Mexican-American music. The Spanish-language press, once so influential in the political and cultural life of the Southwest, virtually disappeared, and Spanish became exclusively an oral language.

"Americanizing" the Mexican-American child became a major function of the public school system.[52] Children were punished for speaking Spanish during school hours, and many who persisted were suspended from school. The curriculum was stripped of materials on Mexican or Mexican-American history. Even though the numbers of Mexican-American teachers steadily increased, they were forbidden to use Spanish in teaching Mexican-American children. Even in courses such as music and dancing, Mexican-American folk music and dances were repressed in favor of the square dance and the folk music of Appalachia. This forced acculturation, regardless of the emotional, educational, and social costs paid by the Mexican-American school child, enjoyed the support of the "new" middle class. Apparently, both Anglo-Americans and middle-class Mexican-Americans felt that Americanization was the *sine qua non*. And yet, the flow of Spanish-speaking children into the schools never ceased.

Even though the traditional position of Mexican-Americans as second-class citizens was only slightly modified during the 1950s, the Mexican-American community itself underwent profound changes. The Mexican-American was now an urban being. A massive migration had carried hundreds of thousands from soil to city. Standards of living improved somewhat. The isolation of Mexican-Americans vanished. Those left behind in the rural villages of northern New Mexico[53] or as migrant workers in the Southwest sank further into poverty—thanks to the cumulative impact of accelerated land loss, discrimination by the National Forest Service against the small Spanish-American farmer and rancher, and the erosion of migrant farm jobs due to agriculture.[54]

A once rather simple society, marked by a few educated, fairly well-off bilingual Mexican-American families mediating between Anglo-Americans and non-English-speaking, impoverished, un- skilled, and semiskilled Mexican-Americans disappeared. Two important, relatively new social strata appeared: (1) a rapidly increasing semiacculturated urban professional, white-collar, and business stratum, quite familiar with English and with Anglo-American values, social and economic systems, and proce- dures; and (2) an even larger class of less acculturated skilled workers and independent artisans. Among both groups, a belief that education was essential had spread widely. The number of Mexican-American school children attending elementary and secondary schools, colleges and universities rapidly increased. With this shift in social position came a shift in religious attitudes. The ancient tie to Catholicism was loosened as many Mexican-Amer- icans began to join Protestant denominations. The Pentecostals especially gained ground among both urban workers and rural villagers.

Even though many Mexican-Americans improved their social standing and levels of living during the 1950s, a very large number still remained in poverty. These were composed of: (1) the semiliterate, semiskilled Mexican-American migrants from rural areas, (2) new Mexican immigrants, and (3) Mexican-American urban residents who, for one reason or another, had not been able to move up the socioeconomic ladder.[55] Although the partially acculturated middle class experienced little poverty, police brutal- ity, or open discrimination, the poor Mexican-Americans, living in urban barrios, did. Furthermore, the spread of television through the poor neighborhoods made every poor Mexican-American very much aware of the contrast between his living conditions and those of the middle-class Americans as portrayed on the tube. Awareness of the differences stirred discontent, unrest, and a desire for social and economic change.

Recent Rise of Unrest

From the end of World War II until the early 1960s, a period marked by the emergence of a new Mexican-American generation, the Southwest was characterized by an uncertain social peace. Socioeconomic conditions, except for the migrant workers in south Texas and the Spanish-Americans of northern New Mexico, improved substantially. The rapidly growing number of small businessmen, professionals, and skilled workers were oriented toward acculturation into Anglo-American society. The number of Mexican-American high school and college students increased substantially. Mexican-Americans continued moving in large numbers from the rural areas of the Southwest to the urban centers of the Midwest, the Rocky Mountains, the Southwest, and the Pacific Coast. Massive numbers of legal and illegal immigrants continued to cross the United States-Mexico border. In general, the Mexican-Americans were quietly digesting the substantial progress of the post-war period.

This peace, however, was not fated to last into the 1960s. As yet, few scholars have attempted to make any systematic analysis of the fundamental causes of the unrest of these years or of the movements that arose to direct it. Although specific factors varied from area to area, certain factors were present in the entire region. Among them were: (1) the influence of the Negro Civil Rights Movement, (2) the political activities of the Kennedys, (3) the programs of President Johnson's War Against Poverty, and (4) the appearance of two charismatic Mexican-American leaders, César Chávez and Reies López Tijerina.

The rise of the black Civil Rights Movement in its protean forms—nonviolent freedom rides, sit-ins, court cases, protest demonstrations, the intervention of the federal government, and urban rioting—caught the interest of Mexican-Americans throughout the Southwest. The spread of television and radio throughout the region after World War II brought the events of "The Movement" into Mexican-American homes. From my own observations, most Mexican-Americans at first were not especially sympathetic toward the blacks. But as they became more familiar with such dynamic black leaders as Martin Luther King, as they learned about the conditions of segregation, discrimination, and poverty against which the blacks were struggling, they became more sympathetic. They were especially impressed by the favorable intervention of the federal government and the outpouring of cash into black communities. Many Mexican-Americans began to take a new look at the conditions in which large numbers of their own people were living in the Southwest—conditions not very different from those in which the blacks were caught—and soon came to the conclusion that they also had just grievances and unmet needs. The many ways in which the black Civil Rights Movement influenced the Mexican-Americans is another chapter to be researched and written.

The entrance of the Kennedys into the Southwest in the late 1950s awakened many Mexican-Americans. Snubbed by the conservative Democratic politicos in the Southwest, the Kennedys put together alternative organizations made up of minority groups, liberals, union members, and other "outs." The Kennedy coalition went to work to register voters, get out the vote, and conduct campaigns among groups largely excluded from the policy-making Democratic and Republican party machinery. The rapport between the Kennedys and the Mexican-Americans was love at first sight. "Viva Kennedy" clubs sprouted like mushrooms throughout the Mexican-American Southwest.

The Viva Kennedy clubs attracted a broad following: the old line Mexican-American politicians, smarting over their limited admission into inner Democratic party circles; ambitious young professionals and small businessmen scenting power and political positions; eager Mexican-American youth from colleges, high schools, the barrios, and rural villages attracted by the hope that Kennedy stirred among them; and, finally, those Mexican-Americans attracted by the Kennedy charisma. Kennedy organizers provided funds to finance political activities; they offered technical assistance in registering voters, getting out the vote, organizing neighborhoods, and conducting political campaigns. The Kennedy operation was a school in which large numbers of Mexican-Americans learned the know-how of politics.

A deep personal friendship sprang up between John Kennedy, his brother Robert, and many Mexican-American leaders such as César Chávez. The Kennedys, long after the assassination of John Kennedy, continued to provide technical assistance and funds in a very quiet manner to Mexican-American leaders. The Kennedys were also a liaison with sympathetic liberal and labor people across the country.

The antipoverty programs sponsored by the Kennedy and Johnson administrations were heralded with the blare of trumpets. Mexican-Americans believed that both Kennedy and Johnson were making good on their promises to eliminate poverty and discrimination if the Mexican-Americans voted for them, which they did en masse. News of these programs and their goals penetrated almost every section of the Southwest. For the first time in their lives, Mexican-Americans came truly to believe that the federal government was interested in their welfare. The old cynicism and apathy toward government vanished. Mexican-Americans responded enthusiastically. Mexican-Americans were drawn into program design, proposal writing, program funding, and administration. These programs sponsored by the Equal Employment Opportunity Commission were also a school in which thousands of Mexican-Americans enrolled. Through on-the-job experience, agency training, and assistance from regional representatives of the Office of Economic Opportunity (OEO), they learned how to organize a neighborhood, how to get to the root of a problem, how Anglo-Americans operate, how their community was structured. They learned the role of Washington in the lives of their own people; the art of negotiating, mediating, confronting, and maneuvering with government agencies and private organizations. Whatever cultural and social isolation may have existed in the Southwest was torn to tatters by the antipoverty programs.

Although these programs did not eliminate mass poverty, they did assist thousands of Mexican-Americans to move out of poverty. They provided employment for additional thousands of Mexican-Americans. Many among the latter moved up through these programs to become program directors. If they were successful directors, they were often pulled into regional and national OEO offices where they secured an advanced training in organizing, national politics, and the diverse roles of local governments. Traveling widely, they came to know conditions among Mexican-Americans throughout the United States and made contacts with local Mexican-American leaders. Many of them moved upward to important positions in permanent government departments and agencies. While a number abandoned government service for corporation employment, many organized their own successful consulting firms. On the other hand, a good many, becoming disillusioned with antipoverty programs that did not seem to eliminate poverty, returned to their own neighborhoods to create locally based organizations designed to change the status quo. By the late 1960s, few urban Mexican-American neighborhoods or rural villages were without well-trained, committed organizers drawn from the antipoverty programs.

In the late 1960s, many of these disillusioned former antipoverty workers began to challenge Anglo-American dominance. During the 1940s and 1950s, Mexican-Americans running for political office on both Democratic and Republican tickets were usually pitted against one another on the ballot. Seldom did they run against an Anglo-American. Except in New Mexico, most Mexican-American political candidates were slotted into political positions that carried little real power. By the late 1960s, however, this pattern began to break down. Mexican-Americans began to run for any and all positions in both the Democratic and Republican primaries. As they gained political experience, they began to win elections against Anglo-American candidates. The ancient ethnic arrangements began to disintegrate.

This breakdown was accelerated by the rise of two charismatic, although quite different, Mexican-American regional leaders: César Chávez[56] in California, and Reies López Tijerina[57] in New Mexico. These were among the first Mexican-American leaders to organize statewide or regional organizations, to present serious, systematically sustained challenges to Anglo rule, to capture the attention of young Mexican-Americans, and to secure the rather unwilling, suspicious attention of government agencies.

César Chávez, perhaps the best known and most acceptable Mexican-American leader to Anglo-Americans because of his nonviolent philosophy, has still not managed to organize more than a fraction of the Mexican-American migrant workers, even in California. Reies López Tijerina was not able to secure the return of any of the Mexican and Spanish land grants to the village people, the goal of his "Alianza." Instead, he went to jail. Yet, both men have had a most profound impact on Mexican-Americans in the Southwest. They captured the attention and devotion of the area's youth, spread the leaven of protest and helped to organize multitudinous protests, provided a voice for Mexican-American aspirations, and completely changed the intellectual and emotional environments prevailing in the Mexican-American rural villages and barrios.

It would be interesting to know, from a scholarly standpoint, why the first successful Mexican-American protest organizations, the National Farmers' Union organized by César Chávez in California, and the "Alianza Federal de las Mercedes" (the Federal Alliance of Land Grants) organized by Reies López Tijerina in New Mexico, arose among the most culturally isolated, and the most impoverished elements among Mexican-Americans: the rural migrants in California and the rural villagers of northern New Mexico. Why did not these organizations first arise in the cities, on the campuses, in industrial plants, or urban slums?

Perhaps motivated in part by the example of the migrants in California and the rural villages in northern New Mexico, Mexican-American high school students in 1968 began a series of strikes that started in California and then flickered across the entire Southwest.[58] Most of the striking students were from poorer urban neighborhoods.

The protest was directed against punishment for speaking Spanish on school grounds; against prejudiced Anglo teachers, counselors, and principals; against lack of Mexican-American school personnel; against antiquated buildings and inadequate educational equipment; but most of all, against the use of schools to anglicize Mexican students. The student strikers demanded the use of Spanish as an instructional tool; more Mexican-American teachers, counselors, and principals; curriculum units in Mexican and Mexican-American history and culture; and discharge of prejudiced teachers.

In Los Angeles the student strikes drew the concentrated wrath of Los Angeles law enforcement agencies, the most hated, except for the Texas Rangers, in the entire Mexican-American world. The strikes led to the organization of the Brown Berets and similar student organizations, patterned after the Black Panthers. The student strikes divided the Mexican-American neighborhoods into the middle class on the one hand, who in general opposed the strikers, and the poorer groups on the other, who, while not fully understanding the issues, supported the student strikers. Most Mexican-American political and social organizations, however, did provide support to the students. The brutality of the police in Los Angeles shocked all segments of Mexican-American society and radicalized many in all social classes.

Mexican-American college students did not participate in militant movements until almost the end of the 1960s. Coming from the middle class, they above all desired admission to the on-going system.

However, the rapid expansion of drug addiction among many Anglo students; the rise of hippie and radical student movements; the change in hair styles, dress, and personal behavior; the growing sexual freedom among them and their sharp attacks on American society caused a strong moral revulsion among both Mexican-American students and their parents. Throughout the entire Southwest, Mexican-American students and members of the middle class began to question the values of Anglo-American culture. The strong persistent drive toward acculturation and assimilation weakened as students and other Mexican-American groupings began to reevaluate their own social systems and values and came to the conclusion that they might well be superior to those of the Anglo-Americans. At any rate, the assumed moral and cultural superiority of the Anglo-American over the Mexican-American culture was shaken by behavior patterns of young middle-class Anglo-Americans.

Today, almost every American university with more than a dozen Mexican-American students possesses one or more Mexican-American student organizations. The names, organizational structure, goals, membership, and leaders of these organizations change with amazing rapidity. This fluidity reflects: a) the changing class composition of the Mexican-American student body with more and more coming from low-income levels; b) the accelerated evolution of the role played by student organizations on campus and in the Mexican-American community; c) the emerging position of the Mexican-American community in the United States; d) agitation among students by off-campus militant organizations; e) the lightning-like exchange of ideas and personnel between one campus and the other; and f) the interaction with black and radical Anglo student organizations. In general, Mexican-American students, except for some California groups, have avoided involvement with non–Mexican-American militants. Mexican-Americans prefer to do their own "thing." On some California campuses, Mexican-American students have joined black, Asian, and radical Anglo-American students in "Third World" movements of undefined ideology that tend to be vaguely antiwhite, anti-American, anticapitalistic, and left wing.

Out of the student movements in the late 1960s emerged the commonly called "Chicano" movement.[59] The word Chicano has been used in the border regions for a long time. Originally, it was employed in a contemptuous way to refer to a person of the lower class: a poor, uneducated, illiterate, ragged, and often badly behaved individual of questionable morals. Some Mexican-American students from lower-income neighborhoods turned the term around to make a proud affirmation of identity. Anglo-Americans have picked the word up without realizing its original meaning and have used it to refer generally to all Mexican-Americans, unaware that the term is still quite offensive to many of them.

As used by students and young people in the barrios, the term refers to an individual committed to the Chicano movement. The Chicano movement has many subtle connotations from place to place. In general, the term refers to the physical and spiritual liberation of the Mexican-American people from poverty, welfare, unemployment, a self-image of inferiority, and Anglo-American dominance. It includes both of the concepts defined by the slogans "Black Power" and "Black Is Beautiful." The term carries with it a fierce pride in being Chicano, living with Chicanos, and maintaining Chicano culture. Chicano "culture" usually refers to the poor barrios and often excludes the more acculturated Mexican-American middle class who have compromised with Anglo-American society. Whatever is called Chicano is acceptable; what is non-Chicano is to be rejected.

As one might expect, many gray areas exist. For example, in much of the Southwest, a person who does not speak the local barrio Spanish or a similar dialect is not Chicano. In those areas of the West and Midwest where the young no longer speak Spanish, they still consider themselves to be Chicanos although feeling guilty about not being able to speak Spanish.

The spiritual home of the Chicanos is "Aztlán," a Nahuatl term that refers to the homeland of their earliest ancestors. Aztlan was the Aztec term for the mythological land of their origin. Chicanos believe that the American Southwest was the Aztlan of the Aztecs—the spiritual and physical turf of the Chicanos.

Recent Politics

To many Mexican-Americans, Crystal City is their Bunker Hill. It was in Crystal City, the spinach-growing center of Texas, populated by low-income Mexican-Americans dominated by an Anglo elite, that one of the most decisive actions took place in the Mexican-American movement. In two 1960 elections, Mexican-Americans in Crystal City outvoted Anglo-Americans to take over the town and school district. The victory was won despite constant harassment by the county sheriff, his deputies, and the Texas Rangers. Before these elections, there were no Mexican-Americans in any governing agency. Since then, municipal services to Mexican-American neighborhoods have been improved. The school system has abandoned punishment of students for speaking Spanish, hired Mexican-American school personnel, developed a curriculum specially directed to the educational needs of Mexican-American children, and experimented with using Spanish as a teaching language. In essence, this was the first successful Mexican-American uprising in the Southwest since the coming of the Anglo-Americans.[60]

The events at Crystal City electrified the entire Mexican-American population of Texas and traumatized the Anglo-American elites. It was hard for both groups to realize that an organization of poor, unskilled workers had actually dared to challenge the existing political system and that they had even managed to defeat and dethrone a dominant Anglo-American political organization.

Following Crystal City, the old superordinate-subordinate system of Anglo-American dominance in south Texas has been challenged. In many sections of Texas where a majority of the population is Mexican-American, political groupings have been organized, winning elections against the old machines. The consequent prospects are that the dominant political element in south Texas will be Mexican-American within a generation. This does not mean, however, that Anglo-American dominance is ended.

Anglo-American landowners, businessmen, and professionals still control the economy of Texas. Many Anglo-American landowners and businessmen are grooming compliant Mexican-American politicians and candidates—simultaneously trying to buy off some present leaders or to intimidate others. Anglo-American landowners and politicians have successfully defeated an attempt by César Chávez to organize migrant workers in Texas. Furthermore, it is likely that differences among various Mexican-American classes and ideologies will surface, with Mexican-American workers battling Mexican-American sheriffs, deputies, and county courts. Yet Crystal City still signifies the power of the Mexican-Americans at the grass roots of politics in south Texas.

Shortly after Crystal City illuminated the potential of the Mexican-American vote, ambitious Mexican-Americans began to organize throughout south Texas a party called "La Raza Unida." The strategy was simple: in areas where Mexican-Americans predominated, they would enter their own candidates in elections. In other regions where Mexican-Americans composed a substantial element in the population, they would run their own candidates where they could, but would support either the local Democratic or Republican party that would run the greatest number of Mexican-American candidates and advocate programs to improve socioeconomic conditions.

La Raza Unida parties have come into existence in Colorado, New Mexico, California, and other states in the West. In states such as California and New Mexico where Mexican-Americans have been quite active in politics, a political struggle is developing between La Raza Unida, usually a bit more militant than the older political groupings, and Mexican-Americans active in the two major political parties. Whatever happens with La Raza Unida, Mexican-Americans will play a far more important role in the political life of the Southwest (and ultimately other regions) than they have before.

In the past, Mexican-American political groupings have formed temporary political alliances with black and liberal Anglo-American political organizations in Texas, California, Utah, and elsewhere. These alliances have been effective in specific elections, but inevitably they have not lasted because of conflicts over issues and candidates. It would be a mistake to assume that tensions do not now exist between Mexican-Americans and blacks. They do, and they may well reach serious proportions in California as Mexican-Americans perfect their own organizations. In New Mexico and Arizona, it is quite possible that tensions and conflicts may also develop between Mexican-Americans and American Indians. (Some Indian leaders have already facetiously asked what role the Southwestern Indian would have in the Chicano Aztlán.)

The most recent of the significant historical events involving Mexican-Americans in the United States is the Los Angeles riots of the early 1970s. These were the first urban upheavals to involve Mexican-Americans. The initial riot took place in the fall of 1970, followed by the second within a few months.

Representatives from the majority of Mexican-American communities across the United States had gathered in Los Angeles in the fall of 1970 to protest the disproportionately high rates at which Mexican-Americans were drafted into the army and killed or wounded in Vietnam. Representatives from almost every major Mexican-American organization in the United States who came to march, fraternize, and discuss found themselves charged, beaten, and jailed by members of the Los Angeles sheriff's department. Stories of the encounter were carried back into almost every Mexican-American community in the country. The resulting wave of indignation was heightened by the senseless, brutal murder by deputies of Ruben Salazar, perhaps the most prominent Mexican-American journalist in the United States. Salazar was not even at the scene of the riot at the time of his assassination. His death caused a noticeable shift of support among middle-class Mexican-Americans toward acceptance of more militant tactics and leaders. In Los Angeles, these police tactics drove a deep wedge between the low-income Mexican-American neighborhoods of Los Angeles and many government agencies.

At the present time, Mexican-American communities throughout the United States are in ferment. The intensity and form of the ferment vary from one section to another. New ideas, forces, and expectations are challenging old accommodations. Anglo domination is challenged wherever Mexican-Americans are strong enough to do so. The longing for acculturation and assimilation of Mexican-Americans into Anglo-American society has lost its lure. The melting pot is being replaced by cultural pluralism. Mexican-Americans in the Southwest are demanding that their language be given equality with English and their values equality with Anglo standards. In areas where Mexican-Americans are a majority, they are fighting for political dominance and a greater share of the economic pie. In areas where they are the minority, they want a proportionate share of the good things of life. Sporadically, violence has broken out in Texas, New Mexico, and California. The Mexican-Americans are no longer a "quiet, forgotten minority." Once more, the ancient Southwest is the arena for clashing cultures.

At such a moment, a society that seeks to maintain its integrity must have an understanding of the peoples involved in the conflict. A first step in such a mission should be a rediscovery of the lost episodes in the life of the Mexican-American people—the history that makes them what they are today. In their past lies the key to an understanding of their potential for the future.

NOTES

1. Leonard Pitt, *The Decline of the Californios* (Berkeley and Los Angeles: University of California Press, 1971).

2. For fairly comprehensive listings of studies on the Mexican-Americans, see Ralph Guzman, *Revised Bibliography,* Mexican-American Study Project, Division of Research, Graduate School of Business Administration (Los Angeles: University of California, 1967); and Ernie Barrios, Bibliografía de Aztlán: An Annotated Chicano Bibliography (San Diego: Centro de Estudios Chicanos, 1971).

3. Among Mexican-American scholars who are publishing today are: Ernesto Galarza, Julian Samora, Manuel P. Servín, Tomas Atencio, Rudolph Gomez, Julian Nava, Ralph Guzman, Felicio Rivera, Y. Arturo Cabrera, Octavio I. Romano, Fernando Penalosa, Armando B. Rendon.

4. Clark S. Knowlton, "Culture Conflict and Natural Resources," in William R. Burch, Jr., Neil H. Cheek, Jr., and Lee Taylor, eds., *Social Behavior, Natural Resources and the Environment* (New York: Harper & Row, 1972), pp. 109–45.

5. Edward Simmen, ed., *The Chicano: From Caricature to Self-Portrait* (New York: New American Library, 1971), pp. 15–26.

6. Arthur J. Rubel, *Across the Tracks* (Austin: University of Texas Press, 1966), p. 140.

7. Margaret Mead, *Cultural Patterns and Technical Change* (New York: The New American Library, 1955), pp. 151–77.

8. Carey McWilliams, *North from Mexico* (New York: Greenwood Press, 1968); Leo Grebler, Joan W. Moore, and Ralph C. Guzman, *The Mexican-American People* (New York: The Free Press, 1970).

9. D. W. Meinig, *Imperial Texas: An Interpretive Essay in Cultural Geography* (Austin: University of Texas Press, 1969).

10. McWilliams, *North from Mexico,* pp. 19–114; Richard L. Nostrand, "The Hispanic-American Borderland: Delimitation of an American Culture Region," *Annals of the Association of American Geographers* 60 (December 1970):639–61; Lynn I. Perrigo, *Texas and Our Spanish Southwest* (Dallas: Banks Upshaw & Co., 1960), pp. 15–95; Odie Faulk, *Land of Many Frontiers* (New York: Oxford University Press, 1968), pp. 5–125.

11. Edward H. Spicer, *Cycles of Conquest* (Tucson: The University of Arizona Press, 1962), pp. 187–209.

12. Charles I. Kenner, *A History of New Mexican-Plains Indians Relations* (Norman: University of Oklahoma Press, 1969); Jack D. Forbes, *Apache, Navajo, and Spaniard* (Norman: University of Oklahoma Press, 1960).

13. Clark S. Knowlton, "The Spanish Americans in New Mexico," *Sociology and Social Research* 45, No. 4 (July 1964); idem, "One Approach to the Economic and Social Problems of Northern New Mexico," *The New Mexico Business Review* 17 (Sept. 1964); Nancie L. González, *The Spanish Americans of New Mexico* (Albuquerque: University of New Mexico Press, 1969); John H. Burma, *Spanish-Speaking Groups in the United States* (Durham, N.C.: Duke University Press, 1954), pp. 3–34.

14. Knowlton, "The Spanish Americans in New Mexico"; idem, "One Approach to the Economic and Social Problems."

15. Fabiola Cabeza de Baca, *We Fed Them Cactus* (Albuquerque: University of New Mexico Press, 1954), pp. 72–75; William A. Keleher, *The Fabulous Frontier* (Albuquerque: University of New Mexico Press, 1962), pp. 83–96; J. Evetts Haley, *Charles Goodnight* (Norman: University of Oklahoma Press, 1949), pp. 217–89; Wayne Gard, "Rivals for Grass," *Southwest Review* 33 (Summer 1948):266–73.

16. Burma, *Spanish-Speaking Groups;* McWilliams, *North from Mexico*, pp. 63–80; Clark S. Knowlton, "Area Development and Planning in New Mexico: Implications for Dependency and for Economic and Social Growth," New Mexico Conference on Social Welfare (1961–62).

17. Olen E. Leonard, *The Role of the Land Grant in the Social Processes of a Spanish American Village* (Albuquerque, N.M.: Calvin Horn Publisher, Inc., 1970); J. J. Bowden, *Spanish and Mexican Land Grants in the Chihuahuan Acquisition* (El Paso, Texas: Texas Western Press, 1971); Clark S. Knowlton, "The Land Question in New Mexico," Committee on Rural Development, House of Representatives, 90th Congress, 1st Session, *Effect of Federal Programs on Rural America* (Washington, D.C.: U.S. Government Printing Office, 1967).

18. Hugh G. Calkins, *Tewa Basin Study,* vol. 2, *The Spanish American Villages,* Soil Conservation Series (Albuquerque, N.M.: U.S. Department of Agriculture, 1935); idem, *Federal Relief Expenditures for Labor in Three Sub-Areas of the Upper Rio Grande Watershed During 1935–1936* (Regional Bulletin No. 41, Albuquerque, N.M.: U.S. Department of Agriculture, 1937); idem, *Village Livelihood in the Upper Rio Grande Area and a Note on the Level of Village Livelihood in the Upper Rio Grande Area* (Regional Bulletin No. 44, Albuquerque, N.M.: U.S. Department of Agriculture, 1937); Soil Conservation Series, George I. Sanchez, *Forgotten People* (Albuquerque, N.M.: Calvin Horn Publisher, Inc., 1967); Charles P. Loomis and Olen E. Leonard, *Culture of a Contemporary Rural Community* (Washington, D.C.: Bureau of Agricultural Economics, U.S. Department of Agriculture, 1941; Leonard, *The Role of the Land Grant;* Sanford M. Mosk, "Influence of Tradition on Agriculture in New Mexico," *Papers Presented at the Second Annual Meeting of the Economic History Association,* Williamstown, Mass., Sept. 4–5, 1942; Ernest E. Maes, "The World and the People of Cundiyo," *Land Policy Review* 4 (March 1941):8–14.

19. Frances L. Swadesh, "Hispanic American of the Ute Frontier from the Chamas Valley to the San Juan Basin, 1694–1960," (Ph.D. diss., University of Colorado, 1966); González, *The Spanish Americans of New Mexico.*

20. Howard R. Lamar, *The Far Southwest, 1846–1912* (New Haven: Yale University Press, 1966), pp. 65–70.

21. William J. Parrish, *The Charles Ilfeld Company* (Cambridge: Harvard University Press, 1961), pp. 150–57.

22. Lamar, *The Far Southwest*, pp. 136–70, 185–98.

23. Calkins, "Federal Relief Expenditures"; idem, "Village Livelihood."

24. Allan G. Harper, Andrew R. Cordova, and Kalervo Oberg, *Man and Resources in the Middle Rio Grande Valley* (Albuquerque: University of New Mexico Press, 1943); Hugh G. Calkins, *Reconnaissance Survey of Human Dependency on Resources in the Rio Grande Watershed*, Soil Conservation Series (Albuquerque, N.M.: U.S. Department of Agriculture, 1935); idem, "Federal Relief Expenditures"; idem, "Village Livelihood"; Knowlton, "The Land Question in New Mexico."

25. *Albuquerque Journal*, Nov. 9, 1967.

26. Knowlton, "The Spanish Americans in New Mexico"; idem, "One Approach to the Economic and Social Problems"; Thomas J. Maloney, "Recent Demographic and Economic Changes in Northern New Mexico," *New Mexico Business* 17 (Sept. 1964).

27. Knowlton, "Culture Conflict and Natural Resources," pp. 109–45.

28. Rubel, *Across the Tracks*, pp. 29–51; McWilliams, *North From Mexico*, pp. 98–114.

29. Meinig, *Imperial Texas*, pp. 28–37; David Lavender, "The Mexican War: Climax of Manifest Destiny," in Stephen B. Oates, ed., *The Republic of Texas* (Palo Alto, Calif.: American West Publishing Co., 1968), pp. 32–57; Rupert N. Richardson, Ernest Wallace, Adrian N. Anderson, *Texas, the Lone Star State* (Englewood Cliffs, N.J.: Prentice Hall, 1970), pp. 47–66.

30. Cecil Robinson, "Flag of Illusion" in Oates, ed., *The Republic of Texas*, pp. 10–17; Richardson et al., *Texas, the Lone Star State*, pp. 69–84.

31. Walter Lord, "Myths and Realities of the Alamo," in Oates, ed., *The Republic of Texas*, p. 20.

32. Ibid., pp. 51–64.

33. Will Hale, *Twenty-Four Years a Cowboy and Ranchman in Southern Texas and Old Mexico* (Norman: University of Oklahoma Press, 1959), p. 137.

34. John H. Culley, *Cattle, Horses, and Men* (Los Angeles: The Ward Ritchie Press, 1940), p. 103.

35. Warren A. Beck, *New Mexico: A History of Four Centuries* (Norman: University of Oklahoma Press, 1962), pp. 140–44.

36. Martin H. Hall, *Sibley's New Mexico Campaign* (Austin: University of Texas Press, 1960), pp. 57–65, 68–99, 102–3.

37. Clarence C. Clendenen, *Blood on the Border* (New York: The MacMillan Co., 1969); Charles C. Cumberland, "Border Raids in the Lower Rio Grande Valley—1915," *Southwestern Historical Quarterly* 57 (July 1953–April 1954); Charles W. Goldfinch, "Juan N. Cortina, 1824–1892: A Re-Appraisal" (M.A. Thesis, University of Chicago, 1949).

38. José T. Canales, *Juan N. Cortina Presents His Motion for a New Trial* (San Antonio, Texas: Artes Gráficas, 1951); William A. Hager, "The Plan of San Diego: Unrest on the Texas Frontier in 1915," *Arizona and the West* 5 (Winter 1963).

39. Américo Paredes, *With His Pistol in His Hand* (Austin: University of Texas Press, 1958).

40. Allen Gerlach, "Conditions Along the Border—1915: The Plan de San Diego," *New Mexico Historical Review* 43, No. 3 (July 1968):195–212.

41. Rubel, *Across the Tracks*, pp. 25–40.

42. Ibid., pp. 41–46.

43. Meinig, *Imperial Texas*, pp. 54–57, 83–84; Rubel, *Across the Tracks*, pp. 46–51.

44. Clark S. Knowlton, "Violence in New Mexico: A Sociological Perspective," *California Law Review* 58, No. 5 (October 1970):1054–84.

45. Spicer, *Cycles of Conquest*, pp. 152–275.

46. Nelle Spilsbury Hatch, *Colonia Juarez* (Salt Lake City: Deseret Book Co., 1954); Thomas C. Romney, *The Mormon Colonies in Mexico* (Salt Lake City: Deseret Book Co., 1938).

47. Calvin W. Redekop, *The Old Colony Mennonites* (Baltimore: The Johns Hopkins University Press, 1969).

48. Goldfinch, "Juan N. Cortina"; Paredes, *With His Pistol in His Hand.*

49. Knowlton, "The Spanish Americans in New Mexico," pp. 3, 15–22.

50. William Madsen, *The Mexican Americans of South Texas* (New York: Holt, Rinehart and Winston, 1964), pp. 355–61.

51. Paul M. Sheldon, "Community Participation and the Emerging Middle Class," in Julian Samora, ed., *La Raza: Forgotten Americans* (Notre Dame, Ind.: University of Notre Dame Press, 1966), pp. 125–57; Madsen, *The Mexican Americans of South Texas,* pp. 35–43.

52. Thomas P. Carter, *Mexican Americans in School: A History of Educational Neglect* (New York: College Entrance Examination Board, 1970), pp. 35–63.

53. Knowlton, "Violence in New Mexico," pp. 1054–84; González, *The Spanish Americans of New Mexico,* pp. 116–35; Calkins, *Tewa Basin Study.*

54. *Migrant and Seasonal Farm Workers' Powerlessness,* Parts 1–7, Hearings of U.S Senate Committee on Labor and Public Welfare (Washington, D.C.: U.S. Government Printing Office, 1970); Rev. William E. Scholes, "The Migrant Worker," in Samora, ed., *La Raza,* pp. 63–94.

55. Walter Fogel, *Mexican Americans in Southwest Labor Markets* (Los Angeles: Mexican-American Study Project, Advance Report 10, Division of Research, Graduate School of Business Administration, University of California, 1967).

56. Steve Nelson, *Huelga: The First Hundred Days of the Great Delano Grape Strike* (Delano, Calif.: Farm Worker Press, 1966); John Gregory Dunne, *Delano: The Story of the California Grape Strike* (New York: Farrar, Strauss and Giroux, 1967).

57. Clark S. Knowlton, "Tijerina, Hero of the Militants," *Texas Observer* 61, No. 6 (March 28, 1969); Richard Gardner, *El Grito* (New York: The Bobbs-Merrill Co., 1970); Peter Nabokov, *Tijerina and the Courthouse Raid* (Albuquerque: University of New Mexico Press, 1969).

58. Rona M. Fields and Charles J. Fox, "Brown Berets," *The Black Politician* 3 (July 1971): 53–63.

59. Abelardo Delgado, "The Chicano Movement: Some Not Too Objective Observations," unpublished manuscript, 1970.

60. John Shockley, "Crystal City, Texas: Los Cinco Mexicanos," unpublished article, 1972; idem, "Crystal City—La Raza Unida," unpublished article, 1972.

3

Mexican Immigration

JULIAN SAMORA

Dr. Samora is Professor of Sociology at the University of Notre Dame.
Among the many works he has authored on Mexican-Americans and
Mexican immigrants are *La Raza: Forgotten Americans* and *Los Mojados:
The Wetback Story.* He has also been a consultant to various government
commissions and private foundations including the U.S. Commission on
Civil Rights, Ford Foundation, and National Endowment for the Human-
ities. Dr. Samora is a native of Pagosa Springs, Colorado.

It is a truism to say that the United States is a nation of
immigrants, yet of all the people who have contributed to its
development, few have contributed more and received so little in
return as the Chicanos. This essay will be concerned with the
development of the Chicano population through immigration as
well as the use and abuse of Mexicans in the cheap labor market.

Most immigrants to this country are here because of the social,
political, religious, or economic conditions in their native country
that compelled them to leave, the attraction of opportunities for a
better life or, as in the case of the blacks, pure coercion. For most
immigrants, leaving their country meant a long journey (with the
exception of Cubans and Canadians) and physical separation by a
body of water. Visiting their home country even once has generally
been financially prohibitive and often politically undesirable. Most
immigrants have therefore been unable to maintain strong ties with
the mother country. Those who were pushed out of their homeland
or who came in search of opportunity and a better life more often
than not arrived with an assimilative resolution to become

This paper draws heavily from the following sources: Gilbert Cardenas, "Mexican
Immigration: An Historical Overview" (unpublished paper, 1970); Julian Samora and Jorge
A. Bustamante, "Mexican Immigration and American Labor Demands," a paper presented
at the Center for Migration Studies, Brooklyn College, March 13–14, 1970, and later
reproduced in: The Senate Committee on Labor and Public Welfare, 1969–70, *Migrant and
Seasonal Farmworker Powerlessness,* Hearings before the Subcommittee on Migratory Labor
of the Committee of Labor and Public Welfare, April 15, 1970; and Samora, "Mexican
Immigrants and the Chicano Community," a paper presented at the National Conference on
Bilingual Education, Texas Education Agency, April 14, 1972.

"Americans" or at least to adapt or accommodate socially and culturally to the nation's dominant culture.

Chicanos in the United States, on the other hand, present a story quite different from other immigrants. The ancestors of the Chicanos (both Indian and Spanish) were in the Southwest before the United States was born. They lived under the flag of Spain from the early explorations of the 1500s until 1823. When the colonists of New Spain revolted from the mother country, the people of the Southwest became Mexican citizens from 1823 to 1849. Some came under the flag of the Lone Star State between 1836 and 1846. When the United States, through an unjust war, defeated Mexico and conquered the Southwest, the Mexicans in this region, through no effort or desire on their part, became American citizens in 1849.

Other factors suggest that Chicano history, as viewed from an immigration perspective, is different from that of any other group in the United States. Among these factors we can cite Mexico's proximity to the United States, which has permitted people to go back and forth between the two countries with great ease; the common history of the region; and the extremely long border between the two nations, which was entirely open up to 1924. There were also the prejudices, tensions, and hostilities which developed between the two peoples as they interacted with one another, beginning in the 1800s; and the subjugation of one nation by another, placing Mexico in a position of subordination following the conquest of its territory.

Still other factors suggest the uniqueness of this situation: the economic and political relationships which have developed between the two countries; the intertwining economy in the border region; the historical accident which placed a developing nation contiguous to one of the most economically and politically powerful nations in the world; and the imperialistic tendencies and actions of the United States as directed toward Mexico.

Immigration to the United States: An Overview

The United States has always viewed itself as welcoming people from other countries, particularly the poor, the oppressed, and the suffering. This humanitarian view has persisted off and on up to the present time. Paradoxically, when immigration policy was codified, the United States consistently discriminated against immigrants, partly based on race and partly on social and cultural characteristics. Moreover, the United States, from its early development to the present time, has constantly required a supply of cheap labor. And again paradoxically, while desiring, and inducing, and even welcoming a certain class of people to perform the cheap labor, its policies reflect that this type of person is more than welcome as a laborer, but not necessarily desirable as a resident and citizen.

One need but reflect briefly on slavery, its conditions and its consequences, to reinforce the above point. Immigration from southern Europe presents other examples. The bringing of the Chinese and their subsequent exclusion is still another example. Having excluded them, we then turned to Japan, the Philippines, and finally to Mexico as the source of cheap labor.

Before 1882, in our first immigration period, the immigrants were mainly from northern and western Europe. They and their descendants pushed the frontiers ever westward and merged rapidly into the mainstream of American society. Throughout this time there were few if any federal restrictions against immigration, and it was during the 1880s that many Chinese came here, as mentioned above.

The second period was from 1882 to 1923. Immigration from northern and western Europe declined, and the Chinese were excluded. Japanese immigration began and was later stopped. The Italians, Russians, and Poles became predominantly the "new" immigrants as the British, Irish, and Germans had been the "old" immigrants.

The third immigration period beginning in 1924 is characterized by the quota system favoring northern and western Europe; the large immigration from Western Hemisphere countries; and the admission of large numbers of political refugees in recent years.

The fourth period was initiated by the immigration law of 1965, which went into effect in 1968. During this time, the quota system by country was abolished; instead, broad quotas were established for the Western Hemisphere (120,000) and the Eastern Hemisphere, (170,000 with a 20,000 limit per country), with applicants from each country being admitted on a first-come-first-served basis. We have yet to see the implications of this last policy.

Americans have both welcomed and resented immigrants. As early as 1850, American laborers resented the competition which was provided by immigrant labor,[1] because it threatened the standard of living, the wage rates, and the employment of domestic labor.

The Irish in the 1800s were both welcomed and resented. They were considered as completely unassimilable to American society.[2] The Irish were perhaps the first to receive the scourge of discrimination from the dominant society, a discrimination which was heaped upon each successive ethnic group as they entered the United States. The usual stereotype of the immigrant, in this case the Irish, was that they were dirty, stupid, riotous, intemperate, corrupt, and immoral. This stereotype was used to describe each successive wave of immigrants to this country and is still used today. It is also interesting to note that most immigrants to this country have been discriminated against in employment and wages without regard to their capabilities.[3]

A paradox which we mentioned earlier characterizes the reaction of Americans to immigration. The doors have always been open for unskilled labor to fill unskilled occupations at low wages.[4] There has also been a demand and a necessity for labor for industrial expansion and development, yet negative reactions to these workers have been expressed in forms of prejudice and discrimination.

It must be remembered that before the 1880s, when the country was young and there was still a frontier, when urbanism was beginning and industrialization in its early stages, when the population was relatively small and the western region was in its formative years, the nation could and did absorb innumerable immigrants without much difficulty. Yet in these early years the nation became apprehensive of the type of immigrants being admitted to its shores, and one of the first immigration laws to be formalized was in 1875 in which the admission of convicts and prostitutes was prohibited. In 1882 the first general immigration statute was passed, placing a head tax of fifty cents on each immigrant, barring idiots, lunatics, convicts, and persons likely to become public charges, as well as excluding Chinese. Thus we were becoming selective and ending the open immigration policy. In 1885 we passed the first labor contract law to end the practice of importing cheap labor in large numbers, a practice that was thought to depress the labor market. (We were later to subvert that law through a departmental order of 1918 to bring in Mexican contract labor and again in 1942 for the so-called Bracero Program.)

In the 1890s we tightened our immigration laws to exclude people with loathsome or dangerous contagious diseases, persons convicted of moral turpitude, paupers, and polygamists. We also were to deport all aliens who had entered illegally. The law of 1903 excluded epileptics, insane persons, professional beggars, and anarchists. The statute of 1907 excluded the feeble-minded, those with physical and mental defects, children under sixteen without parents, and we effectively barred, through the Gentlemen's Agreement, the immigration of Japanese.

That same year, the Dillingham Commission was appointed to study immigration policy. This commission produced forty-two volumes by 1911 but no laws. But in 1917, based on the report of the above commission, we added the literacy requirement for immigrants and the automatic exclusion of immigration from Asia and the Pacific Islands. Aside from Asia there was still no numerical restriction on immigration up to this point. In 1921 we established the first quota system based on a percentage of a nation's immigrants in residence in the United States in 1910 and two years later a permanent quota system was established for each nation based on the percentage of their population in the United States in 1920. We further instituted a quota of one hundred for each Asian country. In the 1940s and 1950s the United States became concerned with subversives and otherwise potentially dangerous persons to the point of establishing annual registrations of aliens, fingerprinting of aliens, and expanding the clauses relating to deportation. The Immigration and Nationality Act of 1952 was a general codification of the previous laws; in it we sought to exclude drug addicts, people with two or more criminal offenses, and retain the quota system yet modify it in that the first 50 percent of those admitted under quota should be highly skilled and educated persons and the second 50 percent should be close relatives of the above. In 1965 we passed a general immigration act to become effective in 1968. Its main feature was to abolish the quota system by country and establish broad quotas for the Eastern and Western Hemispheres.

The immigration laws of the United States looked at in historical perspective tend to reveal our fears and our desires, our priorities and preferences, our prejudices and biases, and, most importantly, the values of the society as reflected in the types of persons who can be eligible for citizenship.

A Border without Boundaries

It is estimated that when the Southwest became part of the United States the Mexican population numbered 100,000.[5] Between 1850 and 1924 there was a continual movement of people back and forth between Mexico and the United States until the Border Patrol was established in 1924. At the turn of the century, the Mexican-derived Spanish-speaking population in the United States was estimated at 221,915.[6] It is obvious that a part of this population was made up of immigrants but presumably a larger portion consisted of those people and their descendants who were conquered in the Mexican-American War.

As the frontier was developed with the expansion of agriculture, the construction of railroads, and the establishment of industry and commerce, there was a sharp demand for labor. To the extent that the Chinese and Japanese were excluded from immigrating to the United States the supply of labor then was from southern Europe and Mexico. The latter was the source of labor for the expansion that was occurring in the Southwest. Inadequate as the statistics might be, in the 1880–90 decade, the Mexican-born population was approximately 9,500 and three decades later (1910–20), it was 266,503. (See Table 1.) Between 1900 and 1910, as the economic development of the Southwest continued, the number of Mexican immigrants increased sharply as shown in Table 1, and we find that approximately 12,000 Mexican illegal aliens were deported.

TABLE 1
Foreign-Born Population in the U.S.

	1880-1890		1890-1900		1900-1910		1910-1920	
	Number	Percent*	Number	Percent	Number	Percent	Number	Percent
Born in Asia	5,766	5.4	6,852	6.0	71,236	59.2	46,466	24.3
Born in Mexico	9,454	13.8	25,540	32.8	118,522	114.6	266,503	119.2
Total of foreign born	2,569,617	38.5	1,091,716	11.8	2,920,061	32.9	90,212	0.8

Source: U.S. Census, quoted by Carpenter, 1927:80-81.
*The increase for each decade has been based on the number of persons reported at the beginning and end of the decade.

The Mexican Revolution began in 1910, and in the years that followed it caused many Mexicans to flee to the United States, entering either legally or illegally. Mexico was definitely becoming the chief supplier of labor for the Southwest. The *Corpus Christi Herald* in 1910 was advertising "the cheapest Mexican labor that you can find" as an inducement for investors to the lower Rio Grande Valley. (Sixty years later, in 1969, the Chamber of Commerce of Tucson was advertising the availability of labor at thirty cents an hour across the border.) During this decade the United States also entered the First World War which brought great demands for labor. Thus, the Mexican Revolution, the First World War, and the curtailment of immigration from Asia produced a dramatic increase of Mexican immigration to the United States. Referring to Table 1, the foreign-born Mexican population in the United States during this decade was 266,503; approximately 28,000 Mexican illegal aliens were deported; and through a departmental order of 1918 which abrogated the Act of February 26, 1885, sometimes referred to as the alien contract labor law (which specifically prohibited the importation of alien labor under contract or agreement), 73,000 Mexican nationals were brought under contract to the United States. The laws relating to the head tax and the literacy requirements were waived for the Mexican laborers. Mexican immigration to the United States at this time was increasing at such a rapid pace that Samuel Gompers, president of the American Federation of Labor, was becoming concerned and began speaking against the importation of such labor.[7]

The decade of the 1920s showed a dramatic increase in legal immigration from Mexico, approximately 500,000, and the number of illegals asked to leave the United States rose to 164,000. (See Tables 2, 3, and 4.) The decade of the 1920s was a period of great prosperity following the First World War. Also, the Border Patrol was established in 1924, thus ending the open border and placing greater restrictions and inconvenience on entry into the United States. At the same time the immigration laws were codified and national quotas established for all countries except those of the Western Hemisphere. It was also a period of continuing demand for labor principally from Mexico since, during this decade, immigration from southern Europe was greatly restricted by the quotas. Temporary contract alien labor had been legitimized and a new category of labor from Mexico was established, namely the commuter.°

The establishment of the Border Patrol brought certain complications to the illegal status of the alien. Before the Border Patrol, most illegals who were apprehended were deported. Now a force of men was on the border to inspect persons entering the United States and, owing to a change in the law, those persons who were then caught in illegal status became felons. A new administrative procedure was also inaugurated to accelerate the expulsion of the illegal immigrant. Instead of deportation (which requires hearings and is expensive and time-consuming) the new administrative procedure was called "voluntary departure." That is, if an illegal immigrant who is apprehended does not wish to become involved with the procedure and technicalities of being deported, he can opt for voluntary departure, which means that he is invited to leave the country voluntarily and does not have to go through the legal procedure. The illegal immigrant is now a fugitive from the law and he has become known as a "wetback."

The establishment of the Border Patrol was also accompanied by the formation of many organized methods of smuggling illegals into this country for a fee. The fee in 1926, for Mexicans, was less than $18.00[8] and in 1970 it ranged as high as $300.00 if the alien wanted to reach Chicago.[9] It is also interesting to note that before 1924 salaries and working conditions were established according to the supply and demand for labor. After the establishment of the Border Patrol, illegal aliens were no longer free on the labor market because of the fear and danger of being apprehended. Since anyone (including an employer) can report an illegal alien to the immigration authorities, the alien has few options but to accept a job at whatever wage is offered or face the possibility of being turned in to the Border Patrol.

At the end of the decade, the United States entered a period of depression which had its impact on Mexican immigration in the 1930s. In those years, Mexican legal immigration dropped from the half a million of the previous decade to approximately 27,000. The

---

°The commuter is an alien who has been given an immigrant visa to work and reside in the United States. Many of these individuals desired to live in Mexico and work in the United States, contrary to the law. In the ensuing years through custom and tradition, this practice has become legitimized and we find today a category of immigrant whom we call the commuter or the "green carder."

number of illegal aliens apprehended during this period, however, increased to over 210,000. This situation perhaps reflected the economic conditions in Mexico at the time.

TABLE 2
Mexican Immigration 1869-1969

Year	Total	Year	Total	Year	Total	Year	Total
1869	320	1894	109	1919	28,844	1944	6,399
1870	463	1895	116	1920	51,042	1945	6,455
1871	402	1896	150	1921	29,603	1946	6,805
1872	569	1897	91	1922	18,246	1947	7,775
1873	606	1898	107	1923	62,709	1948	8,730
1874	386	1899	163	1924	87,648	1949	7,977
1875	610	1900	237	1925	32,378	1950	6,841
1876	631	1901	347	1926	42,638	1951	6,372
1877	445	1902	709	1927	66,766	1952	9,600
1878	465	1903	528	1928	57,765	1953	18,454
1879	556	1904	1,009	1929	38,980	1954	37,456
1880	492	1905	2,637	1930	11,915	1955	50,772
1881	325	1906	1,997	1931	2,627	1956	65,047
1882	366	1907	1,406	1932	1,674	1957	49,154
1883	469	1908	6,067	1933	1,514	1958	26,712
1884	430	1909	16,251	1934	1,470	1959	23,061
1885	323	1910	17,760	1935	1,232	1960	32,684
1886	—	1911	18,784	1936	1,308	1961	41,632
1887	—	1912	22,001	1937	1,918	1962	55,291
1888	—	1913	10,954	1938	2,014	1963	55,253
1889	—	1914	13,089	1939	2,265	1964	32,967
1890	—	1915	10,993	1940	1,914	1965	37,969
1891	—	1916	17,198	1941	2,068	1966	45,163
1892	—	1917	16,438	1942	2,182	1967	42,371
1893	—	1918	17,602	1943	3,985	1968	43,563
						1969	44,623

TOTAL   1,525,928

Sources: Period from 1869 to 1898 shows the number of immigrant aliens (Mexican) admitted by country of origin or nationality taken from International Migration Statistics, Vol. I (No. 14), a publication of the National Bureau of Economic Research, Inc., 1929, pp. 384-93. (1886-1893, information not available.)
Period from 1899 to 1909 shows the number of immigrant aliens (Mexican) admitted by race of people (International Migration Statistics, 1929:432-43).
Period from 1910 to 1964 shows the number of Mexican immigrants admitted (Grebler, 1966:106).
Figures from 1965 to 1968 taken from the 1968 Annual Report of the Immigration and Naturalization Service, p. 61.
Figure for 1969 taken from the 1969 Annual Report of the Immigration and Naturalization Service, p. 63.

TABLE 3
Apprehensions of Illegal Immigrants
by the Border Patrol

Period	Apprehensions	Deportations	Voluntary Departures	Total
1892-1900	--------	1,327	-----------	1,327
1901-1910	--------	11,558	-----------	11,558
1911-1920	--------	27,912	-----------	27,912
1921-1930	128,484	92,157	72,233	164,390
1931-1940	147,457	117,086	93,330	210,416

Source: 1966 Annual Report of the United States Immigration and Naturalization Service.

What was more important, however, was that most communities in the United States that had any sizable number of legal Mexican residents began systematically to repatriate them back to Mexico. The arguments presented for repatriation usually stated that it was far cheaper to return these legal aliens to Mexico than it was to support them on welfare since so many other people were also on the rolls. Such a policy produced tremendous hardships for most of the families of Mexican nationals. Many Mexicans, who had been in this country legally for a number of years, had married American citizens and established families. If the individual had not yet obtained his naturalization papers and become an American citizen, he was then subject to repatriation. This practice broke up many a family where one or another member was a Mexican national and the rest were American citizens. It is reported that in the first four years of the 1930s, well over three hundred thousand persons were repatriated to Mexico.[10]

In the 1940s Mexican legal immigration began very slowly (1,914 in 1940) and increased gradually during the decade. Over fifty thousand Mexicans legally entered the United States during this period. The depression was over and the United States was entering a period of prosperity spurred by the Second World War. Although the United States did not enter the war until 1941, it was a supplier of arms and ammunition and other materials previous to its becoming a belligerent. A large portion of the male labor force was either drafted into the armed services or occupied in defense industries. As a result of a labor shortage that was said to exist, the United States entered into an agreement with Mexico in 1942, permitting the importation of temporary agricultural contract labor during the period of the emergency. The bilateral agreement

TABLE 4
Mexican Illegal Aliens Reported*

Year	Total	Year	Total	Year	Total
1924	4,614	1941	6,082	1958	37,242
1925	2,961	1942	DNA	1959	30,196
1926	4,047	1943	8,189	1960	29,651
1927	4,495	1944	26,689	1961	29,817
1928	5,529	1945	63,602	1962	30,272
1929	8,538	1946	91,456	1963	39,124
1930	18,319	1947	182,986	1964	43,844
1931	8,409	1948	179,385	1965	55,349
1932	7,116	1949	278,538	1966	89,751
1933	15,865	1950	458,215	1967	108,327
1934	8,910	1951	500,000	1968	151,000
1935	9,139	1952	543,538	1969	201,000
1936	9,534	1953	865,318	1970	277,377
1937	9,535	1954	1,075,168	1971	348,178
1938	8,684	1955	242,608	1972	430,213
1939	9,376	1956	72,442	1973	577,000
1940	8,051	1957	44,451		
				TOTAL	7,260,130

Sources: From 1924 to 1941: Annual Report of the Secretary of Labor. From 1942 to 1960: Special compilation of the Immigration and Naturalization Service reported to us. From 1961 to 1973: Annual Report of the Immigration and Naturalization Service.

*The Immigration and Naturalization Service was part of the Department of Labor until 1941. Since then it has been within the Department of Justice. Over the years a variety of categories has been used to report Mexican illegal aliens, with some inconsistency. This table then reflects these inconsistencies. Aliens deported is a category that is consistently used for reporting Mexican illegal aliens, but does not include all Mexican illegal aliens apprehended. It refers to those aliens forcefully expelled from the United States under warrant procedures. Mention is made of illegal entrants who are not allowed to remain in the United States. These are reported as departing without the benefit of deportation warrant procedures after having manifested their willingness to depart. The following categories have been used: *Aliens debarred* from entry (Annual Report of the Commissioner-General of Immigration, 1924:12-13;125-29). *Voluntary removals* (Annual Report of the Secretary of Labor, 1931:53-55). *Voluntary departures* (Annual Report of the Secretary of Labor, 1932:73). *Forced departures* without deportation warrant (Annual Report of the Secretary of Labor, 1939:97;1940:110). *Required departures* (Annual Report of the Secretary of Labor, 1940:110). No data were available for 1942. The figures for 1943-60 were given to us by the Immigration and Naturalization Service under Mexican Illegal Aliens Apprehended (this includes deportations and voluntary departures). The figures for 1961-72 are taken from the Annual Reports of those years under the category: Deportable Aliens Found and/or Located. Even within the same report there are inconsistencies in the figures. In 1963, for example, on the same page, two figures are presented for Deportable Mexican Aliens; one is 38,866, the other 39,124 (Annual Report of Immigration and Naturalization Service, 1964:8).

between the two nations contained many contractual provisions relating to health, housing, wages, transportation, food, and the protection of the laborers' civil rights. Students of the subject seem to agree that the provisions of the agreement, which came to be known as the Bracero Program, were violated many times by American employers.[11]

During World War II some 200,000 braceros (temporary alien contract laborers) were brought to the United States to harvest the fields. After the end of the war, the program continued, reaching a yearly peak number of importees in 1957 of 450,422. With the returning veterans and the slowdown of the defense industries after 1946, a legitimate question can be raised concerning the existence of a labor shortage. The program continued, however, for twenty-two years. It was established under executive order in 1942 and through law in 1951 (Public Law 78) and finally ended in 1964. During this decade (1940–50) over 50,000 legal Mexican immigrants entered the country, over 600,000 braceros were brought in, and the illegal Mexican immigrants (who were apprehended) increased to 800,000. With high unemployment in their own country, many Mexicans who were not chosen as braceros, but who had migrated to the border region, crossed the border illegally and found jobs in this country. Many employers obviously preferred illegals to braceros because the former were and are a most manageable labor force not subject to any regulations or stipulations with regard to housing, health, wages, number of working days, transportation, or any other conditions of employment. (See Table 5.)

This trend continued through the 1950s when 293,000 legal immigrants were admitted, over 3 million braceros were brought in, and more than 3.4 million illegal Mexican aliens were apprehended. It was during the 1950s that the United States became alarmed at the number of illegal aliens in this country and in 1954 President Eisenhower asked Attorney General Brownell to propose a plan to get rid of the "wetbacks." General Joseph May Swing (who participated in the expedition that invaded Mexico in 1916) was named Commissioner of Immigration and Naturalization Service and put in charge of "Operation Wetback." In July of 1954 General Swing stated to a group of employers in South Texas: "When President Eisenhower appointed me for this job his orders were to clean up the border. I intend to do just that."[12] Operation

72

TABLE 5
Temporary Contract Labor from Mexico*

Year	Total	Year	Total
1942	4,203	1955	390,846
1943	52,098	1956	444,581
1944	62,170	1957	450,422
1945	49,454	1958	418,885
1946	32,043	1959	447,535
1947	19,632	1960	427,240
1948	33,288	1961	294,149
1949	143,455	1962	282,556
1950	76,519	1963	195,450
1951	211,098	1964	181,738
1952	187,894	1965	103,563
1953	198,424	1966	18,544
1954	310,476	1967	7,703
		1968	6,127
		TOTAL	5,050,093

*Figures correspond to fiscal years. Although the Bracero Program ended in December 1964, figures from 1966 to 1968 correspond to aliens admitted and reported under the category: temporary contract labor.

Sources: Period from 1942 to 1956 based on figures taken from *Mexican Labor Hearings* (House Committee on Agriculture) 1958, pp. 450-52 as quoted by Hancock, 1959:17.

Figures for 1957 and 1958 based on Report of the Select Commission on Western Hemisphere Immigration (1968:98).

Figures from 1959 to 1968 based on data provided by the 1968 Annual Report of the Immigration and Naturalization Service, p. 73.

Wetback was conducted with military efficiency and in 1954 over a million wetbacks were apprehended and expelled from the United States. This did have the effect of curtailing the movement of Mexican illegals until 1961, but in the latter part of the decade a great increase in Mexican illegal immigration into the United States was noted. Up until the end of the Bracero Program in December 1964, the number of contract laborers brought into the United States was 1.5 million. Legal Mexican immigration increased to 400,000, and over 770,000 illegals were apprehended. It is rather sobering to consider the enormous traffic in people that these population movements suggest. All of these statistics are on the conservative side. To summarize the tables we find that at least 1.5 million Mexicans have immigrated to the United States legally. Over 5 million temporary contract laborers° have been admitted to the U.S. and over 7 million Mexicans°° without proper documents have been expelled from the country.

To complicate the situation further, there exist other categories of aliens who reside in the United States. One such category is the commuter or the "green carder" who crosses the border daily to work in the United States and then returns home to Mexico. Some of the green carders are not daily commuters but come to the United States for periods of several months and then return to Mexico when their jobs terminate or when they feel a desire to go back. Many of these work in agriculture for extended periods or at other jobs. The estimates for the daily commuter run as high as 60,000 (this is considered to be a conservative figure), and Senator Muskie has estimated the number of commuters to be between 100,000 and 400,000.

Another category of aliens are what we might call the "border crossers." These are persons from Mexico who have been issued a card which permits them to come to the United States for a seventy-two-hour period for purposes of visiting, business, or pleasure. These persons should not work in the United States but many do. If they should be apprehended while working, then presumably they become "wetback" statistics. Thousands of these cards are issued every month along the border and hundreds are revoked when the cardholders are caught working when they should not be. Well over a million persons have such cards on any given day. In the year ending June 30, 1970, 907,514 such persons were admitted through the land border ports from Mexico.[13] The number arriving at airports was 173,243 and those disembarking at seaports for the same year was 4,630.

The magnitude of the intercourse between Mexico and the United States can best be shown by the statistics on the movement

---

°Again, these figures do not necessarily represent different individuals since an individual might have to come as a bracero to the United States on more than one occasion and would have been counted separately each time.

°°We will never know how many illegal aliens have come into the United States year by year. Depending on how the statistics are gathered, all that we know is those that were either reported, expelled from the country, deported, or apprehended. The problem of even estimating how many illegal aliens are in the country today remains unsolved. It should also be noted that these figures do not necessarily represent the same number of individuals. It is quite possible for an illegal to be apprehended more than one time in successive years.

of aliens and citizens across the international boundaries. Each
entry of the same person is counted separately, thus these figures do
not necessarily represent different persons but rather the total
number of border crossings. In 1970 there were over 144 million
border crossings from Mexico. Of these, 86.7 million were aliens
(presumably Mexicans) and 57.7 million were United States
citizens. Between 1961 and 1970, 1.2 billion crossings were
reported of which 735.1 million were aliens, and 489.7 million
were United States citizens. The figures for the last forty years,
1928–70, indicate 2.6 billion such crossings, of which 1.5 billion
were aliens and 1.1 billion were United States citizens. Thus, the
figures for the last ten years represent almost 50 percent of the total
crossings over the last forty-two years.[14]

Analysis and Conclusion[°]

Immigration of Mexicans to the United States appears related to
a number of factors. Without implying either causality or order of
importance, the following are suggested: 1) the demand for cheap
labor in the United States; 2) the high population growth in
Mexico; 3) Mexico's inability to keep up with this growth by
providing opportunities for employment, housing, and education,
despite tremendous advances and rapid economic development
during the past thirty years; and 4) the internal rural to urban
migration in Mexico terminating in the Federal District (Mexico
City) and the northern border cities.

Table 6 shows that Mexico's population, using the 1960 census,
will double by 1980.[15] Such growth suggests the need for great
economic development which will provide the employment,
housing, and education necessary to accommodate this growth.
Since economic development has not kept up with population
growth, the rural population in the less developed areas has been
moving to the urban or more developed areas. This migration had
its beginning at the turn of the century and its direction has been
more and more toward the Federal District and the cities of the
northern border.[16] Between 1950 and 1960 the Federal District
received 48 percent of the migrants from other Mexican states,

---

[°]This section is taken in large part from Samora and Bustamante, 1970.

TABLE 6
Population Change in the Mexican Border States
(1950 to 1960 and projections to 1980)

State	1950	1960	Percentage of Change	Projection 1980
Baja California	226,965	520,165	129.1	2,408,100
Chihuahua	846,414	1,226,793	44.9	1,620,000
Coahuila	720,619	907,734	25.9	2,870,700
Nuevo León	740,191	1,024,182	42.6	2,657,600
Sonora	510,607	783,378	53.4	2,085,400
Tamaulipas	718,167	1,024,182	42.6	2,219,000
TOTAL	3,762,963	5,486,434		13,860,800

Source: Mexican Census, 1960 and Benítez and Cabrera, *Proyecciones,* pp. 123-75.

whereas the border states of Baja California, Chihuahua, and Nuevo León received 38 percent of the migrants.[17] Table 7 shows the increase (1940 to 1967) of the four largest *municipios* on the Mexican border (a municipio is similar to a county). Benítez and Cabrera have stated that the population of the six border states was 5,486,434 in 1960. Their projections to 1980 for the six states are 13,860,800.[18] If the 1967 population of only the municipios along the border was close to 3 million, then it is clear that the cities along the border are the destination for this northern migration. The border cities have long served as a magnet which has attracted millions of people, many of them hoping to jump the border and find employment in the United States. This then constitutes the cheap labor pool which we have been stressing in this paper.

TABLE 7
Population Increase of Mexican Border Municipios

Municipio	1940	Years 1960	1967	Percentage of Change
Tijuana	21,977	165,690	347,501	1,481
Mexicali	44,399	281,362	540,300	1,117
Juárez	55,024	276,995	501,416	811
Nuevo Laredo	31,502	96,043	140,818	347
TOTAL Mexican Border Municipios	976,693	2,363,728	2,709,136	

Source: Unpublished figures, U.S. Department of Labor.

With such an abundant supply of labor on the border willing and even eager to work, it is not difficult to exploit it, considering the economies of the two countries. If the unemployed Mexican could get a job in his own country his wages in all probability would not exceed $2.50 per day ($2.00 per day being the minimum). If he is offered between 50 cents and $1.00 per hour in the United States he would be doing very well by Mexican standards. United States citizens, however, would find it difficult to stay above poverty even at $2.00 per hour.

We hypothesize that the demand for cheap labor in the United States, particularly in the agricultural, service, and unskilled occupations, complements the movement of Mexicans to the border, resulting in the subsequent seepage into the United States. As legal and illegal aliens come across by the thousands, wage levels are kept low and the domestic labor force (mainly Mexican-Americans) becomes unemployed and many leave the area in search of employment. For years Mexican-Americans from the border area have been the chief source of supply for the agricultural migrant streams° throughout the United States.

Unfortunately, few sociologists, economists, political scientists, or historians either in the United States or in Mexico have taken a very serious look at the border region as a topic for research. We have, then, only scattered information, quite often in obscure journals, relating to the importance of the border region for both Mexico and the United States.

The Border as Magnet

It must be understood that even though Mexico is developing rapidly, it still has millions of poverty-stricken and unemployed people. In addition it borders the United States which is the richest country in the world. It should also be understood that Mexico's largest concentrations of industry and population are in the central part of the country around the Federal District which is hundreds of miles away from the northern border. Mexico's northern border, as we have stated before, has historically been sparsely populated

---

°The buildup of the Mexican-American population outside of the Southwest can be noted, as they drop off the migrant stream.

except for a phenomenal population growth during the past ten years and here again mainly in cities along the border. This region, then, has not been particularly important to Mexico's economy nor to its social and political life. This region has had low priorities with regard to economic development and it has been largely ignored by the central government. It has been only in recent years that the Mexican government has begun to take account of its northern border and instituted a program of national border development through its Programa Nacional Fronterizo.

We have argued that with the cessation of immigration from Asia and from southern Europe at the turn of the century, and the establishment by the 1920s of immigration quotas for all but the Western Hemisphere countries, Mexico became the chief source of cheap labor for the United States. Since there has been widespread unemployment in Mexico over the years and since the United States is the richest nation in the world and does present some opportunities for employment, the northern border has always been a magnet for Mexicans from the interior.

There has always been free movement of peoples and goods across the U.S.–Mexico border. The establishment of the Border Patrol in 1924 restricted, to a degree, this free movement, but relatively speaking, this still remains an open border. We have shown some data revealing the tremendous intercourse between the two nations based on border crossings.

We have shown also that whenever employment opportunities prevail in the United States, the border attracts many more people from central Mexico than the available employment opportunities. This has been shown with the Bracero Program. When the employment of braceros was at its height, the entrance of illegal aliens was also at its highest.

Wages and Employment

There is no question that when a large surplus labor pool exists, wages will be depressed unless other forces are at work. In the case of the border region the availability of such large numbers of unskilled workers has perennially kept wages on the U.S. side of the border relatively low. This means, too, that the unemployment statistics for the border region in the United States have always been much higher than they have been for the rest of the nation. The result of this has been the actual displacement of Americans in the labor market, in particular Mexican-Americans, because citizens of the United States cannot compete effectively with alien workers, whether legal or illegal, at the going wages. The unionization of American workers along the border region has also been hindered by the excessive labor supply of Mexicans, both legal and illegal.

Other Considerations

The given situation has contributed to a large amount of smuggling of both goods and bodies along the border. The smuggling of bodies has been a one-way process from Mexico into the United States but the smuggling of goods has been a two-way traffic between the two countries.

The recent attempts on the part of the Mexican government to industrialize the border region by permitting American industry to set up "twin plants" on the Mexican side for the exploitation of labor through their labor-intensive productions has not, in our estimation, particularly helped economic development in Mexico, because again the border remains a magnet and many more people are drawn to the area, exceeding the available jobs. Secondly, the work is labor-intensive and it employs primarily women, which undoubtedly will affect the family and social structures. Thirdly, as soon as the particular productions can be automated it will no longer be to the interests of American industry to remain in that region.

Other considerations are the favorable import status which these industries receive when the goods are returned to the United States and the reduction of jobs for American labor when such plants are established in a foreign country.

The northern border thus remains a magnet, resulting in phenomenal population growth in northern Mexican cities; wages are lowered in this country because of the seepage of Mexicans across the border; Americans are displaced and in many instances their only recourse is to move north away from the region, quite often in the migratory agriculture labor streams; unemployment rises on the U.S. side; unionization of labor is hampered; and smuggling of bodies and goods is encouraged. When American industry can move easily from one country to another for the exploitation of cheap labor; when employers are permitted, without penalty, to employ illegal aliens; when commuters can live in Mexico and work in the United States; when the two countries are not seriously considering a regional economic development program; then this U.S.-Mexico border region remains an enigma for both societies, with far-reaching consequences.

Since we are concerned with the understanding of the status of Mexican-Americans in the United States, we argue that we cannot fully comprehend this population and the problems they encounter, in either the Southwest or the rest of the nation, without intensive and serious consideration of the border region.

A Brief Chronology of Mexican Immigration to the United States

The history of Mexican immigration to the United States is related to the rise of great regional and national industries, i.e., agriculture, railroads, and mining as well as the corresponding demand for a reservoir of cheap labor; the special administrative and legislative consideration given to immigration from the Western Hemisphere, particularly from Mexico; and the internal developments and changes in Mexico.

1850–1889: Undesirability of Mexicans for labor or settlement corresponded to the importation and utilization of European and Asiatic laborers and settlers.

1900–1919: Increased use of Mexican laborers was related to the decreasing volume of European immigration, World War I mobilization, rise of defense industries, completion of railroads linking the interior of Mexico to the United States, and the revolutionary conditions in Mexico.

1920–1929: Quotas established. European and Asiatic immigration continued to decrease. Mexican immigration increased, reaching a peak in 1924. Increased restrictions affect immigration which decreases in late 1920s. Illegal Mexican aliens average 4,000 per year.

1930–1939: Effects of Great Depression. Mexicans repatriated. Legal Mexican immigration continues to decrease. Illegal Mexican aliens increase and average 10,500 per year.

1940–47: World War II. Tremendous increase in demand for labor. United States and Mexico make agreement for temporary contract labor (Bracero Program). Numbers of illegal Mexican aliens greatly increase. Mexican legal immigration increases slightly.

1948–1951: Illegals legalized to become braceros. "Braceros" increase. Mexican immigration remains stable. Public Law 78 enacted. Mexican illegal aliens greatly increase.

1952–1959: Korean War. Demand for labor. Braceros, illegals, and Mexican immigration increase dramatically. Illegal Mexicans constitute a high of 1,075. One hundred sixty-eight apprehensions when Operation Wetback inaugurated. Illegals expelled by the thousands.

1960–1970: Bracero Program terminated (1964) due to public pressure. Illegal Mexican aliens on a dramatic increase again. Mexican immigration steadily increasing. New immigration law (Public Law 86.236, passed in 1965, effective July 1, 1968) restricts immigration from Western Hemisphere.

Source: Julian Samora, *Los Mojados: The Wetback Story* (Notre Dame, Indiana: University of Notre Dame Press, 1971).

NOTES

1. Carl Wittke, "Immigration Policy Prior to World War I," *The Annals,* The American Academy of Political and Social Science (Philadelphia, 1949):8.
2. Ibid., p. 7.
3. Ross A. Eckler and Jack Zlotnick, "Immigration and Labor Force," The American Academy of Political and Social Science (Philadelphia, 1949):96.
4. Ibid.
5. Lyle Saunders, "The Social History of Spanish-Speaking People in Southwestern United States Since 1846," *Southwest Council on Education of Spanish-Speaking People* (Albuquerque, 1950):2.
6. Manuel Gamio, *Mexican Immigration to the United States* (Chicago: The University of Chicago Press, 1930), p. 2.
7. Samuel Gompers, "United States–Mexico–Labor–Their Relations," *American Federationist* 23, No. 8 (1916):633–34.
8. Gamio, *Mexican Immigration,* p. 10.
9. Julian Samora, *Los Mojados: The Wetback Story* (Notre Dame, Ind.: University of Notre Dame Press, 1971).
10. Emory J. Bogardus, *The Mexican in the United States* (Los Angeles: University of California Press, 1934).
11. Ernesto Galarza, *Merchants of Labor: The Mexican Bracero History* (Santa Barbara, Calif.: McNally & Loftin, 1966).
12. John G. McBride, *Vanishing Bracero* (San Antonio, Texas: The Naylor Co., 1963), p. 5.
13. *Immigration and Naturalization Annual Report,* 1970, p. 77.
14. Ibid., p. 81.
15. Zenteno Raúl Benítez and Gustavo A. Cabrera, *Proyecciones de la población de México, 1960–1980* (México D. F., Banco de Industriales, 1966).
16. Galarza, *Merchants of Labor,* p. 28.
17. Benítez and Cabrera, *Proyecciones,* p. 112.
18. Ibid., pp. 123–75.

4

The Economic Condition of the
Mexican-American

FRED H. SCHMIDT and KENNETH KOFORD

Before retiring in October 1973, Mr. Schmidt was Senior Lecturer at the Graduate School of Management and Researcher in Industrial Relations at the Institute of Industrial Relations, UCLA. Mr. Koford is a Research Assistant at the Institute of Industrial Relations, and a graduate student in the Department of Economics, UCLA.

This essay examines the economic condition of Mexican-Americans in the Southwest—a population group that scarcely has a statistical existence under that designation in official accounts. It would be fortunate for this work if there were a way to extract from census reports a precise record of the social and economic characteristics of Mexican-Americans. However, information on them must largely be wrung from present and past tabulations made for more broadly defined groups and areas, such as those of "Spanish language," "Spanish surname," "Spanish origin or descent," "Spanish-American," "Spanish-speaking," or other variants. Census tables that focus on the nation's second largest and fastest growing minority are hedged about in a definitional thicket, one through which the statistics on Mexican-Americans can only be seen with their edges blurred, when seen at all.[1]

Despite the vagueness of official records and the confusion that comes from the use of other names that have been applied to Mexican-Americans from time to time and place to place, the impressive outlines of this group can be seen. These outlines have become somewhat sharper as government agencies, social scientists, and politicians respond more and more to the demands of the group for an acknowledged identity, an identity not to be found in the traditional white-nonwhite records kept on the population.

Many a quibble can be made as to the precise composition of a population as heterogeneous as the Mexican-Americans, whatever factors may be taken as denominators common to their identity. Just as it can be said that all Negroes are nonwhite, but all

81

nonwhites are not Negroes, so it is that Mexican-Americans are generally recorded as white, although some of them have chosen to be recorded as nonwhite. All Mexican-Americans are considered to be of Spanish origin, but may not have Spanish surnames. The 1970 Census includes two definitions in its count of persons of Spanish heritage: (1) those of Spanish origin or descent, and (2) persons of Spanish language as a mother tongue, or in families whose head or wife were of such tongue, or, if not of that language, those of Spanish surname, provided that they reside in the states of Arizona, California, Colorado, New Mexico, or Texas.

As explained elsewhere in these papers, most of the 6.1 million persons of Spanish language in the Southwest who sift through the census' definitional screening have lingering ties with Mexican culture or with Mexico itself. And it is the presence of these people and the historic roles of their forebears since precolonial days that have given these five states identity as a region. They lend to the Southwest an ambience that is different from the rest of the United States. Yet, for a century and a quarter, they have been subsumed within a dominant Anglo society which has seldom concerned itself with how they fared.

The persons identified by the census as being of Spanish heritage constitute the only minority in the United States whose numbers continue to grow through large-scale immigration. It has been over a century since the last blacks were infused into the population; it has been well over three-quarters of a century since the Chinese Exclusion Act made it unlawful for Chinese laborers to come to this country, and it has been almost that long since the "Gentlemen's Agreement" with Japan barred from the United States and Hawaii all laborers, except "settled agriculturists." Almost a half century ago, Congress shut to a trickle the gate valves through which millions of European workers, today's "ethnic minorities," streamed into the nation's labor force. Since 1925, the entry of all of these and other racial and ethnic minorities has been severely restricted. But this is not so with respect to Spanish-Americans, a group whose number is steadily being enlarged from outside the United States at a rate which can, within foreseeable years, make it the nation's largest minority.

The annual reports of the Immigration and Naturalization Service give no measure of the actual number of persons of Spanish heritage entering the country from year to year. Puerto Ricans, of course, are not restricted from entering or taking up residency at will, and the legal constraints against the entry of Mexican nationals are quite often lost in the realities of the Southwest. Official reports do show, year by year, the number of Mexican immigrants who have been accorded some form of legal status to enter the country, and they also reveal the number of apprehensions and deportations of illegal entrants during a given year. But they never have arrived at a figure on how many Mexican nationals are now in the country or continue to enter without legal papers. These last, then, are the "invisible people," those who incessantly infiltrate the United States population from Mexico, a process that was examined with scholarly care by Julian Samora in his study, *Los Mojados: The Wetback Story.*[2]

The Border Economy

This situation has always been regarded as merely a regional, or border area, phenomenon, not a matter of national concern. It has been difficult to impress persons outside the Southwest with the gravity of the problem. Indeed, a succession of recent national administrations has been peculiarly indifferent, even resistant, toward examining, much less changing, a situation that persistently mocks national immigration policies. The scope of the problem can be summed up in one statistic: from 1939 through 1969, a period during which 7.4 million persons legally immigrated to the United States from countries all over the world, *more* than 7.4 million Mexican nationals entered the country unlawfully and were apprehended and expatriated to Mexico.[3] The latter figure includes only those persons who were caught and returned to Mexico, not the number who entered the country. This distinction is important. David North has estimated for the U.S. Department of Labor, as have others who have studied the problem, that for every illegal alien caught working there must be another one working who is not caught.[4] North's method of making this estimate appears faulty, since it compares a figure for a period of time to one prevailing at a given time. Nonetheless, there is a consensus that only a fraction of illegal entrants are apprehended by the Border Patrol, and that there are a very large number of unauthorized Mexican nationals working in the country at any given time.

The pressures that prevail on low-income Mexicans, inducing them to seek in the United States some improvement in their economic condition, however furtively this must be done, can be stated in one set of stark figures. The per capita annual gross national product in the United States, as we are accustomed to knowing, is the highest in the world, $5,353 (at this writing). Sweden ranks second, with $4,749, and the only other nation with which we share a border, Canada, is third, with $4,497. Other countries can be arrayed below these figures until one comes to Mexico with its $717.[5] The figures reveal the startling disparity in the economies of the two countries. Nowhere else on earth is there an income disparity between the peoples of two bordering nations equal to that between the U.S. and Mexico. This is what makes the U.S.-Mexico border unique in the world. This economic condition constitutes the attraction—and the unrelenting pressure—which induces Mexicans to enter this country, whether temporarily or permanently, whether legally or surreptitiously. They largely do so to seek a change in their economic fortunes.

Those who enter the country without legal papers must live with uncertainty, no matter how long their residence here. Every representative of civil authority—whether welfare worker, employment service agent, census enumerator, school official, or the like—becomes a potential threat to their tenuous status. And for those in the labor force, the ire of an exploitative employer can be the gravest threat of all.

Given the uncertainties of their lot it is clear why such persons should wish to become "invisible" to all agents of authority. Their elusiveness contributes to the acknowledged undercoat of the census, suggesting that in the Southwest there is a shadow labor force whose number and characteristics are not fully reported in any official documents.[6] The Census Bureau for the first time in 1973 began collecting and tabulating monthly labor force data for what it styles "Hispanic Americans," as part of its ongoing Current Population Survey. Even so, it will be about 1976 before a sufficient data base has been established to make seasonal adjustments in the data, as is done for other employment and earnings figures published by the Census Bureau and the Bureau of Labor Statistics.[7]

The Mexican-American Study Project

Only once has a comprehensive and rigorous effort been made by researchers to learn precisely how Mexican-Americans fare in the larger society of the Southwest. That effort, the Mexican-American Study Project at the University of California, Los Angeles, revealed or confirmed many things about Mexican-Americans. Its conclusions about their economic condition were succinctly summarized:

> As a group, Mexican Americans in the Southwest are highly differentiated from the dominant society on nearly every yardstick of social and economic position. A profile of their main demographic characteristics . . . reveals large variations from the Anglo "norms." Their educational attainment shows an especially notable gap. Associated with this gap is an unfavorable occupational structure and a low average income. Their housing conditions reflect not only poor earnings but the pressures resulting from extremely large families.[8]

The Mexican-American Study Project published its final report in 1970. By that date, the economic data from the 1960 census used in the inquiry were a decade old. But that inquiry provides an important baseline against which changes occurring during the last decade can be measured. This article is an effort to examine such changes by taking an early look at the 1970 census reports which have just become available, and then only partially, for the five-state area of principal interest to this review. It must be noted that the definition of "Spanish Surname" in 1960 is different from the 1970 definition of "Spanish Language/Spanish Surname," and it is possible that the change in definition is part of the reason that the Spanish Language/Spanish Surname group shows improvement relative to that of the Spanish Surname in 1960.

It goes without saying that Mexican-Americans are dispersed in large numbers in many other states, but just as the Mexican-American Study Project had to focus on the Southwest we must largely do so here. The 1970 census' identification of the Spanish-language or Spanish-surname population is of little use outside of the Western states in determining the characteristics of the Mexican-American population, since the survey of persons of Mexican origin was considerably less complete than that of the Spanish Language/Spanish Surname population. This is so because of the large number of Puerto Ricans and other Latin Americans in states outside the West and Southwest who are, of course, included in the Spanish Language/Spanish Surname population. Furthermore, 85 percent of the Mexican-Americans are concentrated in the five states of the Southwest. The remainder are largely in the Great Lakes region and scattered throughout the West.

The Mexican-American Study Project demonstrated graphically the income gap between Mexican-American and Anglo families in the Southwest. For example, when the median income of the Anglo family was set at an index of 100, that for the Spanish-surname family stood at 65, indicating that the median income of Anglo families was one-half again as high as that for Spanish-surname families. This disparity became even more pronounced when incomes were related to the number of persons in the families of the two groups: with the $2,047 median income per person in the Anglo family representing an index of 100, the $968 median income per person in the generally larger-size Spanish-surname family stood at an index of only 47.3, or less than one-half that of an Anglo family member.

This income gap was especially extreme in Texas, where the comparable index for the Spanish-surname family member stood at only 35.5, about one-third that of the Anglo family member. At the time, this was on the order of the difference in per capita income between the populations of the United States and Venezuela. Using the then generally accepted poverty line of $3,000, the study found that 35 percent of the Spanish-surname families fell below that standard in 1960, as compared to only 16 percent of the Anglo families.

It is significant that the above differences in earnings could not be accounted for wholly in terms of the relative social development of persons in the two groups. It is true that a considerable education gap existed between them, amounting to five years in the median school years completed by persons over twenty-five years of age (12.1 years for Anglos and 7.1 years for those with Spanish surnames), but this education gap did not fully account for the income gap.[9] When adjustments were made for the differences in the educational attainments of Spanish-surname males and Anglo males of comparable age, it was found that factors other than schooling operated to cause part of the income gap. Indeed, it was found that income differentials tended even to widen when comparisons were made at the higher levels of educational attainment.

Whatever factors worked to thwart the popularly held belief that an individual's investment in education brings its own reward by placing him on a par with others in the competition for income, the impact of those factors varied from state to state. When median incomes were adjusted for schooling and age differentials, it was found that incomes for the Spanish-surname males in California stood at 88:100 vis-à-vis the Anglo; in Texas this was 72:100. Thus, differences in schooling alone accounted for some, but not all, of the lesser incomes of the Spanish surnamed. However, these comparisons did not take into account differences in the quality of education, which in many cases might make it unreasonable to assume that the educational achievement of Mexican-Americans was on a par with their years of schooling attained. Thus, in the case of Mexican-Americans the years-of-schooling *underestimates* the amount of difference in income accounted for by the difference in education.

The study also showed that the lower incomes received by Spanish-surname persons contributed to a host of other inequalities between the two groups. For instance, whereas only 7 percent of Anglos in metropolitan areas lived in deteriorated and dilapidated housing units, 30 percent of the Spanish surnamed did so; where only 8 percent of Anglos in such areas lived in overcrowded housing units (having less than one room per person) 35 percent of the Spanish surnamed did so, a situation considerably worse than that which prevailed for nonwhites in those areas.

Just as differences in educational attainment did not explain away all of the income gap existing between the two groups, neither did their relative desire and availability for employment. If labor force participation rates—that is, the percentage of persons over fourteen in the population who were either employed or were actively seeking employment—can be accepted as a measure of commitment to work, the slight differences in this rate between the two groups could not be used to explain the income gap between them. Spanish-surname males had a labor force participation rate of 77.5 percent, compared to the male Anglo rate of 79.5 percent. The difference in the rates for females was larger, 28.8 percent and 34.1 percent, respectively—but, again, the study found that this difference was insufficient to account for all of the gap in income. In this regard, it should be noted that in California, where employment opportunities were generally more promising for all groups, the positions of Anglo and Spanish-surname persons with respect to their labor force participation rates were reversed or considerably narrowed: 79.6 percent for Anglo males and 79.9 percent for Spanish-surname males; for females it was 35.6 percent and 32.2 percent, respectively. Thus, the differences that prevail in the other four states might be due to the less favorable employment opportunities available to Mexican-Americans in those states.

In 1960, the overall occupational positions of male and female Spanish-surname workers as compared to those of Anglos were similar to the income gap between the two groups. When indexes were constructed to examine the average value of all occupations held by Spanish surname and those held by Anglo males in the different states, and when a comparison was made of the ratio of earnings of those in the former group to the latter, it was found that these ratios ranged from .86 in New Mexico to .82 in Arizona, meaning that the occupational experience of the Mexican-Americans was as unfavorable as their income experience.

This last comparison may well have overstated the occupational position of Spanish-surname persons. There is an imprecision in constructing a job hierarchy from the census' broad occupational categories, which group together widely differing jobs into single categories. The range of earnings for jobs grouped into the same category is often very large, and if Mexican-Americans are clustered in the lower-paying jobs of a given occupational category, their earnings may well be considerably less than those of the average worker in that category.

Perhaps the most vivid representation of the Mexican-American's position in the occupational structure in 1960 compared to Anglos was shown in the study by the contrast in the percentage each group had placed in low-skill manual and in white-collar occupations. Only 26.3 percent of urban Anglo males were low-skilled manual workers, whereas 57.0 percent of the urban Spanish-surname males were so classified; 46.9 percent of the Anglo males were in white-collar jobs, but only 19.0 percent of the Spanish-surname males were in such jobs.

Another important indicator of how Mexican-Americans then

fared in the labor markets of the Southwest was their unemployment rates as compared with those for Anglos. When the rate of unemployment for Anglo males in 1960 (based then on persons fourteen years of age and older) was only 4.5 percent, it was 8.5 percent for Spanish-surname males. The comparable figures for female workers in the two groups were 5.0 percent and 9.5 percent, respectively.

It should be noted here, however, that both the rate of unemployment and labor force participation rates leave much to be desired as indicators of work opportunities and of the dispositions a group of persons has toward seeking work. These indicators often conceal as much as they reveal, an observation to be considered in what follows:

The Mexican-American Study Project concluded that Mexican-Americans, in 1960, stood considerably lower by every economic yardstick than did Anglos in the Southwest. The project issued a series of advance reports beginning in 1965, and released its final report in 1970, all expressing alarm over the findings. Other investigators have since pursued the inquiries, adding new information useful to those seeking to redress the social and economic problems of the Southwest's largest minority.

The decade of the 1960s was one of pronounced governmental commitment to programs designed to improve employment opportunities for minority groups, assure their civil equities, raise their education and skill levels, and correct some of the grievous effects of inadequate incomes. When these programs began, Mexican-Americans were seldom mentioned as a "client" community to which such efforts should be directed. In the national councils and administrative offices responsible for the programs, black urban ghettos—not Southwestern barrios—were considered the prime target communities. That this was a misplaced emphasis in the case of the Southwest took several years to assert, but the assertion was successfully made during that decade by Mexican-Americans themselves, as they laid hold of new concepts of "La Raza," "Chicano Power," and "Aztlán," this last being the assertion that the Southwest's indigenous people (both in this country and Mexico) were united anthropologically and should disregard any political boundaries separating them. What changes, then, if any, have occurred in the economic condition of Mexican-Americans in the past decade?

One of the early instruments forged by Congress to provide information on the employment progress of minorities was contained in Title VII of the Civil Rights Act of 1964. This Act requires certain employers to report annually to the Equal Employment Opportunity Commission (EEOC) on the pattern of minority employment in their firms. However, these reports contain serious deficiencies in advising us of the progress of Mexican-American workers, more so than of other minority workers. At best, they provide an incomplete picture.

First, the reporting requirement of Title VII applied only to firms employing one hundred or more persons in 1969, the latest year for which reported data are presently available. This numerical cutoff for determining which firms need to report leaves much of agriculture and related enterprises out of the Commission's reports. Less than one-half of the total employment in construction, trade, and service industries is reflected in the reports, while no data are shown for household domestics, temporary or casual employees, government workers, or employees of small businesses or single proprietorships. Furthermore, about one-fourth of the employers who were required to report failed to do so in 1969, and, of course, the reports of those who did constitute, at best, the self-assessments and anthropological judgments of the employers themselves, not the findings of a government commission.[10]

However, inasmuch as the limitations of the 1969 employer reports also hold for the earlier years since reporting began in 1966, possibly these data can be used to indicate some of the changes occurring since passage of the Civil Rights Act.

These reports reveal the extent to which the private firms regard Mexican-American males as being essentially blue-collar workers. Although less than half of all male employees of Southwestern firms reporting in 1969 were in blue-collar occupations, over three-fourths of their Mexican-American male employees were in such occupations.[11] In each state, this proportion was considerably higher than that of Negro males shown as blue-collar workers. The percentages of Mexican-Americans in either blue-collar or service occupations in the five states were: Arizona—84.8; California—82.8; Colorado—87.5; New Mexico—74.1; and Texas—81.5. Thus, in each of these states only a small minority of Mexican-Americans were in white-collar jobs—while the percentage of Anglos in such jobs ranged from 59.0 percent in Colorado and Arizona to 66.0 percent in New Mexico.

The occupational caste system in the Southwest has been described as a wall between blue- and white-collar jobs, one which constitutes a barrier difficult for minority workers to surmount. This barrier appears to exist even where many white-collar jobs require less skill than some of the blue-collar jobs in which minorities have already gained parity representation according to their size in the local labor force.[12] An analysis of 1966 EEOC reports clearly showed that the representation minorities had in an occupation descended as the job hierarchy ascended—a case of down-the-up-staircase for minority workers.

Changes since the Mid-60s

The Manpower Report of the President for 1972 presented tables showing how the percentage of "Spanish surnamed Americans" and other minorities throughout the nation in firms of more than one hundred employees had increased in different occupational categories from 1966 to 1970.[13] The increases for Spanish-surname workers in the period ranged from 39 percent in the laborer classification to 58 percent in all white-collar classifications. Such increases seem phenomenal, until it is considered that they represent changes from very low starting bases. The actual increase, for the Spanish-surname workers, for instance, in the white-collar classification was from but 1.2 percent to 1.9 percent of all workers in those classifications. In the same period this group increased its share of jobs in the laborer classification from 6.1 percent to 8.5 percent, for a representation in that classification four and half times as great as it had in all white-collar jobs in the reporting companies. This is a distribution far out of proportion to how the overall U.S. labor force is distributed between white-collar and laborer jobs.

However, the gains shown by the tables in the Report for the Spanish-surnamed, as well as other minorities, may signify something quite different than the efficacy of public policies requiring equal employment opportunities. The instructions given to employers by the Equal Employment Opportunity Commission was that they could acquire minority group information either by visual surveys or from past employment records as to the identity of employees. The fact that the tables indicate that the number of total Spanish-surname workers in the reporting companies increased by 61 percent, from 1966 to 1970, is itself a denial of what our senses tell us from street-level observations. These figures are suspect and may in large part be but a reflection of changes in company record keeping, or perhaps just the increased color sensitivity true of the general population since the middle of the last decade.

There is an interesting and inexplicable variance between the 1969 EEOC reports and the occupational data of the 1970 census involving the entire labor force. The percentage of white-collar workers among all Anglos and in each state's entire labor force shown in the census is almost identical to the data supplied by the reporting employers for their work forces in those states. However, in each state the EEOC reports show a significantly smaller percentage of Spanish-surname white-collar workers and a much higher percentage of blue-collar workers in these private firms than the census shows for them throughout the state. In other words, there is a higher percentage of Mexican-American white-collar workers in all public and private employment in the Southwest than there is in firms specifically required by law to offer equal employment opportunity.[14] Generally, Anglos in the reporting companies have more than twice the percentage of their total numbers employed in white-collar jobs than do either Negroes or Mexican-Americans.

The most surprising feature of the EEOC reports is that they cover such a small fraction of the Mexican-American labor force. The coverage of jobs held by Mexican-Americans is considerably less than it is for Negroes, Anglos, and others, ranging from only 26.0 percent of all Mexican-American wage and salary workers in New Mexico to 33.0 percent in Arizona. This contrasts with the greater coverage shown in EEOC reports for jobs held by Negroes, ranging from 33.0 percent in New Mexico to 58.0 percent in California.[15] Thus, whatever the pressure of law to gain the upgrading of minority workers in the reporting firms, that pressure could have been exerted on behalf of only one-third—or less—of each state's Mexican-American labor force, since no more than that were employed in these firms. Recent changes in Title VII have, of course, broadened its coverage.

The industrial mix varies from state to state, producing different distributions of the labor force among occupations. However, while there is in all five states a similarity in the principal Anglo occupations, no such similarity exists for Mexican-Americans and Negroes.[16] Selecting from the census' occupational categories the five in which the largest number of workers from each group are employed, the principal Anglo occupations are shown to be: "Professional, technical and kindred workers"; "Clerical and kindred workers"; "Craftsmen, foremen and kindred"; "Managers and administrators"; and "Service workers" (largely because this category includes food service workers).

The pattern for Mexican-Americans and Negroes is different and varies among the states. A listing of the top five occupations for Mexican-Americans must include either "Operatives" or "Laborers." In no state is the category of "Managers and administrators" among the top occupations for Mexican-Americans, and the inclusion of the "Service worker" category results from their having large numbers employed as cleaning service workers. The situation for Negro workers is somewhat similar, but in three states, Arizona, New Mexico, and Texas, the category of "Private household workers" must be included among their five principal occupations. Most surprising, however, is the fact that although agriculture was one of the top five industries in which Mexican-Americans were employed, in no state, in 1970, was the category for farm laborer one of their top five occupations, as it would have been in 1960. This contradicts a prevailing stereotypical view which so often sees Mexican-Americans predominantly cast in farm laborer roles.

Perhaps the most significant shift in the last decade was the increase in the proportion of Mexican-Americans holding white-collar jobs. Their proportional gains were greater than the overall rate of growth in such jobs. In 1960 the percentage of Mexican-American workers in white-collar jobs in the five states ranged from 18 to 28, and by 1970 increased to a range of 30 to 38 percent. Their largest gain in this regard was in Arizona, increasing from 18 to 30 percent, while in California the increase was from 24 to 34 percent, and in Texas from 22 to 32 percent.

At the other end of the job spectrum the proportion of Mexican-Americans in farm work declined rapidly during the same period, decreasing by more than one-half in each of the states. By 1970 the percentage of Mexican-Americans in farm work in the states ranged from 3 to 7 percent, the latter figure being for

Arizona where the largest drop was experienced from the 1960 figure of 24 percent.

Overall, Mexican-Americans made substantial gains in occupational position over the decade, although they are still far behind the population as a whole. A crude measure of occupational difference shows around one-fourth of the gap closing between 1960 and 1970. However, Mexican-Americans usually receive lower earnings in the same occupation, so that even if this gap were closed, they would doubtless have lower average earnings than the general population.

Mexican-Americans are found in all occupations and all industries. However, they tend to cluster more in those offering low- or middle-range earnings, rather than being evenly distributed throughout the spectrum of jobs. Probably this and the fact that a substantial proportion of the jobs they hold do not offer year-round employment account more for their relatively low annual earnings, than the large numbers of them that are holding the lowest-paying jobs in the labor market.

The percentage of Mexican-Americans who are in full-year work (50–52 weeks) is lower than that of Anglos in each of the states; this is true for both male and female workers.[17] The difference is greatest in California, the state offering the highest *rates* of earnings, where only 68 percent of Mexican-American males of ages twenty-five to sixty-four have full-year work as compared to 76 percent of the Anglo males in that age group. In the case of female workers ages twenty-five to fifty-nine, the figures are 42 percent and 49 percent, respectively.

Another factor depressing the earnings of Mexican-Americans throughout the region is their consistently higher rates of unemployment compared to the Anglo rates. At the time of the 1970 census, these rates ranged from a low of 4.1 percent in Arizona to a high of 7.0 percent in Colorado and California, whereas the Anglo rates ranged from 3.4 percent in Arizona to 5.5 percent in California.

While there were no great differences in these rates of unemployment between the time of the 1960 census and the taking of the 1970 census, a decided change occurred in each state in the ratio of the Mexican-American unemployment rates to the Anglo rates. For both males and females, this ratio improved in each state. For instance, in 1960 Mexican-American males had a 9.5

percent rate in Colorado, compared to the Anglo males' 3.4 percent, or 2.8 times as high. The rates stood at 7.0 and 3.5 percent, respectively, in 1970, making the Mexican-American male unemployment rate only twice as high as the Anglo male rate.[18]

It is possible that this indication of more balanced employment prospects for Mexican-Americans vis-à-vis those for Anglos is illusory, however, because important changes were made in the definition of unemployment during these years. Changes made by the Bureau of Labor Statistics in the definition result in a significant amount of present unemployment being masked, deferred, or ignored.[19] For example, now all enrollees in the Neighborhood Youth Corps' out-of-school programs and some other manpower programs count as employed, although such enrollees establish their eligibility for the programs by being unemployed. At the same time, members of the Job Corps were simply counted as "not in the labor force." To the extent that Mexican-Americans are disproportionately represented in these programs, as compared to Anglos, it can be seen that this factor alone could improve the ratio Mexican-American unemployment rates had to the Anglo rates. The placement, for instance, of but fifteen hundred Mexican-American males in Colorado NYC, Job Corps, or other manpower programs which remove enrollees from the unemployment statistics, would be sufficient to account for lowering the 1960 9.5 percent unemployment rate to the 7.0 percent figure for 1970.[20] In this connection it is interesting to point out that in the manpower work and training programs administered by the U.S. Department of Labor the number of Mexican-American enrollees is two and three times the number of Anglos in some states and exceeds that of Anglos in each state. The total enrollment of Mexican-Americans was 68,748, compared to 52,025 Anglos, as of June 30, 1972.[21]

The median income of Mexican-American families rose in the 1960–70 period, as it did for other broad segments of the population. In no case were the dollar amounts of such increases comparable to increases in Anglo median family income, however, although the overall ratio of Mexican-American family incomes to those of Anglos did improve.[22]

The median annual family income for Mexican-Americans in 1960 ranged from $2,913 in Texas to $5,532 in California. By 1970, the range was $5,897 to $8,791, again with Texas and California representing the lowest and highest amount among the states for

Mexican-Americans, contrasting with the range for Anglos of $9,430 to $11,360. It goes without saying that much of the increase for both groups was a consequence of a generally inflationary period, hence it did not represent an increase in real income in the amounts shown.

There was improvement in the ratio of Mexican-American incomes to Anglo incomes in each of the states, except California. With the median Anglo family income set at 100, the ratio of Mexican-American income relative to this figure rose during the decade from 68 to 76 in Arizona; 67 to 73 in Colorado; 57 to 64 in New Mexico; 52 to 62 in Texas; but, oddly, it declined from 79 to 77 in California. It can be speculated that because California attracted more Mexican-American in-migrants than the other states during the ten-year period, it had more persons newly entering its labor markets who were just beginning their trajectory of upward job mobility and, hence, received relatively lower earnings. This speculation appears to be likely in view of the fact that the Mexican-American population more than doubled in California in this ten-year period, increasing by a phenomenal 117 percent!

Even so, in 1970 there were proportionately fewer Mexican-American families in California with incomes below poverty levels than there were in the other states. The poverty definitions used in the 1970 census contained income cutoffs that were adjusted for family size, rural and urban residency, number of children under eighteen years of age, and other factors. These factors rendered the 1970 enumeration of poverty not comparable to earlier years, when such statistics were based on a simple standard of $3,000 annual income per family. At the time of the 1970 census, the percentage of Mexican-American families below the poverty level was 14.0 in California; 20.9 percent in Colorado; 31.4 percent in Texas were below; and in Arizona and New Mexico, there were 20.2 percent and 29.4 percent, respectively. Comparable figures for Anglo families below the poverty level ranged from only 6.3 percent in California to 8.5 percent in Texas. Thus, the incidence of poverty among Mexican-American families in these states was more than two to three times as high as it was among Anglo families.[23]

It is seldom recognized that poverty statistics do not include many of the poorest persons, those who receive income from public income maintenance programs. Although such persons get subsistence allotments only because they are poor, these welfare payments often raise their annual incomes above the poverty standard, with the result that they are then no longer counted as poor. Therefore, the figures on the incidence of poverty should be examined together with those for public assistance.

In the Southwest the difference in the proportion of Mexican-American and Anglo families who receive public income assistance is indeed great. The percentage of Anglo families ranges from 2.0 in Arizona to 5.9 in Colorado, whereas for Mexican-American families it goes from 8.4 percent to 14.9 percent in the same states.[24]

Family size also is an important factor in determining the extent of poverty. In this context, it should be noted that the trend toward smaller families and smaller households that characterizes the general U.S. population applies to Mexican-American families as well. In the 1960–70 decade, the mean size of Mexican-American families declined in most of the states by three-tenths of a person; the mean size of households dropped slightly more than this. These decreases were less in California, but it appears that Mexican-Americans in the other states were simply approaching, by 1970, the family and household sizes that the Mexican-Americans had reached in California by 1960, where their families and households were the smallest among the states. The downward trend in the size of Anglo families and households continued only very slightly in the censal period.[25]

Family size has been declining for two reasons: fewer children and other relatives are living together in the same household, and women are bearing fewer children. The "fertility ratio," which compares the number of children to the number of women of childbearing age, is declining for both Anglos and Mexican-Americans. The ratios show that while a Mexican-American mother has a greater number of children than an Anglo mother, this number is falling for her more rapidly than for the Anglo mother.

These trends have some significance with respect to the incidence of poverty. It was shown in the Mexican-American Study Project that the burden of family poverty among Mexican-Americans, when compared to that of other groups, was more severe than it appeared on the surface because of their larger family size. The dependency ratio—the number of persons being supported by one person with income—was much higher among

Mexican-Americans. This means that the proportion of Mexican-American individuals in poverty was greater than it was for their families.

Whatever slights Mexican-Americans may experience with respect to their incomes, these become a serious plight for a disproportionate number of their elderly. Senator Frank Church, Chairman of the Senate's Special Committee on Aging, has commented that not only are they among the most economically deprived of the population, but are also the least likely to receive benefits from existing federal programs.[26] This is true not only because of the crucial language barrier, the extent of functional illiteracy among their aged, and their consequent lack of knowledge of such programs, but sometimes also because of residency and citizenship requirements that have been written by law into some of the state programs. Some of these laws have only recently been struck down in the courts, yet even the federal Medicare Part B insurance program does not allow aliens to participate unless they are lawful permanent residents and have resided in the country for five years.

Time and again, when analyzing the distinctive elements in the social and economic conditions of Mexican-Americans in the Southwest, one is confronted by the fact that the most central factor contributing to these conditions is the steady addition of more Mexican nationals to their number. This itself creates a process in which those who start with considerable social and economic disadvantages in the economy of the Southwest are the very ones who must bear the greater burden of competing with the poverty that persists in a neighboring country.

It goes without saying that Mexican nationals upon entering this country seek out those urban and rural barrios in which they feel a cultural compatibility and kinship. If they have a dubious legal status as immigrants, such places provide a setting in which they quickly can find some protective means enabling them to elude whatever official curiosity might exist as to their presence. Whether they are lawfully in this country or not, it is apparent that by settling in such communities they are joining an existing local labor market and tapping the same informational grapevine which always served as the principal means by which most workers get their jobs. The overwhelming majority of American workers get their jobs through friends and relatives, not through the highly structured public and private employment services. This simple fact about the functioning of labor markets explains how it is possible, in the 1970s, that there exists in the country a sizable "underground railroad" to whisk workers from one setting to another and place them in the labor force. It is unlikely that the arrangements which existed in pre–Civil War days, moving escaping blacks from the South to the North, could match the subtle intricacies and clandestine arrangements that now serve to place Mexicans in the U.S. labor force.

Mexican and Mexican-American workers have always lined up at the same ports-of-entry for jobs in the labor market. This can only result in a loose labor market—one in constant oversupply, one having a depressing effect on wages. Those institutional arrangements or deterrents to mobility which tend to tighten the market for most jobs and influence wage determination upward in this country simply do not prevail in a significant part of local labor markets on which so many Mexican-Americans depend.

This can best be seen by examining the differences that exist in two Mexican-American communities, one of which has a considerably higher proportion than the other of recent arrivals from Mexico. An opportunity for making such an examination is provided by recent, very detailed, surveys by the Bureau of the Census in eleven urban areas in the Southwest; the one in Los Angeles is useful for making this examination.[27] A very high percentage of Mexican newcomers to the Los Angeles metropolis presently settle in the south-central portion of the city in a section north of the area that came to be known in the past decade as Watts, a designation properly belonging to only one relatively small subdivision in south-central Los Angeles. Less than one-tenth of the Mexican-Americans in this section, including infants and children, were born in Los Angeles; three-fourths were born outside of the United States and one-half came to Los Angeles within the five-year period prior to the survey, principally from Mexico.[28]

The labor force participation rates for both males and females are higher in this section than in Mexican-American communities in the city of Los Angeles populated by smaller proportions of the foreign-born from Mexico. And a higher percentage of them work full-time than is true of persons in other sections. Clearly, their attachment to the labor force is strong. And their success in finding employment, as shown by their lower rates of unemployment for both males and females, seems to be better than is found in sections where longer established groups of Mexican-Americans reside in Los Angeles. Even so, their earnings are substantially less, both in weekly pay and in annual terms. As a consequence, a higher percentage of their families have incomes below the poverty line—almost one-fourth—than is the case among the longer established Mexican-American families in Los Angeles. Also, their housing conditions are decidedly inferior, whether compared to Negro or other families in the same neighborhood or to Mexican-Americans surveyed elsewhere in Los Angeles.

It is of interest to note that the survey found that even in jobs of a kind, such as common labor jobs, the median earnings of Anglo males exceeded that of Mexican-Americans. It also showed that the wage expectations of Mexican-Americans, both male and female, who had experienced unemployment in the preceding year were less than their Anglo counterparts of the same age in the same neighborhoods. The gap in these expectations was greatest for males over sixty-five years old who were out of the labor force. For Mexican-Americans, a median weekly wage of $102 was acceptable for returning them to work, while for Anglos in the same neighborhoods it would have to be $202 a week.[29] This last difference may be a function of Anglos having more adequate Social Security benefit coverage with its accompanying penalty for retiree earnings above the maximum allowable amount.

Although less than one-fifth of the workers in Los Angeles are employed in manufacturing, the majority of Mexican-Americans in the Los Angeles survey areas work in manufacturing industries and in operative or craftsmen occupations. This is true for both males and females.[30] This very fact puts into question a rather commonly held image of the Mexican immigrant, that upon entering this country's labor force he is relegated only to entry-level, unskilled, or common-labor type employment. At least in the urban complex of Los Angeles, this does not appear to be true. There are employment opportunities for the Mexican immigrants in Los Angeles, and the fact that significant numbers of them appear to have entered operative and craftsmen jobs indicates they are indeed competitive with domestic workers in that labor market, not only for unskilled jobs, but operative and craftsmen jobs as well. The proportion of Mexican-Americans in the Southwest who are self-employed, including those who are so employed as unpaid family workers, is less than one-half of what it is for all Anglo workers, being less than 7 percent. The bulk of those so employed are in retail trade and service occupations: small food stores, gas stations, and eating and drinking establishments.

The number of U.S. firms owned by Mexican-Americans is almost insignificant—less than one percent of all firms and representing less than two-tenths of one percent of the gross receipts of all firms.[31] Clearly, the economic turf that Mexican-Americans have established within American business enterprise is minimal. Their economic base is overwhelmingly one of dependency on the employer-employee relationship in firms they do not own or direct.

Many Mexican-American workers who are dependent on jobs within their local labor market are caught up in a situation in which there can never be any tightening of the labor supply so long as the flow of new immigrants from Mexico continues. Consequently, external market forces that might tend to raise wages in the jobs they hold are significantly nullified. A century ago American labor leaders began their long and successful efforts to relieve other groups of U.S. workers from the competitiveness of unrestrained European and Oriental immigration. They sensed correctly that an effective trade union movement could never be established so long as employers were free to tap foreign labor supplies. Such efforts on behalf of Mexican-American workers have not yet succeeded.

Early evidence from the last decade shows that Mexican-Americans, as a group, have progressed somewhat economically, advanced their educational achievement levels considerably, and abandoned any quiescent attitudes that once left them largely unnoticed when legislative programs and appropriations were under consideration.

There has been a dramatic improvement in the level of schooling among Mexican-Americans over the years. This improvement continued during the sixties, so that the median years of schooling of Spanish-surname persons twenty-five years of age and over in the five states moved from averages of 4.8 to 8.6 years in 1960 to 6.7 to

9.7 years in 1970, with Texas the low state and California the high state in both cases.

Since the years of schooling of Anglos rose much less, Mexican-Americans were able to narrow much of the gap between the two groups—closing 19 percent of the gap that existed in Texas in 1960 and 24 percent of the gap that existed in California. However, this gain still left Mexican-Americans far behind the Anglo population—in fact, in each state they are also behind the Negro population in years of schooling.

The very substantial gains of the past decade, following several previous decades of rapid improvement, provide hope that eventually these gains will be translated into higher incomes and a better life for Mexican-Americans to a greater degree than has been true in the past. Of course, it may take a decade or more for even occupational advances made possible by higher education to be fully translated into gains in earnings and incomes. This is so because higher earnings are also a function of work experience and time on the job.[32]

It is doubtful that most of these gains can be viewed as a direct consequence of legislation passed in the last decade providing for more equal job and housing opportunities, federally sponsored remedial education and job training programs, or programs to eliminate poverty. There is evidence that much of the gains can be attributed to the mobility of Mexican-Americans by their moving away from areas of more limited economic opportunity and of more deep-seated discrimination. For instance, by 1970 over one-third of Southwestern Mexican-Americans were in the four metropolises of Los Angeles, San Antonio, San Francisco-Oakland, and Houston. Generally, the Mexican-American population has become more urban in the Southwest than has the Anglo population. The 1950 census showed 72.0 percent of the Anglo population living in urban places, contrasting with only 66.4 percent of the Chicano. By 1970 these figures read 81.1 percent and 86.0 percent, respectively.[33]

It can also be shown from the 1970 census that almost without exception those Mexican-Americans who have moved out of the Southwest to other Western states enjoy more of a parity of family income, as well as median years of schooling, with Anglos than is the case in the five Southwestern states. This is true in Missouri,

Minnesota, Iowa, Oklahoma, Nebraska, Kansas, Oregon, Montana, and Utah. The exceptions to this are found only in Washington, Wyoming, and Idaho, where family income parities with Anglos are slightly below those prevailing in California and Arizona.[34]

On balance, it can be ventured that the decade was at least a holding action for Mexican-Americans, leaving many of the social and economic inequities that accumulated for them in earlier years yet to be settled. Whether these can ever be brought into some semblance of balance with the larger U.S. society depends, again, on what is done about the problem of the border. And for this there is no easy, uncontested solution.

The problem is not just the geographical setting of the border —the fact that this is our only border with a country having large numbers of people seeking to enter as economic refugees, or that many parts of its eighteen-hundred-mile length can often be walked or waded across; there are other considerations.

Mexican-Americans themselves are deeply divided on what to do about restricting entry from Mexico. There are those who would seal the border, or require everyone to carry papers proving citizenship or lawful status, and penalize employers who hire uncredentialed persons. Then there are those who argue that the Treaty of Guadalupe-Hidalgo ending the war with Mexico in 1848 drew no boundary that morally or legally should be recognized, that the "People of Aztlán" should have free passage over their ancestral lands, or, at the least, that amnesty should be offered to all those presently in the country whose status is questionable under immigration regulations.

Whatever is done in these regards, it is clear that present problems are less ones of how to rerun history, or restore ancient equities, but rather ones of improving and equalizing the economic opportunities of all the diverse people of the Southwest, here and in Mexico. Many of these people are direct descendants of those indigenous groups inhabiting the Southwest before the culture and technology of Western Europe confronted them in their land; many others are the racial and ethnic amalgam resulting from that confrontation. It has been 475 years since Henry VII gave the first Letters Patent to the English-speaking Genoese, John Cabot, and his sons, or their heirs and assigns, the right in the King's name "to subdue, occupy and possess all such towns, cities, castles and isles of them found, which they can subdue, occupy and possess, as our vassals . . ." Just as feudal notions of vassalage, subservience, or subordination are scarcely defensible in our society, neither can there be any defense of residual consequences of former vassalage. To the extent that individuals and groups may choose for themselves to remain on the fringes of the developing post-industrial society, there is a growing acceptance of the notion that they should not be interfered with in doing so, that multifarious cultures within a country add to the amenities of our lives. Commitments to equal opportunity for all must include the freedom for people to be different and not thereby be denied a just and full share of what the economy can provide. Mexican-Americans have valued their differences from the host society and for that have all too frequently not enjoyed equality of opportunity, as shown in this book's other essays. Because of this the case can be made that there is reason for the nation to give to Mexican-Americans the same specialized attention accorded other regions and groups of people when their problems come into national focus.

President Franklin Roosevelt gave such attention when he tagged the South "The nation's number one economic problem"; President John Kennedy did it when he instituted massive new programs solely for Appalachia and for workers displaced as a result of our foreign trade policies; Former Senator Ralph W. Yarborough and Senator Joseph M. Montoya attempted to do it when they introduced the Southwestern Human Development Act of 1967, a piece of legislation largely addressed to the economic problems of Mexican-Americans. The funds sought were small compared to what the last three administrations have already expended on training, relocating, and sustaining Cuban refugees.

The argument here is that if it serves the national interest to assist Cuban aliens, or persons floundering in the cultural and economic backwaters of Appalachia, or persons made jobless by national trade policies, or those disadvantaged by the mechanization of agriculture in the South, then surely it will serve the national interest to assist Mexican-Americans in increasing their ability to live their lives as they wish and to improve their place in the economic and social spheres, so that they may claim a more just and full share in what the economy can provide in the Southwest and elsewhere.

Notes

1. The maximum proportion of persons in the Census Bureau's Spanish Language/Spanish Surname category who properly might be styled as Mexican-Americans varies considerably from state to state. While this proportion will vary from 93 to 97 percent of the SL/SS category in Texas, Arizona, Colorado, and New Mexico, it is only 82 percent in California. It must be remembered that there are substantial numbers of persons in these and other states whose origins were in Cuba, Puerto Rico, or elsewhere in Latin America and who would, of course, speak Spanish and for the most part have Spanish surnames. See 1970 Census PC(1)-C, Table 49.

2. Julian Samora, *Los Mojados: The Wetback Story* (Notre Dame, Ind.: University of Notre Dame Press, 1971).

3. Jorge A. Bustamante, "The 'Wetback' as Deviant: An Application of Labeling Theory," *American Journal of Sociology* 77, No. 4 (January 1972):709.

4. David S. North, *Alien Workers: A Study of the Labor Certification Program,* (Washington, D.C.: Trans-Century Corporation, 1971), p. 69. (Study PB 202 827, available from National Technical Information Service of U.S. Department of Commerce.)

5. Agency for International Development, Statistics and Reports Division, *Gross National Product,* Washington, D.C., May 10, 1972.

6. The Bureau of the Census estimates that 5.7 million persons were unenumerated in 1960, mainly men from minority groups between 20 and 50 years of age. See Deborah P. Klein, "Determining the Labor Force Status of Men Missed in the Census," *Monthly Labor Review* 93, No. 3 (U.S. Department of Labor, Washington, D.C., March 1970):26–32.

Affidavit of San Jose (California) Survey of December 1971, in the case of *Confederacion de la Raza Unida, et al., v. George H. Brown, Director of the U.S. Census, et al.* (N.D. Cal., #C-71-2285), states that 17 percent of Mexican-Americans in East San Jose, Santa Clara County, in a random door-to-door survey stated that they were never contacted in the 1970 census, and 55 percent gave indication of reasons to believe the Census Bureau failed to accurately count them. See: Court documents available from Mexican-American Legal Defense and Educational Fund, Inc., 145 Ninth Street, San Francisco, California, 94102.

7. *Monthly Labor Review* 95, No. 12 (December 1972):15.

8. Leo Grebler et al., *The Mexican-American People* (New York: The Free Press, 1970). Also, the eleven Advance Reports of the Mexican-American Study Project at the University of California, Los Angeles, Division of Research, Graduate School of Management, UCLA, 1965–1968.

9. Ibid., p. 13. Professor Walter Fogel estimated that the years of schooling accounted for 47–85 percent of the differences in income in Texas and California in 1960. See Walter Fogel, "The Effects of Low Educational Attainment on Incomes: A Comparative Study of Selected Ethnic Groups," Institute of Industrial Relations, Reprint #166, 1967.

Our own calculations for New Mexico, Arizona, and Colorado show 35 percent, 45 percent, and 58 percent, respectively in 1970. (computed from U.S. Census PC(1)-D, Table 197)

10. Equal Employment Opportunity Commission, *Equal Employment Opportunity Report—1969: Job Patterns for Minorities and Women in Private Industry,* U.S. Government Printing Office, Washington, D.C., 1972, pp. vii–x.

11. Ibid., pp. 4, 6, 7, 33, and 45.

Note: The service worker category contains such a mixed bag of jobs, ranging from porters to detectives, that it was not considered to be blue-collar.

12. Fred H. Schmidt, *Spanish Surnamed American Employment in the Southwest,* Equal Employment Opportunity Commission, USGPO, Washington, D.C., 1970.

13. U.S. Department of Labor, *Manpower Report of the President*, U.S. Government Printing Office, Washington, D.C., March 1972, Tables G-7, G-8, and G-9.

14. These 1970 census computations were made from PC(1)-C volumes, Table 54, "Occupation of Employed Persons by Race," by subtracting employment figures for "Persons of Spanish language or Spanish surname" from those given for "white" to arrive at employment figures for "Anglo."

15. Ibid., Table 56.

16. U.S. Bureau of the Census, Census of the Population: 1970, *General Social and Economic Characteristics*, Final Report PC(1)-C, U.S. GPO, Washington, D.C., 1971.

17. Ibid., Table 56.

18. Ibid., Tables 46 and 53, and 1960 Census PC(2)-B, Table 6.

19. Charles C. Killingsworth, *Rising Unemployment: A "Transitional Problem?"* School of Labor and Industrial Relations, Michigan State University, East Lansing, Michigan, 1971 (Research Reprint Series No. 122).

20. There were 58,941 males in the Mexican-American labor force at the time of the 1970 census. Thus, enrolling 1,473 males in the programs would accomplish a 2.5 percent lowering of the unemployment rate. 1970 Census, PC(1)-C, Table 53.

21. These figures are for enrollees listed as "Spanish-Americans" by the Department of Labor, compared to the number of "white" enrollees less "Spanish Americans." Taken from a table prepared at our request by the Department.

22. U.S. Bureau of the Census, Census of the Population: 1970, Tables 47 and 57. In the computation of Anglo incomes the median was used as a weighted average. The maximum error of this method appears not to exceed 1.0 percent.

23. Ibid., Table 58.

24. Ibid., Table 58.

25. Ibid., Tables 48 and 58.

26. Quoted in *Los Angeles Times*, June 3, 1972, Part 1, p. 11.

27. U.S. Bureau of the Census, Census of Population: 1970, *Employment Profiles of Selected Low-Income Areas*, Final Report PHC(3)-13, 14, and 15, Los Angeles, California—Area 1, Area 2, and Summary, U.S. Government Printing Office, Washington, D.C., 1972.

28. Ibid., Table C.

29. Ibid., Tables 30a, 30b, 31a, and 31b.

30. Ibid., Table 6.

31. *Minority-Owned Business*, U.S. Dept. of Commerce, Bureau of the Census, Table 4, Part C, 1969.

32. Walter Fogel, "The Effects of Low Educational Attainment on Incomes," pp. 38–39.

33. Mexican-American Study Project, and 1970 Census, PC(1)-C, Tables 81 and 97.

34. 1970 Census, PC(1)-C, Tables 51 and 57.

5

Educational Challenges in Elementary and Secondary Schools

JULIAN NAVA

The author is Professor of History at California State University at Northridge and also has been an elected member of the Board of Education, Los Angeles Unified School District, since 1967. In addition he is active in numerous community projects that vary from television program production to helping build Mexican-style equestrian centers. His background includes education in barrio schools, service in the Navy Air Corps in World War II, and a Ph.D. in 1955 from Harvard University. His teaching experience includes a year each in Venezuela, Spain, Colombia, and two years in Puerto Rico. Dr. Nava's perspective is thus broad and includes the field of publishing (some twenty books), community work, and politics.

Introduction

Economic and educational matters embrace virtually every aspect of life in the Southwest, for everything stems from these activities. This essay has made certain selections from the vast subject area, and it shows the bias of the author. The bias holds that education has the greatest single impact on shaping the course of life, and schools are therefore the most important single influence on children in the formative years.

The Weatherhead Foundation deserves praise for undertaking this effort to promote more knowledge about the culture and society of the Southwest. This essay tries to take into account the other essays in this book, but it is also meant to stand on its own.

Good questions are more important than good answers. From good questions we gain a sharp view of reality and can hope to deal with the problems and issues that confront us. From good questions we can hope to produce good answers. Thus this essay will raise questions, as well as supply answers.

The most important question this essay may pose is, "How does education affect the life of Chicano kids today, and what does this mean for the rest of us?"

Cultural pluralism in the Southwest exists today despite Anglo-American efforts to eliminate it. The Indian and Mexican-American cultures have survived in the face of institutionalized drives to wipe out diversity through "Americanization" programs. Most Anglo-Americans have regarded the cultural differences of the two minorities as a flaw and impediment to their acceptance as full Americans.

Today attitudes toward cultural differences are changing. An appropriate starting point might be a sentence from the *1970 Annual Report* of the Weatherhead Foundation that reads: "The apparent success of pluralism in this region [Southwest] seemed, among other things, to offer worthwhile lessons to other sections of the country, including the cities . . ." It is true that "pluralism" does exist in the Southwest with its mix of Anglo, Indian, and Mexican-American cultures—with variations within each of these categories. But such "pluralism" is far less the result of any *policy* by a governing elite than the outcome of resistance by Indians and Mexican-Americans to abolition or assimilation by Anglo society. Pluralism exists despite, not because of, the official policy of many decades. From this epic of minority cultural survival there are indeed "lessons to other sections of the country."

At present we are in a period of transition concerning the acceptability and utilities of diversity. The debate and dialogue arising from past injuries and future aspirations, from the push-and-pull between minority assimilation and assertion, and from the presence of new ideas in established institutions are nowhere more evident and dramatic than in the schools of the Southwest.

The challenge we face in education can be seen in the lack of understanding about Mexican-Americans among public school educators. The following questions, frequently posed by teachers, illustrate the gap between the Anglo instructor and the Mexican-American pupil.

1. Is the culture of Mexico still alive in those who have been in this country a long time?

2. Why is Mexican-American culture so different from ours?

3. Why do Mexican-Americans show up more in crime records?

4. Why do not Mexican-American families stress education like we do?

5. Why do not Mexican-Americans want to acculturate?

6. Why does the Mexican-American peer group hold back those who try to achieve in "Anglo society"?

7. Should we "Americanize" Mexican-American students at the expense of their own culture?

8. How do you change old cultural patterns in school? (There is usually a negative connotation to "old cultural patterns.")

9. Will not special attention to the Mexican-American "spoil" the group so that they cannot progress on their own?

10. What can I do as an individual teacher to help Mexican-Americans?

Simple misunderstanding is—in too many instances—reinforced by deep-seated prejudice. This applies to many educators who would be surprised to discover that some of their common practices and attitudes teach some children to assume a superior status and others an inferior one. Over the years, millions of Mexican-American school children in California (and the Southwest as well) have been taught by teachers and their schools that they are inferior to "Anglos." They learn this at an early age and know it well by puberty, a mind-set that conditions the rest of their lives. Such stratification is sometimes deliberate and sometimes unintentional. The net effect is the same.

Teaching Stratification

The following material is taken from a 1965 Stanford University doctoral dissertation by Theodore Parsons entitled "Ethnic Cleavage in a California School," which was summarized in *Phi Delta Kappan* (October 1966). The paper is based on conditions in a central California town that is typical in many ways of others in the Southwest. Parsons reports:

1. A teacher, asked why she had called on "Johnny" to lead five Mexican-Americans in orderly file out of a school room, explained, "His father owns one of the big farms in the area . . . one day he will have to know how to handle the Mexicans."

2. Another teacher, following the general practice of calling on the Anglos to help Mexican-American pupils recite in class, said in praise of the system, "It draws them [the Anglos] out and gives them a feeling of importance."

3. The president of the Chamber of Commerce declared in praise of the school principal, "He runs a good school. We never have any trouble in our school. Every kid knows his place. . . . We believe that every kid has to learn to respect authority and his betters."

4. The school principal expounded on the "grouping" and departmentalized reading programs instituted under his administration, "We thought that the white children would get more out of school if they could work faster and not be slowed down by the Mexicans. We thought the Mexican kids would do better work if they were in classes geared more to their level. We thought that maybe we could give them some special attention. . . ."

5. By admitted subterfuge the Chamber of Commerce committee sees to it that the artichoke festival "queen" is always an Anglo, with the Mexican-American candidate in second place as her attendant. An influential citizen told Parsons, "We could never have a Mexican queen represent us at the county fair."

6. Two of the three churches do not accept Mexican-Americans. At the Catholic Church, when both groups are assembled for special occasions, the Mexican-Americans sit in the back or stand if seating is inadequate.

7. At school graduation the Mexican-Americans march in last and sit at the back of the platform. A male teacher explained that this is traditional and "makes for a better-looking stage." Also the Anglos who have all the parts in the program can get more easily to the front. He added, "Once

we did let a Mexican girl give a little talk of some kind and all she did was to mumble around. She had quite an accent, too. Afterwards we had several complaints from other parents so we haven't done anything like that since. . . . That was 12 years ago."

8. The Mexican-American Cub Scout pack was in high excitement at the close of one annual town cleanup drive, when their pile was the highest at the 10:00 A.M. deadline. At 10:40 the garbage collector's large truck arrived and deposited a big load of trash on the Anglo pack's pile, which was then awarded the fifty-dollar prize.

9. A light-skinned Mexican-American high school graduate promptly lost the job as a bank teller she had just been engaged to fill when the manager heard her speak to an acquaintance in Spanish. He said he had not realized she was a "Mexican"—it was not bank policy to employ Mexican-Americans.

Parsons reported that the school teachers, all Anglo, and for the most part indigenous to the area, appeared unanimous in sharing the stereotype of Mexican-Americans—inferior in capacity as well as performance. So firmly set is the pattern that a teacher, in full view of a group of well-dressed, quietly behaved Mexican-American children, could describe "Mexican" children as noisy and dirty.

Sociometric tests conducted by Parsons disclosed that even the Mexican-American children came to share the view constantly held up to them that the Anglos are "smarter" and that their good opinion was of special value.

In general, the Anglo informants characterized the Mexicans as immoral, violent, and given to fighting, dirty, unintelligent, improvident, irresponsible, and lazy. . . . Mexican informants often described Anglos as being unsympathetic, aggressive, interested only in themselves, cold and demanding. Not one of the several hundred people contacted during the field investigation had ever visited a home outside of his own ethnic group.

The dissertation, aptly described as a "complacency shocker," has observations that speak for themselves. Because of the mobility

of people today, schools that do not treat Mexican-American
children this way may still acquire some students who have had
such experiences elsewhere.

Recent reports and publications document the extent of the
problems faced by Mexican-Americans in public schools in the
Southwest. Some are worthy of note as basic points of departure
—Thomas Carter's *Mexican Americans in School: A History of
Educational Neglect* (1970), and the three reports by the United
States Commission on Civil Rights on the size and distribution of
Mexican-American enrollment, the performance of schools in areas
like achievement and holding power, and lastly, the most recent
report, *The Excluded Student: Educational Practices Affecting
Mexican Americans in the Southwest*, No. 3 (May 1972).

The basic problems are the following:

1. Ignorance and indifference of school officials in regard
to Mexican-American educational needs
2. Rejection by schools of Hispanic-Mexican culture
3. Exclusion of Spanish language in schools
4. Faulty educational programs and reluctance to change
5. Inadequate teachers and materials
6. Economic and political motives underlying school board
policies
7. Lack of political power among Mexican-Americans to
affect education

The specific problems that we face in helping Mexican-American school children are closely related to other community
problems, such as poverty, malnutrition, and so forth. These affect
school life and may well be causal factors that lead to underachievement. In the area of drop-outs, for example, it is an open
question how the interrelated problems combine so as to produce a
"push-out" or a drop-out. Among drop-outs, some choose to flee
from a bad situation, while others feel compelled to get a job due to
economic needs. Thus school problems must be faced in light of the
conditions in the community.

Let us look more closely at how schools have affected Mexican-
American children in a variety of ways not felt by other students.
Schools have served to Americanize pupils in the image of the
Anglo-American, who has always been in the numerical majority.

Much of our social history has been slanted or distorted to conform with our apparent success as a people.

Education reflects the attitudes and values of adult society, and this is clearly evident in the uses we make of history. To understand the educational challenges we face in helping Mexican-American pupils and their peers, we must reexamine what we think we know about the past.

Nativism vs. Diversity

Much of the strength of America has stemmed from her racial, religious, and cultural diversity. But although we can see this in retrospect, such a view was not common in our early history when minorities gave rise to fear among the English-speaking, Protestant majority. At our independence, most Western European nations did not give the United States of America a fighting chance to survive, as anyone well versed in late eighteenth-century American and European history can recall. Indeed, among the earliest patriots, fears arose that diversity threatened to break up the country from within if outside dangers did not.

As a result of the zeal to forge a nation, "nativism" appeared in the United States during the 1830s. John Higham in *Strangers in the Land* has described this suspicion of anything, anyone, or any group that stood out as either alien or different from the new "American man." The French traveler, Alexis de Tocqueville, was the first to clearly describe the new American society in his classic work *Democracy in America*. By the 1830s, as an expression of nativism, groups like Royalists (which were still considered a threat), Catholics, secret groups like the Masons, exotic religions like Christian Science and the Mormons, and national or racial groups were identified as "minorities." Thus, the struggle between nativism and "minorities" is deeply imbedded in our nation's history.

The "melting pot" theory has persisted as a major theme in our history. While some of the melting was voluntary on the part of immigrants, much was not. The purpose of the melting pot was to forge one new nation out of a polyglot people. Whatever the motives or means may have been, the melting pot did not fully work, for minorities were not eliminated. In my opinion, the melting pot idea is a myth. What did happen is that New England, Midwestern culture (which we sometimes characterize as "WASP") became the mold into which successive waves of immigrant groups were poured. (This practice still continues in many nations. In Latin America, Africa, and much of Asia today, creating a national identity is a prime purpose. In Latin America one says, *hacer patria*—"make motherland"—because there isn't one; there is simply a political unit.) Historically, in the United States, the general purpose of nativism was understandable. The object was to take immigrants from Scandinavia, Ireland, the Germanies (there was no one Germany until the 1870s), and many other places like southeastern Europe, and make them Americans. Therefore, the minorities shed their clothes, changed names, or dropped accents. Others intermarried. Some even reshaped their noses and, back at the ranch, some said that they were "Spanish"! Of course, not all Spanish-surnamed people are Mexican, but until recently, what passed for "Spanish" cuisine in many restaurants was really Mexican. The motives of all those millions of Americans who tried to hide their past were understandable, although in many cases pathetic. But from the national view, conformity did help forge a nation strong enough to survive the Civil War and later conflicts.

Cultural pluralism in the United States has persisted despite pressures to conform to the Anglo-American model. Currently we find a revival of pride in ethnicity among "white ethnics" like Italians, Swedes, and Poles. More visibility is now sought by ethnic groups and I sense this will increase in the future. Nativism now faces a serious challenge. We may have reached the point where the definition of "American" will change.

Looking back, however, nativism exercised a powerful influence on our nation. The human costs of the melting pot were very high, but those costs were obscured by the territorial, economic, and political success of America that amazed the world. Success gave Americans, mostly Anglo-Americans, the conviction that they were not only superior but virtually invincible. Our "Manifest Destiny" had almost no limits so that America was no longer defensive toward Europe by the beginning of the twentieth century. We were a world power.

The American success story has been told so many times (often misleadingly) that there is little relation between the story and what really happened. By 1900 our superiority complex was such that some proposed a world rule in which United States control would extend around the globe. Indeed, we soon annexed the Hawaiian Islands and established protectorates over Puerto Rico and other overseas places without the consent of their people. At home, cultural minorities like Mexican-Americans faced pressure to assimilate.

Old World Roots of Conflict

The origins of American anti-Mexican feelings are to be found in Europe. Just as it is necessary to study British history to understand the formation of American society, so, too, must we trace to their origin American attitudes about other peoples. The roots and attitudes toward Mexicans go back to earlier events concerning Europeans and Indians.

Harry Bernstein in *The Making of an Inter-American Mind* (1961) traced the development in the United States of ideas about Latin Americans. He depicts the mixed feelings which colonists and our Founding Fathers had about Spaniards, *criollos* (whites of Spanish ancestry born in America), *mestizos,* and other mixed groups in Spanish-American lands. These attitudes were the product of certain events that took place after the discovery of America and after the Protestant Reformation—events that transpired not in the United States but in Europe.

The discovery of America opened a new chapter in world history in ways most Americans do not understand. Our books tell the story with little, if any, attention to the Hispanic perspective on the momentous events. The Anglo (English) bias is clear in the accounts offered in college or teacher training. Most of these betray an anti-Spanish point of view, a bias seen in acts of historic commission or omission. As Salvador de Madariaga put it, "Spain had to be wrong so that England could be right in what she did around the world for some three centuries." In addition to this bias against Spain, virtually all historical accounts omit reference to the great debate that raged there over the Indian question and its resolution. Spain's mission in America *(las Indias Occidentales)* is usually grossly misrepresented as well. In short, the discovery of America has been interpreted through hostile English eyes.

The vilification of Spain and Portugal has been referred to as *"la leyenda negra"* (The Black Legend). This bias has survived to the present time in different forms. Mexican-Americans are intimately affected by the Black Legend, as we shall see. So, too, are other contemporary Americans.

The seeds of anti-Spanish sentiment sprung from envy and resentment at her phenomenal rise to world power upon the discovery of the New World. When the extent of the new lands became evident in Europe, other nations questioned the legal basis for Spanish and Portuguese claims. Papal recognition silenced most critics as long as Western Europe was nominally Roman Catholic. After the Protestant Reformation, however, national interests merged with religious ideas to challenge the hegemony of Spain and Portugal. Now a Protestant God blessed the territorial ambitions of Protestant princes. With a national church at their side, north European states felt free to confront both papal interests and the Iberian states. Spain under Charles V (grandson of the Catholic Kings), and especially under Philip II, assumed the task of defending Catholicism against heresy. As in the United States' crusade against Communism, Spain interfered in the domestic affairs of nations above the Pyrenees in defense of Catholicism; she had power in northern Europe as well because of the relation of the Spanish kings to the Hapsburgs. Thus for both religious and dynastic reasons Spain, rather than Portugal, became embroiled in central Europe as an imperial power defending the religious status quo. Spanish occupation aroused bitter hostility, which her troops returned in kind. The very word "Spanish" became hateful.

England was at the center of the historical development that led to prejudice against everything Spanish by the end of the sixteenth century. A recent work by William S. Maltby, *The Black Legend in England* (1971), helps fill this historic void. There are also the works on Philip II by Robert Watson (about 1777) and the work by the American writer, John Lathrop Motley, on the rise of the Dutch Republic in the mid-nineteenth century. Each is a classic example of how bitter the feelings were about the Spaniards. Lewis Hanke's *The Spanish Struggle for Justice in the Conquest of America* (1949) and Clarence Haring's *The Spanish Empire in America* (1947) are seminal arguments against the Black Legend that antedate Maltby.

Modern capitalism flourished in northern Europe as the fortunes of Spain and Portugal declined. By most criteria, northern Europeans dominated Western European life that revolved around new and vigorous Protestant religious and cultural values. Color of skin became associated with strength, creativity, and power in the minds of northern Europeans. In ways that are not fully enough explained, but clearly evident, darker Iberian peoples suffered a new negative stereotype. Because of their historic experience, Spaniards and Portuguese did not equate darkness of skin with other forms of inferiority, since much of Iberian culture stemmed from North African and Middle Eastern sources.

Iberian contact with Africans was varied and extended. By contrast, in the modern era, early north European contacts were associated with conquest and enslavement of Africans. The experience with slavery among Protestant peoples had some qualitative differences from those of Spain and Portugal. Because of Iberian experience with darker peoples, and due to the universality of Catholicism, Catholic support for slavery was always qualified, limited, and guilt-ridden. In contrast, Protestant churches were white to start with and remained so. This helps explain the particular ingredients of racism among Protestants. Generally, among Catholics, slavery was a social condition which did not define the inherent quality of the person. Among northern Europeans slavery came to reflect essential inferiority.

Racism is evident also in the differences between the Iberian and north European view about the Indian. After the scathing denunciation made by Fray Bartolomé de las Casas in the early sixteenth century against Spanish treatment of the Caribbean Indians, Spain debated the Indian question for over a decade. The outcome produced the so-called New Laws of 1542. These defined the rights of Indians and asserted royal protection and dedication to their Christianization, stemming from the conclusion that Indians were human beings, equal to Spaniards in the eyes of God and the king. Indeed, African slavery in Spanish America served at the outset to relieve demands on Indian labor. Even then, in both Portuguese and Spanish America, slaves were extended legal rights exceeding those in the English colonies or later in the United States. Spanish and *criollo* guilt over the hypocrisy of black slavery helps explain the virtually unanimous measures to abolish or phase out slavery when new nations emerged in Latin America after 1810.

U.S. Attitudes

When the United States became a nation, its ideas and practices assigned defined roles to culturally different groups. Indians were clearly outside the body politic. Slaves were assigned a statistical value for purposes of representation in which each counted for less than a man—three-fifths to be exact. Although Spain assisted the American Revolution out of spite towards England, our Founding Fathers had mixed feelings about Spaniards and some could see conflicts that lay ahead over Florida and other lands to the west. Early American experiences with Indians and blacks conditioned their attitudes toward others that were not white, Protestant, and preferably Anglo-Saxon. In the course of efforts to forge a nationality and secure a nation, groups that stood out from the emerging Anglo-Protestant majority suffered pressure to conform or suffer the consequences. The rise of nativism influenced American notions about Mexican-Americans.

By the time de Tocqueville wrote, Americans had streamed across the mountains into the Mississippi Valley, encountering Spaniards and Mexicans. Earlier predictions about Florida had proven true as the United States forcibly annexed parts of Florida by 1813 and pressured Spain to give up the rest in 1819. The drive for new land to the west set the stage for the conflict between Mexico and the United States. Most Americans believed that Indians were inferior and that Spaniards and their descendants were vain, arrogant, cruel, and Catholic as well. With such backgrounds, most American politicians doubted whether Latin Americans were capable of self-government. Paternalism toward the new Latin American republics marked much of United States involvement in Latin America. In light of all this, several historians have said that the conflict between the United States and Mexico was unavoidable.

The so-called Monroe Doctrine of 1823 typifies American paternalism toward Latin America and assumption of special rights in the continent. Before long, ideas about American destiny raised the issue to high levels of emotion and produced notions about God's plan for the United States. Manifest Destiny supplied the final justification for American expansion.

The mestizo quality of most Mexicans added a new component to the American racism described above: Mexicans were worse than mere Indians or Spaniards in that they were "half-breeds." Many, of course, were black or mulatto as well as a mix of other elements. Although many Anglo-Americans were attracted by and admired the Mexican way of life, most scorned Mexicans and barely tolerated Spaniards. Leonard Pitt, in *The Decline of the Californios* (1966), traces the decline of the Spanish-speaking Californians in a somewhat typical region of the Southwest.

The separation of Texas from Mexico and the war that followed is common information. However, to understand the historical experience of Mexican-Americans we must review those crucial events from the Mexican, and, hopefully, from an objective position as well. Each nation and its peoples could be charged with bias. However, a comparison of the account of the conflict in United States and Mexican history textbooks is most interesting. Beyond national bias, what distinguishes United States' responsibility is the premeditation and planning that underlay the American role. The planning was such that even if Mexico had been united in its resistance (which it was not), a United States victory was almost certain.

At the time of the Mexican War there really was no Mexico, except in a political sense. The common man was excluded from a significant role in government until the time of Benito Juárez. Indians did not feel Mexican: Spanish was a second language to them and they disliked officials, most of whom exploited them. The national character of Mexico was not yet formed when war with the United States overwhelmed the nation. Thus Californios and New Mexicans did not put up a fight as one might expect. If they had, the contingents of American troops would have been decimated in view of distance, supply problems, and numbers. Some American historians, misunderstanding Mexico's poor showing, attribute it to her "inferiority."

It has been said that history is the account of the victor. This provocative generalization certainly applies to accounts of the Mexican-American after 1848. Cecil Robinson (*With the Ears of Strangers*, 1963) does a fine job of tracing references to the Mexican in American literature, just as Ramon Eduardo Ruiz's short work, *The Mexican War* (1963), helps those who want to reexamine that question in the light of varying sources and interpretations.

"Mexican-American" is a term common since the Second World War. Before that they were just plain Mexicans, if not "greasers" or

some other slang term. In the century between 1848 and 1948
Mexicans had a poor press and received worse treatment. Two
societies developed in the Southwest: an essentially feudal relationship between Anglo-American lord and "Mexican" serf. Social and
political facts reinforced Anglo ideas of superiority, as reflected in
education, cultural, and religious life, as well as economic and
social matters. Few positive references to Mexicans or Mexican-
Americans could be found in American letters, notes Robinson.

The American romance with the ranchos and missions toward
the end of the century did not carry over to a revision of how living
Mexicans were treated. This applied also to the new-found
romance with Southwestern Indians. The mixed blessings of this
romantic movement are clearly evident in Helen Hunt Jackson's
Ramona (1884).

Mexican-American Assertion

Mexican-American resistance to injustice was ignored in history
books, except in a distorted fashion. Mexicans were *bandidos* in the
event of any violence; Anglos were "pioneers" by comparison. The
killing of whites by Indians was a massacre, whereas whites only
"put down" Indian uprisings. The same form of bias affected
Mexicans who fought to protect their property, religion, and rights.
These distortions fill our history books. Notwithstanding the
historical work of Hubert Howe Bancroft in the nineteenth century
or the work of Herbert E. Bolton in the 1930s, few contributed to a
fair understanding of the Mexican people on both sides of the Rio
Grande. Carey McWilliams opened a new perspective in his *North
from Mexico* (1942). Now, Rudy Acuna's *Occupied America* (1972)
opens the door wide to new perspectives on the westward
movement. Since McWilliams' work, reflecting New Deal liberal-
ism, Mexicans have gradually gained stature. The veterans of
World War II, the "G.I. Generation," gained some social acceptance as "Mexican-Americans." With this came renewed efforts to
gain acceptance in the mainstream of Anglo society and reductions
in blatant discrimination.

In the 1960s a new consciousness emerged among Mexican-Americans. Some of those impatient with previous achievements seized
upon the word "Chicano" to describe themselves. Young Mexican-

Americans use the term to show pride in their heritage. Chicanos want to rewrite American history to show their side of the events. Public schools are only beginning to reexamine the role and contributions of Mexican-Americans to the United States and make corresponding changes in their attitude toward the cultural heritage of the Mexican-American.

United States history is being rewritten to include this neglected component.

Re-Viewing Our History

The historical perspective described above opened new doors and raised new questions about how we know what we know about the past. To correct for the exclusion and distortion of Hispanic and Mexican-American culture in education, the following topics can serve as a checklist to measure our awareness of Mexican-American history:

1. What is my understanding about how the New World was formed?
2. How do I view the European settlement of the Southwest?
3. Can I characterize the encounter of Anglo-American and Hispano-Mexican civilization in the Southwest?
4. How does the encounter between Mexico and the United States differ from relations with other countries?
5. How did the Mexican-American become a minority group by 1910?
6. Why does 1910 set off a new era for Mexican-Americans?
7. What's going on today and what lies ahead?

Schools have deprived Mexican-Americans of an accurate picture of their history. This weakened Mexican-American ability to cope with the prejudice and insensitivity around them. Children became unwitting accomplices to a self-fulfilling prophecy. Introducing their Mexican-American cultural heritage into education would go far to meet the critical needs we face today for multicultural education for all school children.

Schools, with rare exceptions, have chosen to deprive minority pupils of a balanced account of their role in United States history. Some groups, like Asians, Jews, and some religious groups, have offered language study and courses in the history of their people during nonschool hours. Poverty and related social problems have made it harder for Mexican-Americans to follow the practice. In the main, schools have failed Mexican-American children in this vital respect for over a century.

The figures from the 1972 U.S. Civil Rights Commission Report III, *The Excluded Student,* reflect conditions in the Southwest as shown by 1,166 questionnaires. The following data reveal the extent to which the Mexican-American heritage is reflected in school curricula:

The query "Does your school provide for special units in Mexican, Spanish-American, or Hispanic History in Social Studies Classes?" brought forth the following percentages of "yes" responses by state:

In Arizona, 40.6 percent of the elementary schools said "yes" and 17.6 of the secondary schools. In California, the figures were 53.9 and 64.5. In Colorado, they were 36.3 and 35.7; in New Mexico, 47.4 and 46.7; in Texas, 36.0 and 36.7; in the Southwest, 46.5 and 47.6.

One problem in teaching Mexican-American history is the procedure to be employed in dealing with the Mexican-American heritage. Setting content and goals aside for now, should it be "separate but equal" or should it be an integral part of the curriculum? It seems that either choice would be better than what we have now. I believe integration should be common at all levels and course electives at the levels when other electives are offered. We must meet the needs differently at the various grade levels.

Spanish in the Schools

The place of Spanish in schools causes heated debate. To date its rejection is one of the greatest problems for Mexican-American children. The teaching of English in public schools has certain social and psychological consequences that many instructors and administrators may not fully realize. Guided by the melting pot theory, it has been an assumption among educators that instruction

Percentage by State of Elementary and Secondary Schools Offering Mexican and Mexican-American History

| | Mexican History | | Mexican-American History | |
	Elementary	Secondary	Elementary	Secondary
Arizona	1.4	5.9	< .5	11.8
California	8.0	3.6	6.6	9.1
Colorado	2.6	10.7	1.3	10.7
New Mexico	1.0	20.0	3.1	13.3
Texas	0.6	2.2	2.1	1.1
Southwest	4.7	5.8	4.3	7.3

< : less than

Source: *The Excluded Student—Report III*, U.S. Commission Civil Rights (May 1972).

Percentage by State of Pupils Enrolled in Mexican and Mexican-American History

Mexican-American Pupils

| | Mexican History | | Mexican-American History | |
	Elementary	Secondary	Elementary	Secondary
Arizona	1.0	1.1	< .5	1.4
California	3.6	< .5	3.5	0.7
Colorado	< .5	0.8	< .5	0.7
New Mexico	< .5	1.7	0.7	0.8
Texas	< .5	1.7	1.8	0.5
Southwest	1.7	0.9	2.3	0.7

Total Pupils

| | Mexican History | | Mexican-American History | |
	Elementary	Secondary	Elementary	Secondary
Arizona	< .5	0.6	<.5	0.8
California	1.7	< .5	1.7	< .5
Colorado	0.6	1.7	< .5	1.8
New Mexico	< .5	2.5	< .5	3.2
Texas	< .5	0.6	1.0	< .5
Southwest	1.0	0.5	1.3	0.6

Source: *The Excluded Student*

was for a basically homogeneous student population which was already English-speaking.

This is not the case in most of the Southwest, where perhaps five million people have Spanish as their native language. For these people, English is a second language. The general objectives of schools and the expectations of teachers are very difficult for Spanish-speaking pupils to satisfy because of their bilingual situation. From kindergarten on, the encounter with an alien tongue (English) produces in the Spanish-speaking child profound impressions that are often destructive. For many children, the encounter with English-language instruction causes greater shock than the child can cope with. A negative pattern is established that impedes this ethnic group from performing according to ability.

Schools teach Mexican-American children that they are inferior by the use of exams which are not only culturally biased but are given in a language many cannot understand. The kids have two strikes against them (cultural differences and language problems with English) when exam time comes. We should not be surprised that so many "strike out," recording poor grades and low I.Q.s. As a functionally trilingual person, I would score as mentally retarded if I took the test in Mongolian. Yet millions of children with little or no knowledge of English have had to face this very situation over the years. Thus school test scores are worth very little, although we continue to use them as scientific data.

The net effect of English-language instruction in early grades often destroys the self-image and ego of many Spanish-speaking children. Their individual needs have been submerged or suppressed in favor of a curriculum and values established to make everyone think and speak alike. Such efforts to suppress certain ethnic strengths result in social maladjustment and underachievement. The outward manifestations of maladjustment to Anglo-oriented schools usually frustrate teachers. Teachers commonly figure the child is wrong and redouble their emphasis on English, warning Mexican-American pupils that they must adjust or suffer the consequences.

We have taken little time to study the reactions of Mexican-Americans to an experience which is so alien to our own. Thus we find it hard to believe that millions of young and sensitive minds see public education as a harmful process that denies and derides a major part of their personality. The sophisticated say that public schools damage the self-image that Mexican-American kids bring to school. Chicano activists say that the schools are killing our kids.

These general observations stem from both professional and personal experience. I have lived through all of this, first as a bilingual child who tried to cope with all the frightening forces to which school experiences subjected me. As an adult, I have looked back in a rational manner to see what happened to me and what is still happening to countless others.

Most teachers of English are so subject-oriented that they find little time to show concern for the negative effect that instruction exclusively in English has on many of their young bilingual students. After all, teaching is judged by the extent to which students acquire certain skills that will help them fit the pattern we have set for our American public school graduates. We leave to overloaded counselors the tasks of dealing with personal problems related to school experiences. Being bilingual has been commonly viewed in schools as a personal problem. Crowded schools only aggravate the situation.

Practically speaking, we tend to assume that something is wrong with the child if he cannot do well in school. It is natural to assume that he is either deficient in intelligence or not properly motivated. In either case there is little we can do beyond keeping the class in order, getting a minimum amount of subject matter across (maybe even some ideas), and surviving another day. We are not paid to change society or play God.

When Sputnik alarmed America to the fact that we were deficient in teaching science, we invested heavily in training our educators to meet the challenge. But we have not owned up to our deficiences in teaching teachers how to relate to pupils as individuals. Teacher training programs are grossly deficient in preparing teachers to appreciate and help the culturally different child.

Mexican-American Differences

Teachers who want to help Mexican-American pupils are often perplexed by the misapplication of Anglo-oriented sociological data. Mexican-American low educational achievement has been explained by oversimplifications that stem from our experience with European minorities and the Negro. The failure of simple explanations has in turn perpetuated critical stereotypes of this group. In many cases, low educational achievement is used as support for prejudice. So many of these children remain aloof from the mainstream and withdraw into a shell that educators despair of helping them—as do their parents. Many teachers will write off a Mexican-American student by such remarks as, "Well, he is better off going to work anyway!" Teachers need help to understand the function of language in the Mexican-American child.

The Mexican-American in our society finds that difficulty with English is at the bottom of the entire complex of problems he faces in gaining acceptance and equal opportunity. The learning ability of all children is vitally affected by sociopsychological factors. The training of teachers in the psychological foundations of education may vary across the country, but most teachers know that, for the child in school, feelings of personal security, acceptance by the peer group, and native curiosity about knowledge are all very fragile blossoms that must be nurtured tenderly. All of these elements in the personality are hurt by hostile environment, sometimes permanently.

For Mexican-American children all these problems are aggravated by the language gap. Lack of communication skills ties their hands and gags them. Their response to learning situations would probably be positive and creative if they could express themselves well in English. Teachers find it difficult to wait for their English to catch up because the teaching schedule must go on.

To visualize what happens, one must imagine that the situation is reversed, that all teaching took place in Spanish with a minority of students speaking only English as learned at home or in their neighborhood. For both national interests and their own, teachers must force the English-speaking minority to speak only Spanish. Of course, many of these children would cling together for mutual assistance and reassurance against the assaults of the foreign language. The same teacher would very likely scold or punish offenders for their poor manners, lack of interest, and so on.

One of the most immediate handicaps for a Mexican-American is the *way in which he speaks English.* An accent has always helped identify certain classes or groups, such as immigrants and minorities. In our country—traditionally bent on making its citizens fit the WASP model—a nonstandard accent brings ridicule or disdain. Thus a British accent is generally an asset. A Jewish or Italian accent is a mixed blessing. A Mexican or Spanish accent is almost always a handicap.

The exclusion of Spanish in school life is more intense in integrated schools and less intense in schools which have been segregated. The latter dot the Southwest and, as "Mexican schools," often suffer disadvantages in staff, facilities, and standards.

In recent years, Mexican-Americans have opted for community control even if it means control over segregated schools and less financial support. Self-determination thus coincides with the desire of some Anglos to segregate Mexican-Americans. Integration is opposed by many Mexican-American activists of the Chicano generation because it will perpetuate a minority status, whereas they believe that segregation, with self-determination, will produce Mexican-American principals, teachers, curriculum: a school life that will focus on Mexican-American concerns.

Beneficial results from English-as-a-Second-Language instruction (ESL) and bilingual education are evident in many places. New curricular materials, teaching techniques, and staff have emerged, with the goals ranging from ethnic separation to full integration. But the benefits of bringing the culture of the home and school closer together are no longer in doubt; personal performance, conduct, and attitudes are improved and school support increases as well.

Exclusion of Spanish negatively affects the community as well as the pupils. Parents commonly do not understand schools and thus give them little support. Some districts have policies that permit notices or messages to parents in Spanish, but the number is very limited as the following table shows:

Percentage of Schools in Districts 10 Percent or More Mexican-American Which Send Notices Home in Spanish as Well as English

	Elementary	Secondary
Arizona	17.6	< .5*
California	27.7	19.1
Colorado	6.7	< .5*
New Mexico	19.8	6.7
Texas	25.2	7.9
Southwest	24.5	11.0

*Although none of these secondary schools surveyed reported that they send notices home in Spanish, some schools not surveyed in these states may follow this practice.

Source: *The Excluded Student*

The figures in the following table illustrate how few schools allow the use of Spanish in PTA meetings. The net effect of this exclusion is to handicap parental involvement in school life, with resulting damage to Mexican-American educational achievement. Children are in effect made to suffer for the linguistic condition of their parents. I will discuss later whether reduction of Mexican-American parental involvement stems mainly from linguistic chauvinism or deliberate attempts to frustrate Mexican-American political power. The fact remains that imposition of English has historically hindered Mexican-American community involvement in schools.

Percentage of Schools in Districts 10 Percent or More Mexican-American Which Conduct PTA Meetings in Both Spanish and English

	Elementary	Secondary
Arizona	2	< .5*
California	5	1.0
Colorado	2	< .5*
New Mexico	9	< .5*
Texas	17	3.0
Southwest	8	2.0

*Although none of these secondary schools surveyed reported that they hold PTA meetings in Spanish as well as English, some of the schools not surveyed in these states may follow this practice.

Source: *The Excluded Student*

Faulty and inadequate educational programs for Mexican-American pupils abound, and the vast majority of districts are doing little to change their ways. Pilot or token programs in ESL, bilingual instruction, bilingual staff, and new curriculum offer some hope, however. In the area of bilingual instruction, for example, if we assume that over a million Mexican-American students could benefit from it, less than thirty thousand Mexican-American pupils received some bilingual instruction in 1970. Fortunately, the size of this program grows every year. The latest regional data for 1970 are included below:

Percentage of Schools Offering ESL and the Percentage of Mexican-American Students Enrolled in ESL Classes by State

State	Percentage of Schools Offering ESL	Percentage of Mexican-American Students Enrolled in ESL
Arizona	9.3	3.8
California	26.4	5.2
Colorado	1.9	.9
New Mexico	15.7	4.5
Texas	15.8	7.1
Southwest	19.7	5.5

Source: *The Excluded Student*

Recommendations

Staff development appears to be a problem impeding bilingual instruction. Most in-service training is brief and superficial. Granted that specialists are hard to come by and higher education is moving slowly to produce specialists, the question remains, "How do we meet the need?" I have seen community volunteers and paraprofessionals make a great difference. What is even more helpful is to assign staff that wants to learn Spanish on its own. Monetary and other professional inducements will go far to encourage self-development among teachers long before colleges produce a significant number of new teachers.

Some school districts appear to give priority to hiring Mexican-American staff, although hard data is scarce. In the last two years, I have visited school districts in each of the Southwestern states, as well as Wyoming, Kansas, and Michigan. In each I found new talent searches which were raiding other districts and placing a premium on Mexican-American staff. The numbers of Mexican-American staff, as far as this one factor goes, is very small, however. Moreover, this staff is young and not usually in positions of power.

In some districts like the Los Angeles Unified School District, boards have bypassed traditional principal and administrative selection procedures to place Mexican-Americans in positions of leadership. Over great opposition much comparative progress has been made, but more must be done. In the newly decentralized Area G, where about 70 percent of Mexican-American students attend schools in the Los Angeles Unified School District, a young Mexican-American now serves as Area Superintendent with great administrative authority. Perhaps only bold measures like these will bring change fast enough to make a difference.

Real progress in Mexican-American education will depend largely on willingness to use general funds rather than to depend upon categorical funding. In numerous cases, grudging acceptance of federal funds has only served to subsidize Anglo schools in a district by virtue of the reduction in local support for minority schools which receive federal categorical aid. This is a serious and reprehensible perversion of compensatory funds. In the late 1960s a new educational and intellectual movement began in the Southwest, as a few leaders of educational reform began to found Chicano studies departments in colleges and universities. By 1974 some fifty of these were offering many new courses and training a group of professionals. These innovative academic efforts followed two patterns: independent departments and the decentralized "center" approach. Frequently, politics were more important than educational goals in determining the structure of the new departments. Generally, cautious or fearful colleges believed they could control the new groups better by decentralizing the new staff, distributing them among the established academic disciplines like education, history, sociology, and the like. In some cases autonomous departments arose, most of them interdisciplinary and gaining their share of college-wide budgets like the other departments.

Chicano studies have reached academic respectability after a painful experience. On the one hand college administrations often tried to hamper development and growth by obvious methods and by devious ones. On the other hand, internal problems among Chicano staff hurt the new areas. Pro-Castro, pro-Mao, and pro-Mexican revolutionary ideas polarized Chicanos and alarmed the college administrations. Most Chicano professors have tried to build a legitimate academic area of value to everyone, leaving political ideologies to the realm of personal freedom of belief and expression, aside from academic responsibilities. Chicano studies are here to stay, although some of the ideological issues and lack of proper support have killed off some and others linger on in name only for the most part.

Chicano studies raise some important questions for us. I believe that realistically they are indispensable. They have produced a good effect overall. Granted, some produce rather chauvinistic students who believe Chicanos are superior to Anglos, and who hate their historical oppressors. This hatred for oppressors in the abstract has often carried over to antipathy for Anglos here and now who may have no connection with the former oppression of Chicanos. In short, Chicanos coming out of these new departments have often applied "guilt by association" to others, just as they have been lumped together by anti-Mexican racists before.

A new generation is emerging which shuns racism in reverse, and which sees the cultural heritage of Hispanic and Mexican peoples as something good in itself. A new humanism among many Chicanos offers the hope that teachers, social workers, and professionals with this background will bring people together rather than pull them apart.

New scholarship is unearthing buried Chicano history, and correcting the bias of "gringo history." Gradually, new history texts are adding portions on the Chicano, and a few have even integrated this group into general American history. This new scholarship has had a similar impact on other academic areas and publications.

Publishers, authors, school districts, and government agencies have passed the buck, blaming everyone else for the deficiency of instructional materials. Each of these groups must contribute to the solution. However, the log jam lies with school boards and staff who can create the market for better materials which the authors will then write and publishers produce. However, the pressure to sell nationally has forced many publishers to water down coverage of subjects that appear to be regional or very controversial for fear of losing the larger market. In California during 1971 the State Board of Education went further than ever by holding up approval of new social science textbooks until they were revised to meet a new state law that all instructional materials correctly portray the role and contributions of minority groups in United States history. Minority demands forced State Board action and most of the textbooks were revised. N.E.A., at the national level, is moving in this area and thus local school districts can expect more pressure and assistance in this regard.

Schools may not choose to wait for normally published materials and can meet the problem head-on by developing their own. From Texas to California much of this is going on. Not all the school-developed materials will stand the test of time, but all help develop the state of the art. Ultimately, the need extends beyond Mexican-American pupils to other groups who need to understand themselves. Mexican-Americans (and other minorities) must be included in basic instructional materials placed before all pupils.

We must break the vicious cycle whereby most educators give no attention to Mexican-Americans because they know little about them. Assuming that educators are professionals whose development is a process rather than a finished product upon certification, new knowledge will then stem from posing some basic questions about the Mexican-American. The following questions are suggestive rather than all-inclusive:

1. What is a Mexican-American?

2. How many Mexican-Americans are there and where do they live?

3. How do Mexican-Americans earn a living and what do they like to do with their leisure time?

4. What have Mexican-Americans contributed to the development of the United States?

5. How do Mexican-Americans fit into your local picture?

6. How do Mexican-Americans regard themselves?

7. How do you regard Mexican-Americans?

When a teacher has made headway in answering these questions, his or her skills in curriculum development can be applied to fitting Mexican-Americans into the general picture. Mexican-American or Chicano studies as such have emerged and have proven to be of great value. In the long run, however, "majority" students must learn about Mexican-Americans in order to check the virus of prejudice. This can be accomplished only by improving the general studies to which all students are exposed.

There are a few seminal works to help educators see Mexican-Americans in a light that other materials have ignored. These are the various works on bilingual education developed by the National Consortia for Bilingual Education in Fort Worth, Texas, which typifies new materials that are now emerging. Other districts are doing the same. There are the new Chicano newspapers and journals that deal with subjects others ignore. *El Grito* (Quinto Sol Publications, Berkeley, California) and *Aztlán* (Chicano Cultural Center, UCLA) are particularly helpful. The most recent bibliographies are by Matt Meier, *A Bibliography of Mexican American History* (1971), and from the University of Houston Libraries, *Chicanos; A Selected Bibliography* (1971). Although outdated, there is a wealth of material in *The Mexican-American; A Selected and Annotated Bibliography, 1969*, from the Center for Latin American Studies, Stanford University.

There are also school texts in social studies that point the way to new materials on the Mexican-American:

The Story of the Mexican American; The Man and the Land (1969)
Elementary Level, Rudy Acuna

Cultures in Conflict; Problems of the Mexican-American (1970)
Elementary Level, Rudy Acuna

Mexican-American Chronicle (1971)
Secondary Level, Rudy Acuna

Mexican-Americans, Past, Present and Future (1969)
Secondary Level, Julian Nava (Spanish version published in 1972)

Basic Readings on the Mexican American (1972)
Secondary Level, Julian Nava

Mexican-Americans; An Anthology of Basic Readings (1973)
College Level, Julian Nava

Mexican Americans: A Brief Look at Their History (1970)
Julian Nava (Informative booklet published by Anti-Defamation League)

Our Mexican Heritage (1972)
Gertrude S. Brown (Student and teacher's edition)

Mexican American Heritage (1972)
Secondary Level, Ernest Garcia and George Shaftel

Rising Voices (1974)
Secondary Level and Adult, Al Martinez (Spanish version: *Voces Que Surgen*)

Bilingual Stories for Today (1974) (8 vols. in Spanish; 8 vols. in English)
Elementary and Secondary Levels, Julian Nava

Recent publications of the Hispanic Urban Center of Los Angeles such as *The Mexican American: An In-Service Program* (1972) are typical of various materials for staff development.

Political Problems

The political circumstances facing Mexican-Americans comprise a major obstacle facing improved education. Mexican-Americans have not participated in politics actively in a manner commensurate with their numbers. However, they have been very important to the political life of the region because they were generally hard-working, nondemanding, and manageable. They helped count for local, state, and federal funding while costing less per capita than their Anglo counterparts. Thus, streets, parks, electrification,

sewers, and schools in the barrios of the Southwest have been of a
lower quality than those "across the tracks." The net effect is that
Mexican-American communities have subsidized the others. Nowhere has this vital political role of Mexican-Americans been more
important than in education.

For those who care about people or about our national future, it
is vital that they help Mexican-Americans in the political arena.
We must do more than simply let Mexican-Americans sink or swim.
Certainly, Mexican-American children should not suffer the rest of
their lives because their parents are politically disadvantaged and
do not make schools meet their children's needs. By helping the
Mexican-American community increase its political power we can
help assure a positive involvement. Although many still fear
"Brown Power," the record shows that Mexican-American political
involvement ultimately helps others as well. Nowhere is this more
evident than in the *Serrano* v. *Priest* court decision which is
bringing reform to the way we finance public education across the
nation. The principle there was simple: Should a child be held to
suffer an inferior education because of the tax-raising potential of
his parents' residence? Such challenges posed by Mexican-Americans (and other minority groups) serve to protect their own
interests, but ultimately help save the majority from itself.

To conclude, schools will supply the answer as to whether
cultural diversity in America will be a liability or an asset, whether
equality of opportunity shall be a reality, and whether our society
will continue its process of renewal. We cannot stand still in the
world today. The question is, in what direction shall we move? In a
shrinking, ever more dangerous, dirty, crowded, and interdepen-
dent world, cultural diversity and untapped sources of energy and
creativity may well help us not only to survive but to thrive more
fully.

As we try to improve the effect of education on social and
economic life we must still wonder if we are asking the relevant
questions. It is quite likely that Chicano efforts to improve
education and fit better into the mainstream of Anglo-American
life are misdirected efforts. Just what is it Chicanos are trying to be
like? What is the "action" which they are trying to become a part
of?

The economic and educational perspectives of Mexican-Americans are still not very bright. Much of their energy is applied to

gaining acceptance into Anglo society, and fortunately some of this energy is also directed to promoting cultural freedom and acceptance of differences among all of us. Certainly we must strive to promote democracy and equality as well as economic well-being. However, the national and world scene is changing so rapidly that we may have to redefine our goals and the methods for attaining them.

Recent studies suggest that a college education is no longer the best economic investment of time, energy, talent, and money. Skilled crafts people and even garbage collectors in San Francisco often earn more money than college professors. I will not even mention truck drivers and plumbers, except in passing. Education may be preparing educated individuals with good earning capacities who are unskilled in human relations and care mostly about success at any cost. "Watergate" serves to illustrate the extent to which success and power figure in the motivations of our leaders, and those who set the moral tone for our society. We must ask ourselves just what it is that we want as a society from education. The *Fifth Annual Gallup Poll of Public Attitudes Towards Education* (1973) paints a picture which is not very flattering of either schools or public feelings about them.

Chicanos have raised some vital questions about education. The questions were motivated by indignation and demands for justice and respect. Answers to these challenges are emerging steadily, although slower than the growth rate of the Chicano population. Meanwhile, we must ask equally hard questions about education in general. Is it possible we are educating young people for occupations which will not exist soon and teaching them values which are in great part outmoded?

The Southwest Intergroup Relations Council published a recent report with the title *The Future Belongs to Those Who Prepare for It*. How appropriately this applies to the Chicano community. The day has long since passed when as a people, we can afford to sit back and just let our professional leadership happen, as has taken place in the past for whatever reasons. If we are to be masters of our own destiny, if self-determination is a serious quest and our goal, if we are dedicated to the breaking of the "hellish cycle of poverty and ignorance," if we are eager to provide a better tomorrow for the greater numbers of our youth who are presently below eighteen years of age, then it is absolutely imperative that all institutions of higher learning be held accountable for their social responsibility in developing leadership for an emerging people.

This leadership will emerge! How and in what form will depend on the Chicano community's access to the colleges and universities. The colleges and universities must carry through the mission for which they were founded—the development of young minds, hearts, and lives. The Chicano youth have made their case, they have made their challenge: The decade of the seventies will record the response of the institutions of higher learning in our country. Will Chicanos be "locked in" or "locked out"? The response may well determine the future not only for Mexican-Americans but for the country as a whole.

6

Higher Education and the
Mexican-American

HENRY J. CASSO

Dr. Casso is Executive Secretary of the National Education Task Force de
La Raza at the University of New Mexico. He received his Ph.D. in
Education from the University of Massachusetts in 1972.

Education must be considered one of the most important es-
sentials in the emergence, development, and self-determination of
any people. This is especially true in the contemporary Chicano°
movement. Any consideration of higher education as it affects the
Mexican-American must therefore be seen in the context of the
Chicanos' quest for a better quality of life, self-determination, and
political and socioeconomic betterment—not only for those actively
engaged in the present struggle but especially for the children who
are to follow them.

The Chicano struggle has been underway for over one hundred
years. It was not until the late 1960s that Mexican-Americans—the
nation's largest Spanish-speaking community—made their most
dramatic and dynamic progress since the Southwest came under
United States control in 1848. Although this struggle took a variety
of forms and challenged many institutions, it was the public
educational systems that received the most attention.

The Chicano community has always, it can be said even almost
blindly, held in high regard the institutions of elementary, secondary, and higher education. However, these institutions often
excluded Chicano children, and in those cases where they were not
denied admission, the schools did not know how to deal with them.

°The terms "Chicano" and "Mexican-American" are used interchangeably in this
chapter.

137

On the average, if the Chicano did not drop out or was not encouraged to abandon school, the calibre of instruction received was so poor that there was little hope of going on to higher education. Frequently, the young, bright Chicanos were counseled against even applying to institutions of higher learning, and if one of them was fortunate enough to be admitted to a college or university, his survival there was improbable.

Historically, Chicanos did not have their own educational systems and, being unable to receive advanced training, the impact on the calibre of community leadership was immediate and obvious. It must be noted that, few as they were, there did exist organizations such as LULAC (League of United Latin American Citizens) which, from the earliest days, provided financial aid and scholarships to young Chicanos. Various religious denominations also sponsored Chicano students. However, the most significant factor to cause a drastic change in educational opportunities for Chicanos was World War II and the resultant GI Bill. Nonetheless, the struggle for equal and quality education had to continue. Organizations such as the GI Forum and the above-mentioned LULAC waged significant fights in and out of the courts. Their struggles were the forerunners for three recent legal decisions which are bound to have an important effect on American public education: *Diana v. State Board of Education*,[1] dealing with the disproportionate placement of Chicano children into educably mentally retarded classes; and the two cases dealing with unequal expenditure of tax dollars for public education: *Serrano v. Priest*[2] in California and *Rodríguez v. State of Texas*.[3]

The Chicano challenge to the public education system was accurately described by Carlos Muñoz as follows: ". . . for the first time, the schools became the foremost symbol of oppression and powerlessness to various segments of the Chicano community and therefore a prime protest target."[4]

In the present struggle for equal and quality education, a two-pronged effort is being waged by the Chicano community:

> 1. It is challenging the elementary and secondary school systems which are not providing quality education, are not teaching the Chicano child to read, are not keeping the Chicano child in school, or preparing him for higher education.

2. It is pushing for greater college enrollment which traditionally excluded the majority of Chicano students, not to mention their almost total absence from the critical graduate and professional schools.[5]

This two-pronged push deals with the reality that Chicanos are underrepresented in college because they are not doing well in schools. Many are not graduating from the elementary and secondary schools, and those that do are not being counseled toward higher education. The few who do receive this counseling are not prepared for college work; others cannot afford it nor are the institutions prepared to deal with them.

It became very clear to the Chicano community that there was a direct relationship between what was happening to the Chicano child in the classroom and the lack of a Chicano presence on college campuses. The realization of this fact is one of the important points this essay wishes to impress upon the reader, the Chicano community, and American public education.

The Chicano youth were the first to react to and expose the failure of the public schools. It was they who pointed out the relationship between the damaging impact of the public schools and the scarcity of Chicano students in institutions of higher learning. As a result, few Chicanos are in the various "critical" professions necessary to sustain normal participation in American society. To state it another way, Chicanos were not in college chiefly because of the failure of our school systems to prepare them for higher education; concomitantly they are not represented in the critical professions. Dr. Julian Nava reported at the Aspen Conference that there were less than one hundred Chicano Ph.D.s[°]—only eight in sociology, one in political science, one economist, and approximately one hundred twenty CPAs.

Historically, the blame for this low educational level, the small college enrollment, and the lack of native professional leadership was placed on the Chicano community itself—especially by the schools. Some of the more frequently heard rationalizations were that Chicanos are "lazy," "shiftless," "disinterested in education,"

[°]In a recent study of Chicano administrators in higher education, Antonio Esquibel found that there were only 210 in the Southwest. Of these, one was a university president, nine were vice-presidents, thirteen were deans, and seventy-seven were department chairmen of public four-year institutions. The rest were found in two-year colleges.

"happy-go-lucky," and "without ambition." Inwardly, we all knew that Chicano children were indiscriminately placed in mentally retarded classes, forced out of school, and then called drop-outs.[6] All too often, they were made to repeat the first grade two or three times (as a way to handle the linguistically and culturally different child); they were relegated to shop classes, vocational training† in unmarketable skills, or counseled to stay away from dope and go straight. But never were Chicanos directed toward the dream and possibility of higher education. The knowledge of fellowships, scholarships, grants, and loans was kept as a closely guarded secret. How often was heard the expression, "you people are good with your hands." The question easily arises in the mind of anyone giving serious thought to the Chicano struggle as to how Chicanos have been able to survive at all as a people.

It was the Chicano youth, probably because they had the most to gain, who seriously challenged the educational system. Their tactics were varied; some were successful and others not. Many of the older generation who had never heard of such activities were too often dismayed and fearful. Some of the younger leaders even thought these tactics were too "militant." But the young Chicanos' forceful actions were justified by the following facts: A high percentage of Chicanos were not finishing school; there were very few in institutions of higher education and even that small number showed a high drop-out rate, even among some of the more outstanding students.

The actions of these young people were direct and forceful. They placed the blame where it rightfully belonged—on the schools. Long before the Mexican-American Education Project Study Report of the United States Commission on Civil Rights, which is publishing the educational outputs of the schools in the Southwest, the Chicano youth called for an evaluation and an accountability from the schools.[7] They did not wait; they made their accusations and then walked out of the schools.

Assuming that it is the role and responsibility of the elementary and secondary schools of the United States to inspire, animate, and prepare the citizenry for higher education, it would seem that the absence of Chicano youth in our institutions of higher learning

---

†Ed Lucero, a CPA and a leader in economic development for the Chicano community, related at the Aspen Conference how he too was placed into vocational education classes.

would be a clear indictment of the educational failure of those systems. Such an observation was made before the United States Senate in its hearings on equal education opportunity:

We have in America the largest public school system on earth, the most expensive college buildings, the most extensive curriculum. But nowhere is education so blind to its objectives, so indifferent to any real goals as in America. The American educational system has aimed at the repression of faults rather than the creation of virtues.[8]

Furthermore, it became very evident from the Mexican-American Education Project Study, the many extensive lawsuits initiated by the Mexican-American Legal Defense and Educational Fund,[9] and the testimony given before the United States Senate Select Committee on Equal Education Opportunity,[10] that not only was there a lack of "creation of virtues," but more so that there was a design "intended or unintended" present which thwarted the access of Chicano youth to higher education.[11] (In San Antonio, Texas, a community of seven hundred thousand, one-half the population is Mexican-American. It is the third largest city in Texas; however, it is only now building a four-year state university, and it is being built in an area of town inaccessible to the bulk of the Chicano community. San Antonio does have four fine but very expensive private colleges.)

From all this new information, it has become very evident that educational decisions and designs—some subtle and others less so—were obstacles in the way of advancement for any Chicano youth who was fortunate not to have been psychologically destroyed somewhere along his or her educational experience. Certainly, there is clearer evidence today that the school systems were not only instilling an inferior education into young Chicanos, but were in fact relegating them to the "vicious cycle of poverty" or to quote Munoz, ". . . relegated to powerlessness."[12] In other words, we pose the question: Is "powerlessness" related to "lack of quality education" and to the resultant absence of Chicanos on the campuses of higher education? This writer affirms that such indeed is the case! It is quite clear that the failure of public educational institutions to provide quality education for Chicanos in the early years, and the many exclusionary attitudes and practices keeping them from colleges and universities have certainly contributed to the paucity of professional and educated leadership which, in turn, has had its effect in creating the "powerlessness" of a whole people. Before giving examples of this powerlessness, it should be stated very quickly that I do not accept, hold, or believe that leadership comes only from the universities. César Chávez, who attended no college, is probably our best example of a successful leader without higher education. However, for the total development of a people's self-determination, it is essential that Chicanos have access to and are actually in those institutions which train people for the critical professions. Some of these professions, to identify a few, are the law, education, economics, the ministry, writing, the media, and political science. I agree with the proposition postulated by Jane Mercer:

> The schools are the primary social institutions allocating persons to adult statuses and roles in American society. The kind and amount of education which a person has, determines to a large extent whether he will participate in the mainstream of American life or be shunted into the byways. Educational decisions which systematically favor one group over another predetermine what group will occupy the seats of power and which group will remain powerless.[13]

It does not require a great deal of insight to conclude that Chicanos are not in the mainstream of American decision-making. They lack any control over even those important things which affect their lives, and are conspicuously absent from seats of power. Chicanos are in fact "powerless." Each of us can point to some individual exception, someone we know—the person who has "made it." The point here is that the vast numbers of Chicanos who make up the statistical data in Fred H. Schmidt's work in chapter 4 have not "made it" and will "make it" only in direct proportion as more of our youth not only receive quality education in their early years, but have access to higher education.

In order to substantiate this conclusion of "powerlessness" and to emphasize the importance of higher education to the Chicano movement, we will consider the situation in California, the state with the largest Chicano population. For our purposes, it must also be kept in mind that of all the states with a substantial Chicano population, it is probably the most progressive.

Chicano Powerlessness in California

Decisions made by top elected and appointed officials influence every aspect of life in a given state. For a people to have self-determination, access to these decision-making positions is most essential. However, even as late as 1971, it was found that of the 15,650 elected and appointed officials at the municipal, county, state, and federal levels in California, only 310 (1.98 percent) were Mexican-American.[14] Presently, the Mexican-American constitutes 16 percent of the total California population.

At the time of the hearings held by the State Advisory Committee to the United States Commission on Civil Rights, in August 1971, there were no Mexican-Americans among the top forty state officials nor the twenty-eight governor's advisors.[15]

Important policy and administrative decisions are made by 4,023 employees in the executive branch of the California state government which includes boards, commissions, and advisories. Of these only 60 (1.5 percent) are Mexican-Americans. (It should be noted that most of these positions are appointive, not elective.)[16]

In city and county government decision-making positions, there are only 241, or 2.2 percent, of the 10,907 employees who are Mexican-American.

The judicial machinery and the administration of justice are vitally important to the well-being of any socioeconomic group. However, as of 1971 there were no Mexican-Americans in any of the top 132 posts of California's judicial system. This includes seven Supreme Court justices, the Judicial Council, the Administrative Office of the Courts, the Commission on Judicial Qualifications, and the State Court of Appeals.[17]

Of the 874 federal-level decision-making positions affecting California—many of which are appointive—only 14 are held by Mexican-Americans. This includes such roles as legislators, judges, marshals, commissioners, and U.S. attorneys and their assistants. None of the 87 U.S. assistant attorneys is Mexican-American. "In the United States Court of Appeals and the United States District Court in California including U.S. judges, referees, probation officers, commissioners, and marshals, there are 262 positions of which only six are filled by Mexican-Americans."[18]

Certainly, it becomes most obvious that the Mexican-American is not proportionately represented in the important judicial branch and one can safely conclude that Chicanos exert no power and little influence in California's judicial process.

In the matter of economic status, the Chicano is equally powerless. In an administrative complaint brought by six Spanish-speaking organizations against HEW in 1970 which, at the time of the complaint, was spending $1.1 billion in California, it was alleged that of the 53,221 persons employed in HEW programs in that state, only 1,635 (3.1 percent) were Mexican-Americans.[19] There were, at the time of the complaint, three million Spanish-surnamed Californians, the majority of whom are Mexican-American.

According to a publication entitled *A Study by Responsible Corporate Action of San Francisco*, there are some sixty-seven corporations in California. It is estimated that in 1969, these corporations grossed over $82 billion. This study revealed that these corporations have assets in excess of $111,732,877,000; enjoy an annual gross revenue of $82,673,471,000; have a net income of $3,087,703,000; and employ 1,552,167 Americans, a substantial portion of whom are Californians.[20]

A scrutiny of the managerial personnel who control such vast wealth, not to mention the economic destiny of so many people, reveals that as of 1970, "of the 1,008 Directors of the Board, and of the 1,268 top corporate officials and Executives, there is no Mexican-American."[*][21]

It is clear from this data that Mexican-Americans have no say in the allocation of this vast wealth and, therefore, must be considered economically powerless.

Chicano Powerlessness in the Southwest: Educational Decision-Making

The one profession where Mexican-Americans are numerically represented to a greater degree than in any other is that of education. In this field—although there are larger numbers of teachers, principals, and superintendents, especially in California —the Mexican-American does not hold such positions in proportion

---

[*]Among the Directors of the Board, one is a Spanish-surnamed Basque and another is a Mexican national resident in California.

to his population. It is precisely in the school system where Chicano youths make some of their first and most meaningful contacts; these offer a wonderful opportunity for role models that will encourage young Chicanos toward higher education. Certainly, it is most important for a child to develop a positive self-image. Table 1 categorizes the major ethnic groups in the Southwest and the fields in which they are employed, in descending order of importance. Thus more Anglos are engaged in teaching in New Mexico than in any other profession; teaching is the second most popular activity for Anglos in Arizona, California, Colorado, and Texas. For blacks, teaching comes in second in New Mexico, third in Arizona, California, and Texas, and fifth in Colorado. Chicano employment in the schools is found in the top five in only two states and in these instances, the Chicano is in third place in Colorado and New Mexico. In the other three states, school employment of Chicanos must be so low it did not show up at all in the employment figures.

Because of the importance of the teaching profession, it would be well to look at some data for the Southwest contained in the Mexican-American Education Project Report:

> Except for those in the positions of custodian or teachers' aides, Mexican-Americans comprise substantially less of school staff than they do of enrollment.

> Mexican-Americans are grossly under-represented among teachers. Of approximately 325,000 teachers in the Southwest, only about 12,000 or four percent are Mexican-American while about seventeen percent of the enrollment is Mexican-American. Furthermore, Black teachers, although they are also under-represented, outnumber Mexican-American teachers by almost two to one, notwithstanding the fact that Black population representation in California is less than that of the Chicano.

> An even smaller proportion of principals than teachers is Mexican-American. Of approximately 12,000 school principals in the Southwest, less than 400 or three percent are Mexican-American. Furthermore, Mexican-American principals are outnumbered by Black principals.

> Employment and school assignment patterns for Mexican-

TABLE 1

	Anglo	Chicano	Blacks
Arizona	Manufacturing Schools Construction Retail Trade Public Admin.	Manufacturing Agriculture Construction Mining Public Admin.	Manufacturing Private Household Schools Personal Services Public Admin.
California	Manufacturing Schools Public Admin. Retail Trade Construction	Manufacturing Agriculture Construction Wholesale Trade Public Admin.	Manufacturing Public Admin. Schools Hospitals Personal Services
Colorado	Manufacturing Schools Construction Public Admin. Retail Trade	Manufacturing Public Admin. Schools Construction Hospitals	Manufacturing Public Admin. Hospitals Entertainment Schools
New Mexico	Schools Public Admin. Retail Trade Mining Construction	Public Admin. Construction Schools Manufacturing Retail Trade	Private Household Schools Public Admin. Personal Services Manufacturing
Texas	Manufacturing Schools Construction Retail Trade Public Admin.	Manufacturing Construction Agriculture Public Admin. Retail Trade	Manufacturing Private Household Schools Personal Services Construction

1. 1970 Census PC (1)-C, Table 55.

Americans in other non-teaching professional positions such as assistant principals, counselors, and librarians is similar to that of Mexican-American teachers and principals . . . to a greater extent, Mexican-Americans are employed as teachers' aides or as non-professionals, especially custodians rather than as professionals.

About fifty of the 480 are superintendents or associate or assistant superintendents. The majority of these are in New Mexico.[22]

In spite of the above figures, it is clear that the Chicano in education is more involved in decision-making than he is in any other profession. Even so, there is a long way to go before proportionate representation is attained even in communities where the Chicano population is substantial. Observations from my own experience as Director of Education for the Mexican-American Legal Defense and Educational Fund can be noted here. In 1971, judging from a review of the applications for MALDEF Educational Law Grants, a sizable number of law school applicants seemed to be from the teaching profession. This new trend is both interesting and encouraging. Interesting from the standpoint that education, up to this point, was considered by Chicanos to be a professional plateau. And it is encouraging in the sense that Chicanos were becoming interested in other professional fields.°

The above data indicate that Chicanos do not participate in decision-making in those very states where they are a significant population group. This is especially true of those crucial areas— education, politics, the judicial process—which are the key to breaking the hellish cycle of economic inferiority, ignorance, and political powerlessness.

It has been well established that entrance into the decision-making levels of American society is possible only through higher education; it is precisely this fact that has caused young Chicanos to concentrate their efforts in this area.

A good example of this is seen in a recent random survey conducted by the College Entrance Examination Board, "Access to College for Mexican-Americans in the Southwest"[23] (July 1972). It shows that between the fall of 1970 and the fall of 1971, Mexican-American enrollment increased 14 percent or double the increase for all other students. This takes on greater meaning when the figures in Table 2 are considered.

Between 1968 and 1970, there was an increase in Chicano college enrollment. This was especially noticeable in data from the Southwest because Mexican-Americans were singled out.

In Arizona, the numbers of Chicano undergraduates increased from 3,565 in 1968 to 4,252 in 1970, an increase of 687 with the percent representation remaining the same 6.9 percent. It must be noted that in 1970, almost one-half of the total Mexican-American undergraduate enrollment was in the freshman and sophomore

---

°In May 1972, the first eighty MALDEF grantees graduated from twenty-four law schools in the United States. Considering that it is from the legal profession where the greater percentage of public officials come, this will be important for Chicano development. Presently, there are over two hundred law students receiving MALDEF grants.

TABLE 2

	Percentage of Elem-intermed Secondary of Total Enroll[1]	Percentage of Undergrads 1968[2]	Percentage of Undergrads 1970[3]	Percentage of Population 1970[4]
Arizona	19.6	6.9	6.9	20.0
California	14.4	5.5	6.2	15.9
Colorado	13.7	3.4	5.2	12.9
New Mexico	38.0	17.5	18.9	40.9
Texas	20.1	7.4	7.5	18.8
Southwest	17.2			

1. *Mexican-American Education Study,* U.S. Commission on Civil Rights.
2. Ibid.
3. Ibid.
4. 1970 Census, PC (1)-C, Table 51.

years. In the graduate schools, there were twice as many in the first year.[*]

To more fully understand the challenge which the Chicano community faced, the above figures must be seen in the light of the total number of students. For example in Arizona, according to the HEW Civil Rights Report of 1968, the Mexican-American represented 20.3 percent (47,723) of the elementary school enrollment, 19.3 percent (6,548) at the intermediate level, and 17.8 percent (17,477) in the high schools, or a total of 19.6 percent (17,748). Representation in higher education was 3,565 or only 6.9 percent of the total school population. (See Table 4.) The percentage of 6.9 percent remained true for 1970. On the other hand, Anglo students represented 71.6 (262,526) percent of the total school population and for the same year had 89.0 percent or 46,212 in undergraduate college enrollment. This indicates that while one in five Anglos went to college only one in twenty Chicanos did so for the same period.

In California, Chicano undergraduates increased from 5.5 percent (31,858) in 1968 to 6.2 percent (35,902) in 1970, an increase of 4,044. Although this was the largest numerical increase in the five Southwestern states, it represents a percentage increase of only .07

[*]Figures obtained from the following: (1) The U.S. Commission on Civil Rights, Mexican-American Education Project Study; (2) 1970 HEW Office of Civil Rights Report; (3) *The Higher Education Chronicle.*

percent. As in Arizona, the largest numbers, approximately 29,594, were in the freshman and sophomore years. In the graduate schools, there were approximately twice as many Chicanos in the first year. These figures dramatize the Chicano movement's concentration on higher education.

In the case of California, whereas the Mexican-American in 1968 represented 15.6 percent (404,750) of the elementary school enrollment, 13.6 percent (104,264) at the intermediate level, and 12.3 percent (137,268) in high schools, or a total of 14.4 percent (646,282), undergraduate representation was 31,858 or only 5.5 percent. On the other hand, Anglo students represented 74.2 percent of the total school population or 3,323,478 in 1968 and for the same year had 84.5 percent or 487,137 in undergraduate college enrollment. This indicates that one in seven Anglos went on to college, whereas one in twenty Chicanos did so for the same period. It can be noted that although the Mexican-American did make a gain of 4,044 from 1968 to 1970, blacks gained 1,003 and Oriental enrollment increased by 5,821. (See Table 3.)

In Colorado, Chicano undergraduate enrollment increased from 3.8 percent (2,709) in 1968 to 5.2 percent (4,284) in 1970, an increase of 1,575 or 1.4 percent. (Note: Anglo enrollment increased in numbers, but lost two percentage points.) Clearly, two-thirds of the Chicano students in 1970 were in the freshman and sophomore years with one-half of the students in the freshman year. In the graduate schools, unlike the situation in Arizona and California, there seemed to be a 100 percent drop in the first year's attendance from the previous one. This is a matter that needs further study.

The Mexican-American in Colorado represents 14.7 percent (43,028) of elementary school enrollment, 12.9 percent (13,734) at the intermediate level, and 12.3 percent (14,587) in the high schools. Of the total noncollege school population, 13.7 percent (71,348) is Mexican-American. Undergraduate representation in 1968 was only 3.4 percent (2,709). Anglo students represented 82.0 percent (425,749) of the total school population and for the same year had 92.4 percent (66,365) of the undergraduate college enrollment. This indicates that approximately one out of every seven Anglos went to college, whereas one in twenty-seven Chicanos did so. (See Tables 2 and 3.)

In New Mexico, Chicano undergraduate enrollment increased from 17.5 percent (5,053) in 1968 to 19.1 percent (5,564) in 1970,

TABLE 3

Number and Percent of Enrollment That Is Mexican-American and Anglo by School Level*

Ethnic Group by School Level	Arizona Number	Percent	California Number	Percent	Colorado Number	Percent	New Mexico Number	Percent	Texas Number	Percent	Southwest Number	Percent
Elementary												
Anglo	164,398	70.1	1,884,277	72.5	236,668	80.6	73,541	49.5	850,928	61.0	3,209,813	68.8
Mexican-American	47,723	20.3	404,750	15.6	43,028	14.7	58,975	39.7	312,299	22.4	866,774	18.6
Black	11,529	4.9	237,436	9.1	11,026	3.8	3,393	2.3	226,881	16.3	490,264	10.5
Other†	10,903	4.6	71,245	2.7	2,739	0.9	12,547	8.5	4,375	0.3	101,809	2.1
Total	234,553	99.9	2,597,708	99.9	293,461	100.0	148,456	100.0	1,394,483	100.0	4,668,660	100.0
Intermediate												
Anglo	24,732	72.9	562,043	73.2	88,607	83.0	32,994	58.2	335,015	68.0	1,043,391	71.6
Mexican-American	6,548	19.3	104,264	13.6	13,734	12.9	19,784	34.9	88,775	18.0	233,106	16.0
Black	962	2.8	80,222	10.5	3,718	3.5	1,234	2.2	68,125	13.8	154,261	10.5
Other†	1,665	4.9	20,934	2.7	739	0.6	2,643	4.7	1,080	0.2	27,060	1.9
Total	33,907	99.9	767,463	100.0	106,798	100.0	56,655	100.0	492,995	100.0	1,457,818	100.0
Secondary												
Anglo	73,395	74.9	877,158	78.9	100,474	84.5	35,556	53.9	431,897	69.3	1,518,480	75.3
Mexican-American	17,477	17.8	137,268	12.3	14,587	12.3	24,235	36.8	104,140	16.7	297,707	14.8
Black	3,292	3.4	70,321	6.3	3,053	2.6	1,032	1.6	84,807	13.6	162,505	8.1
Other†	3,835	3.9	27,464	2.5	720	0.6	5,105	7.7	2,038	0.3	39,162	1.9
Total	97,999	100.0	1,112,211	100.0	118,834	100.0	65,928	100.0	622,882	99.9	2,017,854	100.1
All School Levels												
Anglo	262,526	71.6	3,323,478	74.2	425,749	82.0	142,092	52.4	1,617,840	64.4	5,771,684	70.9
Mexican-American	71,748	19.6	646,282	14.4	71,348	13.7	102,994	38.0	505,214	20.1	1,397,586	17.2
Black	15,783	4.3	387,978	8.7	17,797	3.4	5,658	2.1	379,813	15.1	807,030	9.9
Other†	16,402	4.5	119,642	2.7	4,198	0.8	20,295	7.5	7,492	0.3	168,030	2.0
Total	366,459	100.0	4,477,380	100.0	519,092	99.9	271,039	100.0	2,510,359	99.9	8,144,330	100.0

Source: Fall 1968 HEW Title VI Survey
*minute differences in totals are due to computer rounding
†includes American Indians and Orientals

TABLE 4
Undergraduate College Enrollment by State and Ethnic Group

Ethnic Group	Arizona Number	Percent	California Number	Percent	Colorado Number	Percent	New Mexico Number	Percent	Texas Number	Percent	Southwest Number	Percent
1970[1]												
Anglo	53,738	87.6	477,641	82.3	73,758	90.4	22,168	76.1	242,456	83.5	869,761	83.4
Mexican-American	4,252	6.9	35,902	6.2	4,284	5.2	5,564	19.1	22,131	7.6	72,133	6.9
Black	1,274	2.1	33,317	5.7	1,853	2.3	565	1.9	22,343	7.7	59,352	5.7
Indian	1,382	2.3	5,441	0.9	736	0.9	613	2.1	1,876	0.6	10,039	1.0
Oriental	675	1.1	27,758	4.8	980	1.2	207	0.7	1,467	0.5	31,087	3.0
TOTAL	61,321	100.0	580,059	99.9	81,611	100.0	29,117	99.9	290,264	99.9	1,042,372	100.0
1968[2]												
Anglo	46,212	89.0	487,137	84.5	66,365	92.4	22,481	78.0	237,661	83.4	859,856	84.8
Mexican-American	3,565	6.9	31,858	5.5	2,709	3.8	5,053	17.5	21,071	7.4	64,256	6.3
Black	877	1.7	32,314	5.6	1,053	1.5	518	1.8	21,291	7.5	56,053	5.5
Indian	849	1.6	2,917	0.5	708	1.0	532	1.8	2,972	1.0	7,978	0.8
Oriental	441	0.8	21,937	3.8	1,036	1.4	241	0.8	1,805	0.6	25,460	2.5
TOTAL	51,944	100.0	576,163	99.9	71,871	100.1	28,825	100.0	284,800	99.9	1,013,603	99.9

1. Fall 1970 Survey of Institutions, U.S. Department of Health, Education, and Welfare, Office for Civil Rights.
2. U.S. Department of Health, Education, and Welfare, *Undergraduate Enrollment by Ethnic Group in Federally Funded Institutions of Higher Education,* Fall 1968.

or an increase of 511, a percent increase of two points. It must be noted that the number of Anglo students decreased numerically as well as in percentage points for the same period. Again, the greater numbers were in the freshman and sophomore years. As with Colorado, there was indication of a drop in graduate school attendance in comparison with the previous year. There was growth, however, for Orientals, blacks, and American Indians, although very small. (See Tables 2 and 3.) Chicanos in 1968 represented 39.7 percent (58,975) of the elementary school enrollment, 34.9 percent (19,784) at the intermediate level, 36.8 percent (24,235) in high schools, or a total of 38.0 percent (102,994) of the noncollege school population. Anglos constituted 52.4 percent or 142,092 of the elementary and secondary school population for 1968, and had 22,481 or 78.0 percent in college. (See Tables 2 and 3.) (Note: In each of the five states, a higher percentage of Anglo students appear to be enrolled in colleges or universities than their population representation.)

In Texas, the numbers of Chicano undergraduates increased from 7.4 percent (21,071) in 1968 to 7.6 percent (22,131) in 1970, an increase of only 1,060 with the percent representation going up by only .2 percent. In 1970 nearly two-thirds were in the freshman and sophomore years and a little less than 50 percent in the first year. In 1970, there was a slight forward movement in the graduate schools. (See Tables 2 and 3.)

In 1968, Chicanos in Texas represented 22.4 percent (312,299) of the elementary school enrollment, 18.0 percent (88,775) at the intermediate level, and 16.7 percent (104,140) in the high schools, or a total of 20.1 percent (505,214) of the precollege school population. Representation in undergraduate colleges and universities was 21,071 or 7.4 percent.

In 1968 Anglo students in Texas represented 64.4 percent of the total school population or 1,617,840, and for the same year had 83.4 percent or 237,661 in undergraduate college enrollment. Although the Mexican-American enrollment increased by 1,060, blacks increased from 21,291 to 22,343 for an increase of 1,052, so that in Texas, blacks have a .1 percent higher increase in college in 1970 than Mexican-Americans even though blacks had a lesser numerical representation in the total state population. (See Tables 2 and 3.)

Much can be done with statistics; however, the above data is given in the hope that it will contribute to a greater realization of the awesome task which lies ahead of the Chicano community. A very discouraging note is that the increased gains in four-year colleges and universities for the Mexican-American in 1968 through 1970 did not seem to keep up with this group's total population growth.

The ACMAS survey reported "140,000 Mexican-Americans enrolled in the Southwestern colleges in the fall of 1971,"[24] a figure that I consider too high. In order to begin to reflect proportionately their standing in the population of the Southwest, it is estimated that "over 100,000" Mexican-American students must be enrolled in the area's colleges and universities. What is disturbing about this is that the cost of higher education is increasing, entrance requirements are getting more stringent, graduate schools are more difficult to enter, and the awarding of Ph.D.s is becoming more restrictive.

The ACMAS survey indicates that we can expect to see definite improvement. It found that "between the fall of 1970 and the fall of 1971, the Mexican-American enrollment increased fourteen percent" or "twice the increase for all students." Another increase of 13 percent took place in the fall of 1972 while an increase of 8 percent was noted for all others. It is expected, as in 1968–70, that California will have the greatest numerical increase.[25]

As is found in each of the states discussed above, the greatest increase occurred in the freshman year for 1971. There was a 13 percent increase for Chicanos while "all others" increased only 6 percent.

An important feature of the ACMAS survey was that it classified the ethnic background of participants in colleges and universities so that the Mexican-American is clearly identified. However, it is limited only to the Southwest.* This kind of classification is not given in other reports. This makes it difficult for the Chicano community to accurately know how it is doing.

It appears that in 1971 and 1972 the greatest growth took place in the community colleges. In counties with at least fifty thousand

---

*A damaging result of data depicting the Chicano as being in the Southwest alone is that it tends to give decision-makers the impression that all Chicanos live in that area of the country. In programmatic, economic, educational, and political decisions, the Chicano is then treated as a regional issue rather than as a national one.

Mexican-Americans, three times as many were in community colleges as attended public four-year institutions. It is therefore not unreasonable to expect that Mexican-Americans will attain proportionate representation in higher education, since ACMAS found that Mexican-Americans are thus represented in those community colleges surveyed. Mexican-Americans make up 16 percent of the community college student body, although they constitute 18 percent of the total population.

There have been noticeable increases of Chicano students in colleges and universities both in the undergraduate and graduate schools, as was shown by the 1971–72 data. However, if proportionate representation is successfully attained in the state colleges and universities, as has been accomplished in the community colleges of the Southwest, approximately 175,000 Chicano college students can be anticipated. This is 75,000 higher than the ACMAS survey suggested. The 175,000 figure is supported by the Ford Foundation Report, *Minority Access to College*, which estimates "Mexican-American enrollment in 1970 would have to be increased by 165,000 (from 50,000 to 215,000)—an increase of 330 percent." From a community assessment of present efforts, the accomplishment of this goal is not only realistic, but is essential for the Chicano community. As efforts to attain this goal increase, however, some cautionary notes must be observed:

1. The community colleges must not become the "dumping ground" for Chicano and other minority students. It must be kept in mind that, just as many Chicano youths in junior and senior high school have been directed toward technical and vocational education exclusively, there is also a real danger that the same will happen to them in college. Already it is noted from the ACMAS data that "ninety percent of all Mexican-American students attending colleges in the Southwest enroll in public institutions with more than twice as many attending community colleges and universities."[26] Is it already happening? Why are there twice as many Chicanos in community colleges as in state colleges and universities? Is it that they are more accessible? Are community colleges making greater efforts to attract Chicanos than state colleges and universities? If so, why? If the Chicano community is directed away or directs itself away from state colleges and

universities because of financial reasons, it is difficult to explain that "the typical Mexican-American student attending a public two-year college received $168 in aid, while his counterpart at a public four-year college received five times as much."[27] It is interesting to note that in the surveyed community colleges, over one-half of the aid was in the form of jobs.[28] Either a lot of Chicanos are getting very little pay or very few were being paid sufficiently.

2. There is danger that financial resources, loans, grants, fellowships, scholarships, and assistantships are not made available to the Chicano recruited for college. What value are the recruitment, the slots, and the positions if the students cannot make it financially? That this can be a serious problem is brought out by the ACMAS survey: "Most colleges evidently do not expect any substantial change in their commitment to Mexican-American students over the next two years." Two-thirds indicated "all things being considered, it will probably be about the same as now."[29] (How are the estimated 175,000 Chicano students to enter college or universities?)

3. At a time when a greater number of Chicanos are making more concentrated efforts to get into colleges and universities (in Texas, a little less than 50 percent of Chicano students are in the freshman year), the cost of higher education is making a college education an unattainable luxury for many. The problem becomes more aggravated at the graduate level. Many Chicano students are already too overburdened repaying loans they received for their undergraduate education.

4. Universities and colleges must examine their curriculums with a view toward making them meaningful, applicable, and productive for the needs, desires, and goals of the Chicano students, otherwise dropouts would have merely been postponed from high school to college. Often the young, dedicated, and talented Chicano enters the university seeking to develop skills with which to be able to return to his or her community as a more effective instrument for leadership, but winds up frustrated with only a diploma. Moreover, the young Chicano's self-esteem is questioned, and his value to the community weakened.

Expansion of the ACMAS Report

The ACMAS reports are valuable for the speedy and timely data they provide. Probably because of speed, however, its Higher Education Survey failed to provide more in-depth information in critical areas which constitute serious problems and obstacles for the Chicano. Since the College Entrance Examination Board has an interest in providing needed data, I recommend to them the following:

1. It should assess the whole question of College Entrance Exams and the use of test scores in the undergraduate and graduate schools. These have had the effects of excluding many Chicanos and other minority students from college.

2. It should assess the relevance of curriculums mandated by community colleges, state colleges, and universities.

3. It should come up with current and accurate data as to the use and impact of education and career opportunity grants and other federal educational opportunity programs. One university was known to have turned back $85,000 to the Office of Education, although it is located in a community in dire need of this economic help.

4. It should seek information from Chicano groups in the universities, since the financial aid officers themselves did not consider a number of areas deemed critical to Chicanos such as: "Poor high school academic performance, inadequate information in secondary schools regarding availability of aid, cost of application, test and analysis fees."[30]

A Success Model

There are any number of excellent programs which have been developed at some institutions. One program from my experience embodies the ideal combination of ideas, programs, curriculum design, sensitivity, commitment, and financing. This project is Puerta Abierta of Our Lady of the Lake College, San Antonio, Texas. It is a teacher training program for bilingual, bicultural education. The mean income per family was $4,014 and the mean number of dependent children per family was 5.6. Some of the project's most pertinent findings are:[31]

1. Sixty percent of the students that were admitted into the project during the first year could not qualify for admission to college by the application of the usual measures for admission. Yet these students had a smaller percentage of failures and a smaller percentage on scholastic probation than the freshman class as a whole.

2. The correlation between the College Entrance Examination Board scores and the grade point average was not significantly different from zero for each of the two years of the project for which data were available. In other words, the College Board Test was no better than chance as a predictor of academic success for this segment of the population.

3. Research on the application of ten variables as a predictor of academic success was made. The most significant contributors to the prediction analysis were the motivational ratings obtained by the application of the admission criteria which have been established for the project. These were judgmental evaluations based on the careful application of these criteria, but these ratings had a much higher predictive value than the College Board score.

4. The Sequential Tests of Educational Progress were administered at the end of the freshman year for two successive years. The scores were compared with a control group from the college and with the national norm. The project students compared favorably with the control group within the college and the male students exceeded the national norm. The female students exceeded the national norm in social studies, but fell slightly below it in science.

5. Out of 135 students who have been in the project, only three have been lost because of academic suspension. The project is now in its third year of operation and more than ninety percent of the original enrollees are still in college. Seven of the students who dropped out had family problems.

After three years of experience, the project made the following recommendations:[32]

1. Students from low income families must have adequate and complete financial aid to provide room, board, tuition, fees, books, school supplies, clothing, transportation, personal needs, and some spending money so that they may attend school like other students. They cannot be partially supported financially and told to scratch for the rest, for these students have nowhere to obtain supplementary funds without further deprivation of their already impoverished families. Their work time has been completely consumed by their participation in the College Work-Study Program. To provide the students with less than total financial aid is to create the additional frustration that would make academic success impossible. It took a long period of negotiation and change in the operation of financial aid to fully implement the principle of complete financial aid.

2. A total institutional involvement and commitment is essential to the success of these students. This does not mean a lowering of academic standards, as some of the uninformed quickly assume, but rather a commitment to teaching instead of screening. The learning needs of each student have to be diagnosed and a sequential learning program set up to repair whatever deficiencies may exist. This institutional commitment of the academic faculty must also involve recognition of differences and means of enhancement of the richness of a bilingual society. This kind of institutional commitment cannot be quickly obtained, but with administrative cooperation, it can be developed.

3. Students from low income areas—because of their long communion with frustration, inequities, and failure—must have strong supportive personal counseling to prevent their discouragement and to increase their confidence and self-concept.

Other successful programs have been developed at: San Fernando Valley State College, California, which has an excellent Chicano studies model; the University of Colorado at Boulder, Colorado, where Mecha has instituted a successful recruitment program; and the University of Denver Law School which has a fine Graduate Professional Law Program which can serve as an example for graduate school programs.

In the preceding pages we have been considering the challenge that the Chicano movement has posed for our system of public education. The schools have been called to task for their failure to educate Chicanos and prepare them for college. As a result there has been a lack of Chicano professionals at all decision-making levels, a situation which has rendered the Mexican-American community virtually powerless in American society. It seems imperative that, having considered all of this, a plan of action be outlined.

A Recommended Agenda for Action

1. As an emerging people seeking self-determination, we must not only increase our encouragement of Chicano youth to pursue higher education, but must commit more of our time, energy, resources, and know-how to career and professional development of our youth.

2. It must become mandatory that each major research or development program involving Chicanos that is sponsored by a university or college should develop the expertise of those involved, along with the objectives of the given program or project. This assures the development of skills that will continue long after the program or project has been terminated.

3. HEW, Office of Civil Rights, the Office of Education, the Bureau of the Census, *The Higher Education Chronicle*—anyone having to do with providing important data on higher education—must clearly identify the Mexican-American in their reports. Simply identified under the classification of "Spanish-speaking" or "other minorities," it is impossible to know the exact educational status of the Chicano.

4. Universities and colleges must institutionalize the programs and procedures which have been successful in increasing the skills of young Chicanos. Otherwise, crash programs only benefit the *immediate* directors and administrators, and perhaps a limited number of Chicano students. Certainly, they are of no benefit to the larger Chicano community.

5. Universities and colleges must reassess their social role and responsibility toward American society, especially in providing upward mobility to a people who have been historically excluded.

6. Individual Chicano communities, urban and rural, should actually sponsor the professional development of Chicano lawyers, educators, writers, doctors, media specialists, economists, and clergy from their respective communities by providing fellowships, scholarships, and grants.

7. Chicanos must strive for academic positions as regents, presidents, and deans where decisions for procedures, curriculums, programs, and resources are made.

8. Chicanos must insist on representation proportionate to their population on educational development programs, loans, fellowships, and scholarships funded by government, industry, and private foundations.

9. The Chicano community must become more aware and utilize more effectively new educational programs such as the recent Higher Education Act. The management and allocation of these programs cannot be left unchallenged. It can no longer be assumed that they will be used to the best advantage of the Chicano youth.

10. Chicanos must become more knowledgeable and utilize with greater interest the internships in the Office of Education as OE Fellows, HEW Interns, White House Fellows, and Ford, Rockefeller, and Danforth Fellows. Recipients must also share their experiences and knowledge with other Chicanos.

11. The Chicano youth must recognize their inherent right to seek out, inquire about, and apply for scholarships, loans, and grants.

12. Chicano youths, supported by their families, must be willing to travel to those colleges and universities which have the interest, commitment, resources, and openings available for their professional training. Too often, it is found that these will be institutions outside of the Southwest such as the Harvard School of Law or the University of Massachusetts School of Education. This also brings up the question of those Southwestern colleges with a poor record in responding to the

special needs of Chicanos. It must be impressed upon these institutions that they are not fulfilling a basic responsibility.

13. Students must begin to think, hope, and prepare for higher education; this must begin early in their educational development, certainly at least in junior high school.

14. Parents must continue to develop a deeper appreciation of the value in acquiring a higher education.

15. Chicanos must insist that foundation, government, and industry funds that are provided for minority education be shared proportionately.

16. High school counselors must be held accountable for advice they give to Chicano youths about courses, examination procedures, and resources for higher education. Perhaps counselors should be evaluated on the percentage of Chicanos that go on to higher education from their respective schools.

17. Colleges and universities should no longer recruit Chicanos without also advising them on how to obtain financial assistance.

18. Colleges and universities must assess their curriculums to determine that their courses are "turning Chicano students on" and not "turning them off."

19. The Chicano community must make sure the community college is not a terminal point, but rather another option for further higher education.

20. Colleges and universities must realize that the median age of Chicanos is below eighteen years. The Chicano community has yet to "have its day in the sun" and it will come. Chicano youth must be seen as an untapped reservoir for future professional leadership in linking this country with the two hundred million people of Latin America.

The Southwest Intergroup Relations Council published a report with the title *The Future Belongs to Those Who Prepare for It.* How appropriately this applies to the Chicano community. The day has long since passed when, as a people, we can afford to sit back and just let our professional leadership happen, as has taken place in the past for whatever reasons. If we are to be masters of our own destiny, if self-determination is a serious quest and our goal, if we are dedicated to the breaking of the "hellish cycle of poverty and ignorance," if we are anxious to provide a better tomorrow for our youth who are presently below eighteen years of age, then it is absolutely imperative that all institutions of higher learning be held accountable for their social responsibility in developing leadership for an emerging people.

This leadership will emerge! How and in what form will depend on the Chicano community's access to the colleges and universities. These institutions must perform that for which they were founded —the development of young minds, hearts, and lives, from whose ranks will come the leadership of the future. The Chicano youth have made their case, they have made their challenge—the decades of the seventies and eighties will record the response of our country's institutions of higher learning. American society will know if the Chicanos are really "locked in or locked out." All of us will know if every American truly has access to higher education.

NOTES

1. *Diana* v. *State Board of Education*, Soledad, California, C70-37-RFP.

2. *Serrano* v. *Priest*, California Supreme Court Decision, 96 California Rptr. 601, 5 Cal. 3d584, 487 P.2d 1241 (1971).

3. *San Antonio School District* v. *Rodriguez*, 411-U.S. 1-36 Law. ed. 2nd. 16 93 Sup. Ct. 1278-1973.

4. Carlos Muñoz, Jr., "The Politics of Educational Change in East Los Angeles," *Proceedings on the Symposium on Mexican-Americans and Educational Change.*

5. Henry J. Casso, "A Study of Three Legal Challenges for Placing Mexican American Children into Educably Mentally Retarded Classes" (Ph.D. diss., University of Massachusetts, 1972), p. 4.

6. Ibid., p. 5.

7. United States Commission on Civil Rights, Mexican-American Education Study, *The Unfinished Education: Outcomes for Minorities in the Five Southwestern States, Report II* (Washington, D.C.); *Toward Quality Education for Mexican-Americans, Report VI.* Washington, D.C., 1974.

8. Hearings before the Senate Committee on Equal Education Opportunity, United States Senate, 91st Congress, 2nd Session, Pt. 4 Mexican-American Education, 1970.

9. *Arreola* v. *Board of Education*, Santa Ana Unified School District 150577, California, 1970; *Covarrubias* v. *San Diego Unified School District*, 70-394-T; *Diana* v. *State Board of Education*, Soledad, California, C70-37 RFP, California, 1970.

10. Hearings before the Senate Committee on Equal Education Opportunity, United States Senate, 91st Congress, 2nd Session, Pt. 4 Mexican-American Education, 1970.

11. Ibid.

12. Muñoz, "The Politics of Educational Change."

13. Jane Mercer, "Institutionalized Anglocentrism: Labeling Mental Retardates in the Public Schools," Chap. 10, *Race, Change and Urban Society*, Vol. 5, *Urban Affairs Annual Reviews* (Beverly Hills, Calif.: Sage Publications, 1971).

14. California State Advisory Committee to the United States Commission on Civil Rights, Report of the Committee, Political Participation of Mexican-Americans in California, 1971.

15. Ibid.

16. Ibid.

17. Ibid.

18. Ibid.

19. Casso, "A Study of Three Legal Challenges."

20. Ibid.

21. Ibid.

22. United States Commission on Civil Rights, Mexican-American Education Study, *Ethnic Isolation in Public Schools, Report I* (Washington, D.C.: 1971).

23. College Entrance Examination Board, "Access to College for Mexican-Americans in the Southwest," *Higher Education Surveys*, Report No. 6 (July 1972).

24. Ibid.

25. Ibid.

26. Fred E. Crossland, *Minority Access to College*, A Ford Foundation Report (New York: Schocken Books, 1971).

27. Ibid.

28. Ibid.

29. Ibid.

30. Ibid., pp. 22, 31, 32.

31. Project "Puerta Abierta," a Bilingual, Bicultural Program of Elementary Teacher Education, School of Education, Our Lady of the Lake College, San Antonio, Texas, 1971 (unpublished report).

32. Ibid., p. 17.

7

A Perspective on Mexican-American Organizations

HENRY SANTIESTEVAN

Mr. Santiestevan is a founder, board member, and former National Director of the National Council of La Raza. In addition, he has been involved with and written extensively on the international labor movement with an emphasis on Latin America. Mr. Santiestevan is active in Mexican-American affairs and at various times has been a member of the Los Angeles Community Services Organization, the G.I. Forum, and LULAC. He has also worked closely with César Chávez.

Introduction

Organizations° are created in order to bring about some form of interaction with their environment, usually with the objective of somehow improving it. Generally, the environments with which Mexican-American, or Chicano,† organizations have attempted to interact have been harsh. They have not been conducive to the development and growth of Chicano-organized institutions.

Mexican-American organizations usually have been faced with an "outside" environment of a surrounding, dominant society that was inimical or indifferent to them, and an "inside" environment of a barrio suffering from meager resources and preoccupied with sheer survival.

The repression imposed upon the barrio and its inhabitants by the dominant society for some 125 years has produced internalized pressures and tensions in communities and individuals that have made planned, sustained, and coordinated activities, essential to the life and growth of an organization, extremely difficult.

°Following is the definition of the term "organization" as used herein: An organization is the coordination of differentiated activities by a defined group of persons to carry out planned activities to interact with the environment.

†The terms "Mexican-American" and "Chicano" are used interchangeably.

It is useful, therefore, to get an overview of the broad historical and socioeconomic factors that have gone into the formation of the environments which have influenced the formation, development, or demise of Mexican-American organizations.

An Historical Overview

European expansion, which began its imperialistic march in the fifteenth century, moved in the next two hundred years to dominate the indigenous people of the Americas, Africa, southern Asia, and the islands of the South Seas. First to feel the full impact of European conquest were the native tribes in the Caribbean and North America as Spanish conquistadores added a Nueva España, a "New Spain," to their empire. In rapid order, waves of conquerors from France and England added a "New France" and a "New England" as they claimed large areas of the New World on behalf of their nations.

Thus, under the might of conquest, began the long and uneven efforts, which ranged from tyrannical cruelty to well-meaning paternalism, by the white men from Europe to transform the lives and languages, the religions and the cultures of the indigenous "Americans," whom the conquerors misnamed "Indians."

From the beginning of their march of conquest, the Spaniards identified their attempts to "civilize" the indigenous natives—the "Indians"—as a Catholic-Christian duty. Missionaries as well as the colonial administrators and the military leaders were very conscious of themselves as bearers of civilization. They often used the word "civilization" and in its name brought about changes in everything from religious practice to clothing.

Spaniards, of course, identified "civilization" with their own culture, as is the way of all conquerors. The proper language of civilization was Spanish. The proper homes were permanent structures made of stone or adobe, the men properly wore trousers, and the only form of "civilized" religion was the Roman Catholic form of Christianity.

The Spaniards succeeded in laying the foundations for a culture which still remains in extensive portions of the Western Hemisphere.

After two hundred years of steady advance northward from the Valley of Mexico, the Spanish conquest began to slow down during the last half of the 1700s. As the controlling hand of the Spaniards faltered, rumblings of independence began to increase, particularly among the mestizos who now made up one-fifth of Mexico's population.

In 1810 the population of Mexico was roughly estimated to be 6,000,000 people—40,000 Spaniards, 1,000,000 Creoles, 3,500,000 pure-blooded Indians, and 1,500,000 Mestizos.[1]

The Creoles were whites born in Mexico of Spanish parents or ancestry. Mestizos were the descendants of Spanish and Indian parents and they were beginning to think of themselves not as Spaniards nor as members of separate Indian tribes, but as Mexicans.

On September 16, 1810, Father Miguel Hidalgo y Costilla mounted the pulpit of his church in the small village of Dolores and sounded *El Grito*, "The Cry," now regarded as Mexico's proclamation of independence from Spain. "Mexicanos, Viva México," cried Father Hidalgo, and he was soon joined by thousands of Indians and mestizos who marched with him into the pages of Mexican history. But independence was not to come to Mexico until eleven years later. In 1821, first the empire and later the republic of Mexico replaced the three-hundred-year-old viceroyalty of New Spain.

It was in the southwestern part of what is today the United States that the frontiers of Spanish and English North America met and overlapped. Some two hundred years behind the Spanish, the English conquest had by the last half of the 1700s barely reached to the Mississippi River. But by the early 1800s, some American trappers were moving into the areas of New Mexico and what later became Arizona.

The emerging new nations of Mexico and the United States were to clash first in Texas which, in 1836, had declared its own independence. Ten years later, in May of 1846, the United States responded to the "Manifest Destiny" expansionist program of President James Polk and declared war on Mexico.

On February 2, 1848, the Treaty of Guadalupe-Hidalgo was signed and the war between the United States and Mexico came to an end. The price Mexico paid as the loser was high. Less than thirty years after gaining its independence from Spain, the young republic of Mexico lost California, Arizona, New Mexico, and Texas. In exchange Mexico received a payment of $15 million.

Some five years later, the United States completed its acquisition of the southwestern border states when it purchased the lower portion of New Mexico and Arizona from Mexico for $10 million. The Gadsden Treaty which completed the purchase was signed on April 25, 1854. The long history of the Mexican-American minority had begun.

> Mexican Americans became a minority not by immigrating or being brought to this country as a subordinate people, but by being conquered. . . . The early history of the Mexican Americans beginning in the 19th Century is thus the history of how they became a subordinate people. . . . This early history with its very important variations from state to state set the stage for the large scale immigration from Mexico in the 20th Century; and it influenced the economic, social and political roles Mexican Americans are able to play.[2]

Without moving a single step from their ancestral homes, Mexicans virtually overnight became Mexican-Americans—instant aliens in their own land. According to historical statistics of the United States Bureau of the Census, Mexicans were sparsely settled throughout the Southwest when it was first taken over by the United States. There were an estimated sixty thousand in New Mexico, the southwestern area first penetrated by the Spanish, perhaps five thousand in Texas, no more than one thousand in Arizona, and around seventy-five hundred along the length of California. Also there were some small and isolated settlements in what is today Colorado.

Mexican colonists—that is, Spanish settlers coming from Mexico—generally had entered the Southwest through mountain passes and river valleys. They formed settlements that stretched in a fan-like pattern for more than two thousand miles along its northern edge; in only a few places did the settlements extend beyond two hundred miles north of the present Mexican border.

In the strategic valleys, fertile river areas, and other typical frontier locations in which they settled, early Mexican colonists established small, tight, and defensible communities.

Texas

Probably 80 percent or more of the Mexicans of Texas, who became Mexican-Americans after the Treaty of Guadalupe-Hidalgo, lived in the lower Rio Grande Valley and in the cities along the river. El Paso very early became the most westerly town of any consequence. Mexicans of the Rio Grande Valley and the river towns were numerically dominant, but after the annexation of Texas, the Anglo-Americans quickly took control of the land and became economically and politically dominant. For example, Paul S. Taylor notes in *An American-Mexican Frontier* that all Mexican-owned grants but one in Nueces County, Texas, passed into the hands of Anglo-American settlers between 1840 and 1859.[3]

The economy of this border area of Texas rested upon cattle ranches which were based upon the ownership of livestock rather than land. With the invention of barbed wire in 1875, the large cattle and sheep ranches were very quickly fenced and the owner-control of land became dominant. A great number of small- and medium-size Mexican and Anglo cattle and sheep ranchers who owned livestock but little or no land were very quickly frozen out. Only a few Mexican ranchers were able to retain ownership of the land they worked. Mexican settlers in Texas, now Mexican-Americans, moved on to the large ranches as laborers.

At the same time, large cattle and sheep ranches and cotton plantations began to move slowly into south Texas from east Texas. Steadily moving west in search of cheap land and cheap labor, Anglo-American cotton growers turned to the extensive labor pool of conquered Mexican-Americans and Mexicans crossing the new border.

> The resulting demand for cheap Mexican labor to cultivate cotton either as wage laborers or as tenants was so great that it fixed very nearly in its modern form the economic base of the Mexican Americans and the Mexican old settler in Texas. . . . By 1890 the cotton culture of the deep South was well established in Nueces County.[4]

At this same period a string of mercantile towns were growing up along the Rio Grande—Brownsville, Laredo, Rio Grande City, and Dolores were among them. These towns were almost entirely Mexican-American in population and it was here that there appeared very early the Mexican-American middle-class element which was to be important to the future of the Rio Grande Valley.

By the beginning of the twentieth century, the Anglo-American process of defining the Mexican-American laborer in both rural and urban Texas as an inferior person not entitled to political education or social equality was well under way. Only in some of the commercial towns along the Rio Grande Valley, where Mexican-Americans remained in the majority, did the remnants of social and political equality survive to a limited extent.

The economic destiny of the Mexican-American as a source of cheap labor was thus fixed in Texas by 1900.

California

The Rio Grande Valley in Texas stretching to Brownsville on the Gulf of Mexico formed the most easterly finger of original Mexican settlement. The most westerly was California.

In California, first under Spanish rule and then under Mexican, a mere handful of rancheros held an enormous area which was almost completely separated from the political and economic centers of Mexico. Cut off by the formidable Rocky Mountains and barren deserts, California was so far west that in the early period the Anglo-American settlers came in small numbers. But then gold was discovered in northern California in the late 1840s and suddenly the area was being invaded by multitudes of Anglo-American miners. At least 100,000 miners were arriving each year bringing their Eastern, Midwestern, or Southern racial prejudices with them.

> In the mines remote from any law, Mexicans were taxed, lynched, robbed and expelled in an endless series of incidents. Many of the Mexicans then drifted into California towns and formed a substantial group of landless laborers. The mining troubles were an early and a bad precedent for American-Mexican relations in California.[5]

Gold mining very quickly became less profitable and unable to sustain the large number of new arrivals, most of whom then turned to agriculture. The new Anglo-Americans squatted on the Mexican land grants. Due to the steadily growing numbers and influence of Anglo-American settlers, the Californios (native Mexican settlers) found themselves in the position of small groups of overextended landlords barely able to hold on to their land. Within a few years, they had lost nearly all of their land and economic power in northern California.

The Gold Rush which brought Anglo-Americans into northern California by the hundreds of thousands did not have the same impact on southern California. For nearly a generation after gold was discovered at Sutter's Mill in the north, the situation in the south remained unchanged. Almost all of the arable land was owned by about fifty Californio families, including about a dozen "Mexicanized" Yankee families.

The availability of both cheap land and cheap Indian labor and the lack of economic enterprises tended to keep out Mexican wage laborers. The dry southern California climate proved unattractive to the Anglo land squatter, who preferred the moister climate in the north for the development of family-sized farms.

But racial tensions were growing nevertheless as Los Angeles began to expand with a population of lower-class Mexicans, Indians, Chinese, and Anglos. And the growing Anglo-American influence in the north on the state government was making California less tolerant. The state ceased publishing its laws in Spanish, and in 1855 school instruction in Spanish was banned by law, in violation of the Treaty of Guadalupe-Hidalgo.

Then, in 1862, rancheros in southern California were hit by a devastating flood which was followed by two years of severe drought. The back-to-back disasters practically wiped out the rancheros by destroying their wealth at its source—the land.

It was the railroads that leveled the final blow. By 1869, the railroad had arrived at San Francisco, and seven years later it was completed to Los Angeles. In 1877, another railroad line from the East reached Los Angeles. A rush of Anglo-American settlers resulted.

In one year alone (1887), the railroads brought in more than two hundred thousand Anglo-American settlers; that year there were only some twelve thousand Mexicans in all of southern California. The Mexican majority had become a local minority in one year. A great land boom broke soon after the arrival of the railroads and that brought to an end most of what remained of Mexican ownership of the great ranches. Any chance for the families of the original Mexican settlers to retain any meaningful economic or political influence (much less control) in either southern or northern California was gone.

Los Angeles, however, developed the largest concentration of Mexican-Americans in the United States as successive waves of Mexican immigrants crossed the border and thousands of Mexican-Americans from the border states flowed into the "big city" in the first half of the twentieth century.

For the most part, what they found in Los Angeles was poverty and powerlessness. By this time, the Anglo pattern of economic and political domination was solidly established.

Arizona

The Spaniards attempted to settle Arizona in the seventeenth and eighteenth centuries with a string of missions which opened up the river valleys of the San Pedro, Santa Cruz, San Miguel, and Altar rivers. There was some colonization, mostly in the form of large estates, but it did not "take," because of the persistent opposition of the Indians, particularly the Apaches.

By the mid-nineteenth century, the Indians had gained the upper hand and almost all of the Arizona colonists lived in the fortified city of Tucson. Because of the formidable and continuous resistance of the Indians and the indifference or inability of Mexico to furnish adequate military protection, Arizona remained only sparsely settled by Mexicans, and the shift to Anglo domination in the latter part of the nineteenth century was rapid and fairly smooth.

Indian resistance collapsed by the 1880s, which came at about the same time that large-scale mining and railroad construction started. The small number of Mexicans in Arizona had never had an opportunity to become politically or economically significant, and when the railroads came and mining began, they were drawn into cheap wage labor. But there were not nearly enough workers to satisfy the huge appetite of the railroads and the mines. The result was that thousands more were imported from the cheap labor markets of El Paso and Laredo, Texas.

Thus the Texas pattern of transition to wage labor appeared very early in Arizona and with it the dreary succession of lynchings, unsolved murders, and vigilante actions against a working class population of what was defined as a different race.[6]

The Arizona pattern into which the Mexican wage laborers were channeled was that of numerous, isolated mining towns, nearly all of which developed a large majority of Mexican-Americans. These were company towns, dominated by copper corporations, which appeared in great numbers in the 1880s and gave Arizona such isolated mining towns as Miami, San Manuel, Tubac, Ajo, Morenci, Duquesne, Metcalf, and many others, some of which are still in existence and others which have become ghost towns. Many larger Arizona towns, such as Douglas, Prescott, and Bisbee, received their original impetus from mining.

The geographical isolation of the mining towns meant that they were cut off from the larger American society of the time. Most of them were completely dominated by a single employer, and the workers suffered from all the evils of company-town control, including low wages, harsh living conditions, ruthless exploitation, and severe discrimination along occupational and racial lines. In practice, this meant sharp, company-enforced segregation of Mexican-Americans from Anglo-Americans, including the setting up of separate "Mexican" shopping hours in the company store owned by the Anglo employers.

The racist segregation policies of the Anglo-owned mining companies underlined some of the most bitter confrontations of labor and management in the Southwest when the miners moved in the mid-twentieth century toward the organization of their own unions.

New Mexico

New Mexico generally presented a more congenial political and economic environment for settlers from Mexico than did the other border states. At the time of the signing of the Guadalupe-Hidalgo Treaty, there were about sixty thousand persons in the territory of New Mexico, and practically all of them were Mexicans. Most of this population lived within a fifty-mile radius of Santa Fe or at the headwaters of the Rio Grande and the Pecos River.

Because of the isolation and almost continual battles with the

Indians, Anglo penetration of the territory came very slowly. Mexican colonization was built around three types of inhabited areas: large ranches, a considerable number of small villages, and administrative-military towns, such as Albuquerque and Santa Fe. The Mexican settlers had from the beginning established their political influence and control.

The economic subordination of Mexicans extended west from Texas into the grain and ranching areas of eastern New Mexico (the area is still called "Little Texas"), as large cattlemen began to enclose their land and push out Mexican (and Anglo) sheep ranchers. Several clashes resulted, including the "Lincoln County Wars" from 1869 to 1881. But most of the New Mexicans lived a long way from these border areas and were not much affected by the disturbances.

However, profound economic changes were impinging fairly swiftly on the isolated, and relatively small, Mexican society. The railroads came, and by the end of the nineteenth century, the Indians were overcome and large stretches of land held by Apache raiders were opened up to Anglo settlement.

By 1900, large numbers of small farmers and sheepherders were being forced into wage labor by the consolidation of large ranches, overgrazing and erosion problems, and the withdrawal of large areas of grazing land for federal use, such as national forests, railroads, and homesteading. And immigration of Mexican-Americans and Mexicans from Texas was beginning to swell the wage labor pools and tending to force down wages.

Thus, although the effect would take many years to be deeply felt, by the turn of the century the underlying forces were in motion that forced the New Mexican villager into a long, slow, and losing battle for economic survival.

By 1900, also, American ranching, transportation, and mining interests were flowing into New Mexico, bringing with them increasing numbers of Anglo settlers. The railroads were opening up new markets for meat, hides, and wool which in turn accelerated the development of larger ranches. Smaller cattlemen and sheepmen were the losers.

There was evidence that Anglo penetration was also bringing in another, and ominous, social force: racial prejudice. New Mexico had been notably free from discrimination, with tolerance generally cutting across economic class lines. The territorial legislature was dominated for many years by an alliance between wealthy "Spanish-American" families and Anglo interests in ranching, railroading, and banking.

> Inter-marriage between Anglo men and Mexican women was apparently quite common, and not restricted to any particular social class. . . . Business and commercial mergers between Anglos and Mexicans occurred frequently, and in politics, coalitions of Anglos and Mexicans worked together in each of the major parties.[7]

But economic and social forces were grinding Mexican-Americans into the status of a dependent minority and class distinctions were hardening along racial lines.

It was during that turbulent half century, from the time Mexico turned over huge areas of her territory to the new conquistadores of the mid-nineteenth century, to the time that the victorious Anglo-Americans had consolidated their economic and political control over those vast areas at the beginning of the twentieth century, that the Mexican-American was virtually sentenced to an internal colonial status in the United States.

When the Anglo-Americans took over, they brought in economic and legal patterns that concentrated control of land, labor, and capital in their own hands. They imposed patterns of social and economic segregation which quickly became institutionalized and enforced by organized military and police forces.

For the Mexican settlers entrapped by conquest on "el otro lado"—the other side—of the new border, it was the beginning of sharp separation from the direct historical experiences of an emerging mestizo nation—Mexico—and of the painful denial of free and democratic entry into a developing Anglo-American nation —the United States.

It was the beginning of the profound and prolonged struggle for survival and search for identity of the Mexican-American—the Chicano.

Mexican-American Organizations: The First Century

Mexican-American attempts to organize so as to more effectively combat the oppression imposed upon them began almost as soon as the American conquest of the Southwest was accomplished. The first organizations had a military character; their tactics were violent, and their objectives were direct: to oust the "gringo."

The war between Mexico and the United States formally ended with the Treaty of Guadalupe-Hidalgo. But that did not end the actual fighting. Force was used by the Anglos to gain control, and force was used by the Mexicans to retaliate. There was an almost constant state of guerrilla warfare between sizable "armies" in Texas which, for the next generation, experienced a series of bloody clashes, some reaching the status of international warfare in the 1850s. In New Mexico, an abortive rebellion followed the American occupation.

This was the period during which scores, perhaps even hundreds, of leaders rose spontaneously to lead guerrilla groups ranging in size from small bands to substantial forces against the Anglo. In Anglo versions of history, many of these leaders are called outlaws; among the Mexican-Americans they were considered liberators, fighting for their people. In California, for example, there were Tiburcio Vásquez and Joaquín Murieta, whose lives have since been highly romanticized. And in Texas, there were Juan Flores Salinas and Juan Cortina.

Juan Cortina was perhaps the most successful of these "liberators." He first invaded Texas in 1859 in a series of skirmishes which are now known as the "Cortina Wars." Cortina began his expeditions as a personal vendetta against an Anglo sheriff in Brownsville, Texas. But he soon extended his campaign to a call for a general emancipation of Mexicans from Anglo rule. Mexicans on both sides of the Rio Grande flocked to his camp, and his army engaged United States troops in many battles. Eventually Cortina and his small army were forced to retreat into Mexico. He was still leading raids into Texas as late as the middle 1870s.

However, the end of the Civil War in the United States released troops which were then sent to the Southwest to "pacify" both the Indians and the guerrilla bands of protesting Mexican-Americans. Also, the railroad began to bring in large numbers of Easterners looking for land in the new frontier, and the era of open violence between Mexican-Americans and Anglos came to an end. It was followed by a period of relative quiet.

Thus, organized retaliation, ranging from the guerrilla raids of small bands to the military movement of substantial armies, was an early Mexican-American response toward hostile and threatening environments.

About the turn of the century, Mexican-Americans, still seeking to find some measure of economic and social release from the harsh pressures of a dominant society, turned to the formation of mutual aid organizations. The Alianza Hispano Americana founded in Arizona in 1894 was an excellent example of a mutualist society. It is still in existence and is one of the oldest. Mutualist societies such as the Alianza attracted members by providing small sickness and death benefits. The mutualist organizations were characteristic of an era of adaptation and accommodation which extended roughly from the early 1900s until about the 1930s. Large numbers of Mexican immigrants coming into the United States in the 1910s and 1920s brought about an increased impetus in the development of societies with mutualistic aims. These groups tended to be oriented toward Mexican consulates and emphasized Mexican culture or nationalism. They served as meeting places where members could get together, share experiences, and help each other cope with the American way of life. Among these groups were La Sociedad Mutualista Mexicana, La Sociedad Ignacio Zaragoza, La Cámara de Comercial Mexicana, and La Sociedad Cervantes.

In 1921 one of the most important of these organizations, La Comisión Honorífica Mexicana, was founded in Los Angeles by Eduardo Ruiz, the Mexican consul. The original purpose of La Comisión was to assist immigrant Mexican nationals until consular aid could be attained. However, it later developed much broader goals and was accepted as a community spokesman, especially in cities and towns with a fairly large and recent middle-class Mexican immigration. Subsequent to the formation of La Comisión Honorífica Mexicana in Los Angeles, hundreds of similar chapters were formed throughout the Southwest.

It was no mere coincidence that the mutualist societies began to appear at the same time that a small Mexican-American middle class emerged which was attempting to come to some form of political accommodation with the larger society. These societies did not press for full political participation nor include demands for equality, either between Mexican-Americans themselves, or in terms of the dominant majority.

Thus, only internal citizens of the United States of Mexican or Spanish extraction, either native or naturalized, were eligible to join. This exclusion by citizenship was meant—and used—as an exclusionary mechanism. The implication was that Mexican Americans were more trustworthy to Anglos than Mexican nationals and also more deserving of the benefits of American life.[8]

For example, the "exclusion by citizenship" was a policy of the Orden Hijos de América (Order of the Sons of America), founded in San Antonio in 1921. It is interesting to note that the Comisión Honorífica Mexicana and the Orden Hijos de América were both formed in 1921 and that the former emphasized its relationship with Mexican culture and nationalism, while the latter placed emphasis on its relationship with America, that is the United States, as evidenced by their names.

The founding members of the Order of the Sons of America came almost entirely from the newly emerging middle class. The social and economic positions of these founding members were precarious, and their policy of adaption was undoubtedly a reflection of the painful vulnerability of Mexican-Americans during the 1920s. It was a valid decision by the Order of the Sons of America that, in order to survive, it must be as noncontroversial as possible and openly express declarations of loyalty to the United States of America. The policies of accommodation and adaptation were thus in their own way a response to the social and economic pressures of a surrounding and generally repressive society.

A large number of the members were returning veterans who had seen military service during World War I, an experience that had extended their education and experience outside accustomed barrio environments. They returned with strong motivations to educate their fellow Mexican-Americans about their political rights.

The basic objectives of this organization were to enable Mexican Americans to achieve acculturation and integration, principally through political action. Ultimately, the Order sought to end prejudice against Mexican Americans, to achieve equality before the law, to acquire political representation at all levels and to obtain greater educational opportunities, restricting membership to United States citizens of Mexican or Hispanic background. It strongly emphasized that its members learn English and work toward gaining citizenship.[9]

Thus, the Order of the Sons of America and organizations similar to it laid the groundwork for many of the objectives of the Chicano organizations of today.

The Order of the Sons of America also was to be a forerunner of one of the most enduring of the Mexican-American organizations —the League of United Latin American Citizens (LULAC)—which still exists. LULAC was born as a result of an exercise of statesmanlike leadership that brought about the unification of several Mexican-American organizations faced with fragmentation and dissolution.

The Order of the Sons of America had developed internal conflicts which resulted in the San Antonio councils independently reorganizing as the Knights of America. This separation led several Mexican-American leaders, among them Benjamin Garza, a leading figure in the Corpus Christi council of the Order of the Sons of America, to call a meeting. As a result, in August 1927, a conference was held in Harlingen, Texas, at which time a decision to reorganize was reached. A year and a half later, on February 17, 1929, a unification convention was held in Corpus Christi, Texas, by representatives of the Order of the Sons of America, the League of Latin American Citizens, and the Knights of America. At that convention the League of United Latin American Citizens was born.

Within a few months, LULAC had adopted a constitution stressing the achievement of economic, social, and political rights for all Mexican-Americans as its major goal.

In its objectives, LULAC sought to end discrimination and mistreatment of Mexican-Americans; to achieve equality in government, law, business and education; to promote education in order to produce more doctors, lawyers, engineers and other professional people of Mexican descent; to develop pride in Mexican ancestry; to promote the learning of English by Mexicans as a means of achieving a greater degree of equality; and to encourage the effective exercise of the United States citizenship by active participation in politics.[10]

The participation in politics as defined by LULAC at that time did not call for an aggressive entry into the political arena, nor for any kind of Mexican-American political participation based on a separate ethnic identity, but emphasized education for "good citizenship."

Adaptation and accommodation was the style in the 1920s and 1930s and LULAC conformed to it in that period. At the time LULAC was organized, a debate was going on in Congress and in the press concerning the "rising tide" of Mexican immigration. In 1929 the Great Depression began and brought the emerging, small Mexican-American middle class to a point of extreme vulnerability.

> Thus, in 1929, to protect themselves from social and economic sanctions, the willingness of Mexican Americans to assert even minimum political demands was tempered at all times and in all expressions by a desire to reaffirm citizenship and loyalty to the United States. It is not surprising that there was at this time no pressure for Mexican civil rights particularly if it might have involved any kind of open demonstrations.[11]

Among the expressed aims of LULAC was "to develop within the members of our race the best, purest and most perfect type of a true and loyal citizen of the United States of America." Article I of LULAC's bylaws stated, "we shall oppose any radical and violent demonstration which may tend to create conflicts and disturb the peace and tranquility of our country." Although the development of pride in Mexican ancestry was a primary aim of LULAC and certainly individual members were proud of their ethnic identity, there was no demand upon the dominant society for any form of cultural pluralism.

Such emphasis on conformity to the standards of Anglo society, particularly Texas-Anglo society, must be judged in the context of the political milieu of the United States and Texas in the 1920s and 1930s. Both Mexican-Americans and blacks were kept in "their place" by a repressive society with methods that included lynchings. The paternalistic influence of the Anglo *patrón* was strong, even carrying with it, at least in the eyes of the patrón, the right to dictate to Mexican-Americans which organizations they should or should not join. An example is an excerpt from a letter written by such an Anglo patrón in which he scolded his "Mexican Texas friends" for even forming such a group as LULAC.

I have been and still consider myself as your Leader or
Superior Chief. . . . I have always sheltered in my soul the
most pure tenderness for the Mexican Texas race and have
watched over your interests to the best of my ability and
knowledge. . . . Therefore, I disapprove the political activity
of groups which have no other object than to organize
Mexican Texas voters into political groups for guidance from
other leaders.[12]

The "most pure tenderness" of the letter-writing Texas patrón
was an ironic expression of the most pure hypocrisy. It was written
by a member of a dominant establishment that did not hesitate to
use any means—from paternalism to force—to maintain the Mexican-American in a position of dependence.

LULAC was to survive—and even gain influence—by following
such policies of adaptation and accommodation through the
Depression and World War II years.

The years following World War II were to carry LULAC and
some new, emerging Mexican-American organizations into increasingly aggressive demands for social and political equality. The
development of these organizations in the two decades following
World War II occurred in a period of profound social change for
the Mexican-American population.

World War II brought hundreds of thousands of young Mexican-
American males into the armed services, which took them out of
the confining experiences of their home areas, brought them into
contact with millions of other young Americans, and carried them
literally around the world. Mexican-American young men in the
armed services during World War II found themselves in shoulder-
to-shoulder contact with millions of other Americans and facing the
same dangers, challenges, and demands. They found that not only
could they keep up with Americans from all parts of the United
States but could often excel.

The second factor deeply influencing the development of
Mexican-American organizations following World War II was the
urbanization of the Mexican-American population. The Mexican-
American joined in the sweeping historic movement of the
American people from the rural areas to the cities, and they joined
into it for the same reasons: in search of jobs and economic

security. By the end of 1950, some 80 to 85 percent of the Mexican-Americans were living in urban areas.

Still a third factor important in the development of organizations by Mexican-Americans following World War II was the fact that many of them were now the third, fourth, and even fifth and sixth generations born in the United States. Mexican-Americans now had some one hundred years of historical experience as an emerging and identifiable minority in the United States. While they had clung tenaciously to the cultural heritage of their mother country, Mexico, they had also been subjected to and influenced by the ideas, experiences, and institutions of the United States.

A fourth factor influencing Mexican-American organizations in the 1940s and 1950s was the extension of the Mexican-American population throughout most of the United States. Migratory labor, railroads, and a search for jobs in the industrial centers of the Midwest, particularly in the steel and auto industries, had carried the Mexican-American far beyond his Southwestern home. They had become the second largest minority in the nation.

The stage was set for the emergence of the organizations which would turn the policies of accommodation into programs of action to break through ancient patterns of prejudice and discrimination. The chief method was aggressive and direct participation in political action.

It was in this period that the California-born Community Service Organization (CSO) became an important and meaningful organization. CSO utilized new techniques of larger scale grassroots community organization and put emphasis on appealing to active and increased participation by as many elements of the community as possible. CSO moved to broaden the base of the Mexican-American organization beyond the relatively few and successful middle-class members, as was typical of former organizations. CSO activity recruited blue-collar workers and lower income members, including new arrivals from Mexico. It also admitted some non-Mexican-American members, although these were few.

CSO's intent was to cope with concrete and immediate political, social, and economic problems. An assumption of CSO was that American institutions would be responsive to the needs of the Mexican-American population and changes could be brought about by broad community organization and action. Thus, a prime

objective of CSO was to get large numbers of Mexican-Americans
to register and vote.

The organization put on large-scale community registration
drives, some of which, significantly and probably permanently,
increased the number of Mexican-American voters. In Los Angeles,
CSO registration attempts in its early organizational phase had the
election of a Mexican-American city councilman as its immediate
objective. CSO registered some fifteen thousand new Mexican-
American voters in the Los Angeles area and its efforts to elect its
candidate to the city council were successful.° It demonstrated that
a Mexican-American organization could successfully organize politically and elect candidates. CSO thus pioneered extensive community and political organization and action in the Mexican-American
communities.

Two other political groups founded in the late 1950s developed
similar patterns of political action. The Mexican American Political Association (MAPA) founded in California in 1958, and the
Political Association of Spanish Speaking Organizations (PASSO)
organized in Texas, were formed to negotiate with, influence,
and/or pressure the political system at the party level. Primary
objectives of both MAPA and PASSO were to register Mexican-
Americans and get them to vote, and to elect candidates to
political office.

In the early 1960s, PASSO scored a significant and precedent-
shattering victory by electing the mayor and city councilman in
Crystal City, Texas, successfully deposing a longstanding Anglo
political structure. The Crystal City victory foreshadowed what
Mexican-Americans could accomplish politically in communities
where they had a substantial population.

Another important Mexican-American organization to emerge
after World War II was the American GI Forum. The GI Forum
was formed out of protest when a funeral home in Three Rivers,
Texas, refused to bury a Mexican-American war veteran in 1948.
Formation of the GI Forum was the active response of Mexican-
American veterans notifying the nation which they had served
loyally and heroically in World War II that they would not tolerate
the indignities of prejudice and discrimination.

The GI Forum quickly began to accent political action and

°Ed Roybal, now a Congressman from Los Angeles.

organized intensive "get out the vote" and "pay your poll tax" drives in Texas in the 1950s. Since the repeal of the Texas poll tax, it has continued vigorous voter registration drives and civil rights activities. The GI Forum attempts to be active at various levels of the American political system. Today, it is an important Mexican-American organization with chapters throughout the Southwest and in other parts of the United States.

Thus, the Mexican-American organizations which emerged in the post–World War II period introduced at least three new major factors in their policies and programs:

1. Mass community organization with an across-the-board appeal to all elements of the Mexican-American communities.
2. Direct involvement with the political system.
3. Cooperation with supportive Anglo-American organizations and individuals in the "outside" environment to create supportive alliances for their programs.

The policies of accommodation and adaptation utilized for survival in the midst of a hostile environment by Mexican-American organizations during the 1920s and 30s were dramatically altered by the emerging post–World War II organizations into aggressive demands for civil liberties and political and economic rights.

Instead of accommodating to Anglo-American attitudes and institutions, these post–World War II organizations demanded that those institutions respond to their needs. Mexican-American organizations were thus well on their way to insisting that the American community as a whole accept them and their communities as equals within the American system.

Mexican-Americans and Labor Organizations

Mexican-American workers have a long and consistent history of tenaciously battling against harsh working conditions, discrimination, and substandard wages. They always have played a substantial (and largely unrecorded) role in the organizing of labor in the Southwest, which accompanied the emergence of large cattle companies, commercial farm operations (agribusiness), and development of the railroad and mining industries.

One of the first labor unions in the Southwest, The Caballeros de Labor, patterned after the Knights of Labor, was organized in the 1880s by Mexican-Americans. The Caballeros de Labor made ownership of land a more important issue than wages and hours. ". . . It concentrated its efforts in fighting Anglo land-grabbing schemes, however, with only moderate success. Since its objectives were largely political rather than those of a regular trade union, it had little influence among the masses of Mexican-American workers."[3]

In 1910, a Los Angeles street-railway workers strike began when Mexican-American workers walked off the job and demanded more pay. That strike quickly spread to the brewing industry, leather workers, and metal trades. These strikes were crippled and then broken after the bombing of the building of the strongly antiunion Los Angeles *Times*—a senseless act of violence with which Mexican-American workers had no connection.

In 1927, Mexican-American workers in Los Angeles took the significant step of forming a union of their own. A committee representing the Federation of Mexican Societies in Los Angeles met in November of that year and passed a resolution calling on its affiliates to lend financial and moral support in a drive to organize Mexican-American workers of that area. As a result, several local unions were organized and they formed the Confederación de Uniones de Obreros Mejicanos (CUOM). This new, historically significant, Mexican-American labor organization drew up a constitution and adopted among its objectives the organization of all Mexican workers in the United States. Also included in their objectives were achievement of wage parity with Anglo workers, the ending of discrimination against Mexican-American workers, and the persuading of the Mexican government to restrict the flow of immigrant labor to the United States. They also called upon the government of Mexico to assume a more positive role in meeting the economic needs of repatriated Mexican workers by establishing agricultural colonies in Mexico.

In April of 1928, CUOM held a general convention in Los Angeles attended by representatives of twenty-two unions. The Mexican labor union, the Confederación Regional Obrera Mejicana (CROM) after which CUOM had been modeled, sent a representative to this convention who served as an advisor and remained a month longer to help unionize Mexican-American and Mexican workers in the southern California area.

Unfortunately, CUOM fell victim to the Depression and went out of existence. However, it was very important in the history of Mexican-American activity in organizing labor unions. Mexican-American views and objectives were clearly expressed in its constitution and on issues of importance to La Raza. CUOM also provided leadership training for Mexican-American workers who later helped to establish more successful and enduring labor organizations.

The aggressive attempts by Mexican-American workers to organize unions in two of the Southwest's major industries in which they were —and still are—a major segment of the work force, exemplify their intense and persistent struggles to win economic justice. These industries are agribusiness and mining, both of which employ large numbers of Mexican-American workers and are of central importance to the economy of the entire Southwest.

Mexican-American agricultural workers began to form unions or take some kind of collective action almost from the moment they began to move into the fields in substantial numbers. Soon after the turn of the century in 1903, Mexican-American sugar beet workers near Ventura, California, along with Japanese workers, walked out. After a two-month strike, they won the right to negotiate directly with the grower, rather than with a labor contractor.

In the summer of 1913, Mexican-American workers were involved in a strike against the Durst Ranch near Wheatland, California. This strike was significant because it was at this time that organizers of the Industrial Workers of the World (the "Wobblies"), took a direct part in attempting to organize agricultural workers. A riot was touched off in this strike by a deputy sheriff who was said to have fired a warning shot into the air. At least four workers were left dead in that riot and the National Guard was called in. One hundred migrant workers were arrested and the strike was broken. However, the widespread publicity precipitated by this strike led to one of the first reactions of the California government and a state Commission on Immigration and Housing was formed to investigate. The report of this commission raised awareness of the plight of migratory workers and its recommendations led to some state regulation of the farm labor camps. There were only minimum improvements in working and housing conditions for the Mexican-American farm workers, but for the first time, a governmental body had taken some notice.

In 1928, Mexican-American field workers took another significant step toward collective bargaining. In April of that year melon pickers established the Mexican Mutual Aid Society of Imperial Valley (MMAS) with the assistance of the Mexican Consul in Calexico. The MMAS then served an ultimatum on the growers, including demands for acceptance of their organization as spokesman for the workers and the elimination of the *contratista* or the labor broker. They also demanded pay increases. The melon workers, unwilling to accept compromises offered by the growers, refused to harvest the crop. This was followed by the usual threats and coercions against the workers who were eventually forced to accept the growers' terms. But the action of the MMAS helped to increase the unionization efforts of Mexican-American workers in that area.

Between the Depression years of 1930 and 1935, there were a large number of strikes, especially because wages were falling to all-time lows, below the already near-starvation levels of the 1920s. Mexican-Americans were active in organizing labor and in leading strikes throughout this time. In California, they had effectively organized some forty agricultural unions by mid-1934, but most of these were short-lived. One of the most successful was the Confederación de Uniones de Campesinos y Obreros Mejicanos (CUCOM).

Dissatisfied with wages that had dropped to as little as nine cents an hour, several thousand Mexican-American pickers walked out of the strawberry fields at El Monte, California, in May 1933.

> The strike was characterized by a power struggle for control of the workers between local Mexican American leaders and outside representatives of the radical Cannery and Agricultural Workers Industrial Union (CAWIU), who attempted to dominate the movement.[4]

It was this strike that led to the organization of the CUCOM which rapidly became the most active agricultural union in California. It had some fifty locals and more than five thousand members by the end of 1933.

Throughout the embattled thirties, Mexican-American unions

struggling for survival against intense and often violent opposition were constantly attempting to strengthen and unite their forces. In January 1936, CUCOM led in bringing together several independent Spanish-speaking unions in Los Angeles county. They formed the Federation of Agricultural Worker Unions of America. By April this new federation had called a strike in the Los Angeles celery fields in which some twenty-six hundred workers walked out. Growers, as usual, resorted to strikebreaking techniques but the workers achieved a number of gains, including an improved wage scale.

Mexican-American farmworkers continually pressed their attempts to form larger and more effective organizations. In 1935 and 1936 the CUCOM and other California labor groups held several conferences to form a statewide organization, but they had only small success. In 1937, what is believed to be the first national convention of agricultural workers was held in Denver, Colorado. It attracted many delegates from a large number of the California Spanish-speaking unions.

In January 1941, the last important pre-war farmworkers' strike in California took place in Ventura County where fifteen hundred lemon pickers, mostly Mexican-Americans, organized the Agricultural and Citrus Workers Union, which became affiliated with the American Federation of Labor (AFL). The strike collapsed four months later when the growers brought in strikebreakers. The strikers not only lost the strike, but also their jobs, which in this case were taken mostly by Anglo refugees from the dust bowl of the nation.

In 1946, AFL granted a charter to the National Farm Labor Union (NFLU) which was successor to the Southern Tenants Farmers Union, thus involving the AFL for the first time with farm labor union developments on a nationwide basis. The NFLU involved Mexican-Americans in its membership and leadership. Dr. Ernesto Galarza served as its director of research and education, and he has since become one of the nation's foremost authorities on migrant workers. The NFLU scored some significant success in organizing migrant workers and in 1947 called a strike against the giant DiGiorgio Food Corporation in Kern County, California. The issue was recognition of the union.

The strike was opposed bitterly and violently by the DiGiorgio Corporation, and it was eventually broken, principally by the use of imported farmworkers—braceros—as strikebreakers. Within a few weeks after the strike began, thousands of strikebreakers were imported into the fields. Government officials openly escorted braceros through the union's picket lines.

> On the first day of the strike, the braceros stopped work. This show of solidarity with the domestic farm hands, was as unexpected as it was embarrassing. The sheriff . . . and a representative of the U.S. Department of Agriculture, were called in. What precisely they told the Mexicans is not known. The braceros went back to work.[15]

The loss of the strike brought to an end the NFLU's major effort to organize two hundred thousand California farmworkers.

Until the mid-1960s, the continuous attempts to organize and the countless strikes by Mexican-American farmworkers, particularly in California, were placed in a virtual "can't win" context by the bottomless cheap labor pool made available to the growers by the Bracero Program, an agreement between the United States and Mexican governments to furnish Mexican nationals as field workers to the growers. No enduring successful organizing program could be achieved so long as Mexican braceros were plentifully available to undercut union demands. After long struggles against it by labor organizations, churches, and many civic groups, the Bracero Program was ended by Congress as of December 31, 1964.

Less than nine months later on September 8, 1965, Filipino farmworkers who were members of the Agricultural Workers Organizing Committee, AFL-CIO, walked out of the vineyards in Delano, California, to be followed eight days later—September 16, Mexican Independence Day—by the members of the National Farm Workers' Association, an independent organization composed predominantly of Mexican-American farmworkers and led by César Chávez.

Huelga! (Strike!)

Viva la Causa! (Long Live the Cause!)

The "Grito" of the farmworkers rose from the vineyards of Delano to be heard across the nation. The still unfolding story of the Huelga has become one of the most widely known, dramatic, and dynamic in modern labor history. The United Farmworkers of America, AFL-CIO, formed by the merger of the AWOC and the NFWA, is the first union composed principally of Mexican-American workers to smash through the barriers of isolation and gain the concerned attention of the nation.

In the mining industry, the long and tenacious struggle of embattled Mexican-American miners was waged in the lonely isolation of scattered mining towns, far from the attention of any media and the concern, or conscience, of the nation. The miners and their families in the widely separated company towns were extremely vulnerable to the repressive, and often violent, opposition of the copper corporations.

After decades of intense determination and heroic sacrifice, the copper miners won their fight to organize and bargain collectively. They won far more than the right to organize their unions; they won freedom from oppressive economic discrimination and social injustice. The copper miners were the first large group of substantially concentrated Mexican-American workers to build an enduring organization with effective power to significantly influence and permanently improve their socioeconomic environments.

The mines could not have been organized without the leadership, commitment, and determination of Mexican-American mineworkers. Yet, the story of their struggle and that of their families is virtually undocumented and untold, even in the annals of organized labor. It is the story of an almost continual struggle carried on in the mining towns for more than half a century. A decade before the end of the nineteenth century, the Western Federation of Miners started organizing copper miners. Mexican-Americans quickly emerged to take leadership positions in that struggle.

Mexican-American miners initiated a strike in 1903 to protest a pay reduction in the Arizona copper mining region of Morenci and Clifton. The arrest, trial, and conviction of the strike leaders broke the walkout in 1904. Mineworkers in the same area again went on strike in 1915 in protest over "traditional" pay differentials between Mexican-American and Anglo workers. After five months, a guarantee of equal pay rates was won—and the miners threw out the Western Federation of Miners for supporting the differential and set up their own committees and grievance procedures.

In 1917 and 1918, strikes again broke out among the copper miners in Arizona supported by both Mexican-American and Anglo workers. Vigilante action accompanied by violence against the miners broke these strikes and hundreds of Mexican miners were forcibly deported. Large numbers of Mexican-Americans, including entire families of men, women, and children, were taken out into the deadly deserts by vigilantes and left there without food or water.

The Mine, Mill, and Smelter Workers (MMSW) became a major union of copper miners in the Southwest and Mountain states during the 1930s and 1940s as the result of organizing efforts in which Mexican-Americans played a decisive role.

"If it had not been for the Chicano copper miners, Mine, Mill would not have been organized in Arizona, Texas and New Mexico," said Maclovio Barraza, former MMSW leader who is now an international representative of the United Steelworkers of America, AFL-CIO.

The MMSW merged with the Steelworkers Union in 1957 and Mexican-American copper miners, smelter workers, and steelworkers have become an influential segment in the nationally important Steelworkers Union.

Mexican-American workers made significant contributions to the organization of many substantial unions of today, such as the United Auto Workers, United Rubber Workers, Teamsters, Carpenters, Laborers, Furniture Workers, Electrical Workers, Clothing Workers, and many others.

By far the largest group of organized Chicanos today are in the labor movement. They form a substantial part of the membership of many unions and hold many important, policy-level leadership positions. They are an emerging and growing influence in organized labor. And Mexican-Americans with union experience are active throughout the Chicano movement.

There is a definite and significant historical relationship in the development of both the labor and Chicano movements—each is a continuation of the Mexican-Americans' unceasing search for effective ways to achieve enduring social and economic justice.

The Chicano Movement: The Second Century Begins

The Chicano movement which erupted in the mid-1960s was a breakthrough of forces that had been building for more than a century. It opened the second century of the Mexican-Americans' persistent, active search for equality and social justice as a major segment of the population of the United States.

It was as if the steady flowing of many streams over long years created a churning river that broke out and over old banks into new open areas.

The pilgrimage of the farmworkers from Delano to Sacramento in the spring of 1966, which began as a small stream and flowed as a growing river of human concern into the nation's awareness, serves well as the symbol of the beginning of the Chicano movement. The pilgrimage became symbolic of the long and tortured struggle La Raza has had to wage with all its tribulations, tragedies, successes, and failures. The principal participants were Chicano farmworkers. Their bitter struggle to organize and their Huelga became unifying forces for Chicanos from all economic and social levels.

But, the farmworkers' pilgrimage to Delano was not the only "beginning" of the Chicano movement.

> The exact beginnings of the movement are obscure. There is some evidence that the Chicano movement grew out of a group of conferences held at Loyola University in Los Angeles in the summer of 1966. . . . The Chicano movement is extremely heterogeneous. Its elements have different aims and purposes. . . . The movement cuts across social class, regional and generational lines. Its aims range from traditional forms of social protest to increasingly more radical goals that appear as a sign of an emerging nationalism. . . . The dynamic force of the movement is its ideology—Chicanismo—ideology is advanced as a challenge to the dominant Anglo beliefs concerning Mexicans as well as to the beliefs of Mexican Americans themselves.[16]

Among young adults, the Chicano movement principally has taken the form of new student organizations. Among these groups, which began to appear in 1966 and 1967, are the Mexican American Student Confederation (MASC), the Mexican American Student Association (MASA), and the United Mexican American Students (UMAS). Other student groups are the Movimiento Estudiantil Chicano de Aztlán (MECHA) and the Mexican American Youth Organization (MAYO), which includes young adults at both the college and high school level and from the communities.

A new sense of the dignity and worth of La Raza inspired by the Chicano movement gave impetus to Chicano youth to demand recognition from educational systems. Some of the young leadership turned to direct action and militant confrontation to achieve their goals. Chicano students staged walkouts in the later 1960s in Texas, Colorado, New Mexico, California, and Arizona. Such student walkouts often became the focal point around which La Raza communities rallied forces and extended their activities. In several areas the student walkouts precipitated reaction from the police. Many student leaders were sent to prison, fined, or placed on probation with the result that some of the student organizations were left without effective leadership and with a demoralized membership. But the student groups reevaluated their structures, planned new tactics and strategies, and continued their attempts to get adequate responses from the educational institutions and to improve their communities' quality of life. Their protests and walkouts undoubtedly had a measure of success in changing educational environments. Today some student groups and young adult leaders have become dynamic and effective forces, not only in the area of education, but also in political activity. Some young adults who were former leaders of student walkouts have moved on to become elected to political office on city councils, boards of supervisors, and boards of education. The leadership of MAYO went directly into political action and organized La Raza Unida as a political party.

Young Chicanos have also been active in developing organizations in addition to campus groups and with other objectives in addition to education. One of these is the Brown Berets, organized in Los Angeles, now active in California and Texas. The Brown Berets believe that by giving the example of a disciplined and committed life based on principles of "carnalismo"—brotherhood —they can unite the community. A similar organization is the Black Berets founded in Mountain View, California, in the latter 1960s. Both the Black and Brown Berets in recent years have been involved in action-oriented activities in barrio communities throughout the Southwest.

One of the most active organizations to work with Chicano youth has been the Crusade for Justice, founded in Denver in 1965 by Rudolfo "Corky" González. The Crusade for Justice has had considerable influence on Chicano young people through its annual Chicano Youth Liberation Conference, the first of which was held in March 1969 in Denver.

At the first meeting of the Chicano Youth Liberation Conference, the delegates voted to adopt "El Plan Espiritual de Aztlán," which called for Chicanos to work together to achieve common goals through a revival of the legendary Aztec homeland. Aztlán has become one of the most imaginative and evocative symbols of the Chicano movement. It appeals strongly to Chicanos everywhere and undoubtedly is an expression of the deep psychological need of an alienated and isolated people for a national identity of their own. Mexican-Americans were separated by conquest from one nation, Mexico, and forcibly alienated for more than a century from equal participation and acceptance in another nation, the United States. The Chicanos of today understandably have turned to an image of a "nation" of their own, interpreted through a renaissance of their own historical and cultural heritage.

Thus, the symbol of Aztlán has become the "centerpiece" of Chicano nationalism. Symbols of nationalism of various strengths and types permeate the Chicano movement. The Crusade for Justice and other Chicano organizations make positive use of nationalism to build Chicano identity and pride, and provide an underlying unifying force to organize a wide variety of programs and social services with Chicano perspectives. Among their demands are better housing, relevant education for Chicanos, reformation of the police and courts, greater and more diverse employment and economic opportunities, and land reform.

The issue of land reform thrusts deeply into the history of the Mexican-American. It has been particularly explosive in New Mexico.

In 1963, Reies López Tijerina organized the Alianza Federal de Mercedes (Federal Alliance of Land Grants) in northern New Mexico. By 1964 the Alliance was claiming some six thousand land grant heirs in New Mexico, Colorado, Texas, California, and even Utah, as members. It was expounding a program which emphasized litigation and government action to win the return of land which the Alianza claimed belonged, under old Spanish land grants, to its members or to villages as common land. Most of the problems of Chicanos are derived from the loss of their land to Anglo intruders, the Alianza believes.

By 1966 the Alianza, claiming some twenty thousand members, was laying claim to millions of acres originally owned by Mexican-American village communities. The Alianza proposed to make this land the basis of a secessionist movement through the creation of a Confederation of Free City States. Some of the Alianza members began posting "no trespassing" signs on former village land grants. In October of 1966, members of the Alianza attempted to take over part of the Kit Carson National Forest which they claimed as their own. They proclaimed the Republic of San Joaquín del Río de Chama. Forest Service rangers ignored their claim for sovereignty, however, and several Alianza members were arrested, including Tijerina. Later, Alianza members raided a courthouse in the small northwestern New Mexican town of Tierra Amarilla. The incident brought the Alianza movement national publicity.

Eventually, however, Tijerina was sent to prison and he lost an appeal to the U.S. Supreme Court. He was released from prison in July 1971 after serving two years, and parole was granted on the condition that he no longer hold any official position in the Alianza. When his parole was up in 1974, Tijerina had to return to prison, but he received a full pardon in December 1974. The Alianza continues to press the land issue, demanding that millions of acres claimed as grant land be returned by the federal government. Its activities today are oriented toward filing law suits and publishing educational material on the land issue.

During this period of Chicano activism, a group of youthful leaders in Texas who had founded the Mexican American Youth Organization (MAYO) were trying a form of political action that was unique to Mexican-Americans—forming their own political party. Led by José Angel Gutiérrez—youthful, politically astute founder and former state chairman of MAYO—they established La Raza Unida as a distinct and new political party. La Raza Unida maintains that Chicanos must have their own separate political party in order to achieve self-determination.

> The preamble to La Raza Unida program states the decision of "the people of la raza . . . to reject the existing political party of our oppressor and take it upon ourselves to form La Raza Unida Party which will serve as a unifying force in our struggle for self determination."[17]

Gutiérrez and two other Chicanos ran as candidates of the La Raza Unida Party in the school board elections in Crystal City, Texas, in April 1970, and won easily. It was the first time the school board had had a Mexican-American majority in this community which was predominantly Mexican-American. Gutiérrez was elected president of the board which immediately established a bilingual education curriculum, started a federal free lunch program, and mandated that discrimination against or neglect of Mexican-American students would not be tolerated. The following spring, La Raza Unida ran two more candidates for the school board and again won, thereby guaranteeing its control of the board for several years to come. Crystal City is the same community where, several years before, concerted political action by Mexican-Americans had gained them control of the mayoralty and the city council, only to lose that control when they were unable to consolidate their political position. The significant victories of La Raza Unida in the board of education elections again made Crystal City a symbol to Chicanos of strength through unified political action.

La Raza Unida went on to win the city council and board of education elections in several other communities and has now established itself on the Texas ballot as a statewide political party. Following his school board victory in Crystal City, Gutiérrez said, "Aztlán has begun in the Southwestern part of Texas." His words underscored the dynamic force of the Chicano nationalism that runs throughout the Chicano movement.

The dynamism of the Chicano movement is also affecting the Mexican-American female—the Chicana.

Chicanas are making increasingly effective efforts to organize and assert their own identity and dignity. Among the many active Chicana organizations are the Comisión Femenil Mexicana of Los Angeles; the National Chicana Institute of Tempe, Arizona; the National Chicana Welfare Rights of Los Angeles; the National Institute for Chicana Women of San Antonio, Texas; the National Chicana Businesswomen's Association of Albuquerque, New Mexico; and Barrio Pride, an organization of Chicanas in Phoenix, Arizona, working with subteen and teenage Chicanas.

Emergence of the Chicana as a strong motivating force within the Spanish Speaking community has been in conjunction with that of the Chicano. For this reason her struggle cannot be parallel with the Anglo woman's fight for rights against the Anglo male. Chicanas have fought side by side with their men in the struggle for equal opportunity in all areas of American life. . . . Women have stepped out of the background into the spotlight as spokesmen of various public meetings. School boards, commissions, city councils, to name a few, have felt the sting of the verbal slaps from irate Mexican American women. Chicanas have shown themselves to be alert, forceful and intelligent and they appear to be a major catalyst in the Chicano community. The aggression on the part of the Chicana toward the Anglo has not been condemned but encouraged by the Mexican American male.[18]

The activist Chicana comes well within the historical tradition of Mexican and Mexican-American women. Their traditional image as always docile and submissive does not coincide with historical accuracy. The Spanish conquistadores tell of meeting women *caciques*—chiefs—leading some of the Indian tribes. The story of "Adelita" as a militant revolutionary is one of the best known and most colorful of the Mexican Revolution. And Mexican-American women have always been formidable figures of strength, leadership, and durability in the long painful trek of their people toward full equality and justice in the United States. It is not surprising, therefore, to find Chicana women of today forming their own organizations, asserting their own independence and identity, and defining their own role in the Chicano movement.

The force of the Chicano movement has also surged through prison walls. Convicts and former convicts (known as "pintos" in barrio language) have formed their own organizations. Two such organizations are Empleo and Pintos, formed in California prisons, dedicated to the rehabilitation of prisoners and to prison reform. The appeal of ethnic pride and identity of Chicanismo has brought a new sense of dignity and worth, and with it new motivations to the unfortunate "pintos" among La Raza.

But nowhere is the Chicano movement penetrating more deeply, influencing organizations and their programs more positively, and bringing about more significant changes than in the barrios. A development of major significance in the Chicano movement is the emergence in the late 1960s and early 1970s of the barrio community organizations.

The barrio and colonia° organizations are committed to the improvement of their communities through planned programs in housing, economic development, health services, social services, youth programs, manpower training, and education. These organizations relate directly to problems of the barrios and colonias and involve the community in their organizations and programs. They seek to develop a spectrum of specific programs with identifiable and measurable objectives.

The barrio community organizations are organized as tax-exempt (501-c-3) corporations and seek the support of foundations, corporations, churches, federal government, and concerned individuals. They have learned to apply the professional skills and other disciplines necessary to the development of an effective, programmatic organization and at the same time remain relevant and responsive to the needs of the community and its people. They are autonomous organizations formed by and for the people of the community who determine their own agendas.

Notable examples of successful barrio community organizations are the Mexican American Unity Council (MAUC) in San Antonio; the Chicanos Por La Causa (CPLC) in Phoenix, Arizona; the Spanish Speaking Unity Council (SSUC) in Oakland, California; the Home Education Livelihood Program (HELP) which carries out programs in the rural areas of New Mexico; and The East Los Angeles Community Union (TELACU) and Euclid Foundation in East Los Angeles.

In their short time of existence, these program-oriented community organizations already have scored notable results. Here, briefly, are some of them:

In San Antonio, MAUC, directed by Juan Patlan, recorded a first for local community organizations when it opened a nationally franchised food service drive-in. It has also packaged various other business enterprises, constructed a low-cost housing project, and run a mental health program which achieves unique success in reaching barrio residents.

°A "barrio" is a community, usually in an urban area, which is composed predominantly of Spanish-speaking residents. The term "colonia" is applied to a similar community, usually in a rural area. Because of the poverty and deprivation to which Mexican-Americans have been subjected, barrios and colonias suffer from problems similar to the ghettos, and the terms have tended to become synonymous.

The SSUC, directed by Arabella Martínez, developed a sixty-one-unit low and moderate income townhouse project in Hayward, California, believed to be the first of its type and made possible by a community-based, Chicano group in northern California. SSUC also operates successful and efficiently run youth programs, packages business enterprises, and plays an influential role in the general activities of the community.

The CPLC in Phoenix, Arizona, directed by Ronnie López, is an active barrio development organization that has successfully packaged loans for a Mexican-American bakery, developed a restaurant, has completed several homes in its housing program, and is involved in many other projects. CPLC also works closely with the Barrio Youth Project, directed by Sam Ramírez, which conducts a spectrum of training and other programs for young adults, including a printers' training course in their own print shop.

HELP in New Mexico is oriented to rural development, including such projects as self-help housing, a community-based weaving factory which produces colorful ponchos, wall-hangings, and rugs. It is also involved in farmers' cooperative associations, a manufacturing company which produces camper shells for pick-up trucks, and many other business enterprises. The Executive Director of HELP is Ray López.

In Los Angeles, TELACU and the Euclid Foundation are pursuing similar barrio development programs and have scored notable achievements in housing, packaging of business enterprises, programs for the elderly, and similar activities. Executive Directors of TELACU and the Euclid Foundation are Esteban Tórres and the Rev. Tony Hernández, respectively.

Colonias del Valle, directed by Alejandro Moreno, is developing a system to provide water to fifty-two families of a colonia near Donna in Hidalgo County, Texas. Presently, one-eighth of the county's 181,000 residents do not have access to piped water.

In Homestead, Florida, the Organized Migrants in Community Action (OMICA), directed by Rudolfo Juárez, are attempting to provide decent housing for migrant workers. Recently, OMICA's prompt and vigorous action resulted in bringing in medical and other aid for rural families hit by typhoid fever caused by polluted water in the area.

These barrio community organizations and others like them are concentrating on definable, positive programs to achieve concrete results for their communities. Their directors and leadership, as well as their staffs, are generally youthful, have developed excellent professional skills, and are vigorously committed to the permanent improvement of the quality of life in their communities.

Among other organizations are the Mexican American Education Council (MAEC) in Houston, Texas; the Trinity Chicano Coalition in El Paso, Texas; the Guadalupe Organization (GO) in Guadalupe, Arizona; the Corporación Organizada Para Acción Servidora (COPAS) in Santa Fe, New Mexico; OBECA/Arriba Juntos in San Francisco, California; the Barrio Development, Inc., in Uvalde, Texas; the Arriba Juntos in Corpus Christi, Texas; and the Chicano Federation of San Diego County, Inc., San Diego, California.

These barrio community organizations firmly maintain that they must develop a spectrum of programs so that they will eventually achieve self-sufficiency. They see themselves as developing or facilitating the development of economic bases broad and productive enough so that they eventually will have a major impact on the economy of their communities.

The barrio community organizations, despite the short time they have been in existence, already are having a discernible influence on the direction of an important segment of the Chicano movement. They are developing program-oriented, permanent institutions in the barrios, to serve the needs of the barrios. They are turning around older, outworn policies of accommodating Mexican-American organizations to the attitudes and institutions of the dominant society. They are, instead, developing policies and programs that bring American attitudes and institutions into support of their own agendas.

They are awakening a nation—slowly but steadily—to the creative strengths of a people breaking free from the barriers of prejudice, alienation, and repression forced upon them by a domineering, surrounding environment.

As the nation moves into the last quarter of the twentieth century, Mexican-Americans are moving into their second century as a major segment of its people. They have stepped boldly onto the national scene. They are demanding to be heard, and they are ready.

Mexican-American organizations are now emerging as national bodies, advocating the interests and expressing the concerns of Chicanos to the nation.

One of the first to appear, the National Council of La Raza (NCLR), was developed in close programmatic relationships with the emerging barrio community organizations. NCLR began in 1968 as the Southwest Council of La Raza, with headquarters in Phoenix, Arizona.

In its first four years of existence, the Southwest Council of La Raza moved to a position of national recognition as an effective, new Chicano organization. It assembled training, technical assistance, and funding support for autonomous barrio community organizations, and together with them fashioned a network to channel resources into the barrios.

The field experience of the Southwest Council of La Raza made it clear that Mexican-Americans and the problems they faced were to be found throughout the nation. The Southwest Council of La Raza found it imperative to expand its role to interpret and advocate Chicano interests nationally.

In December 1972, the Council reorganized as the National Council of La Raza and established its headquarters office in Washington, D.C., and its program operations office in Phoenix, Arizona. NCLR now operates as a national advocacy center for La Raza interests. Its headquarters carries out program liaison services with the federal agencies, provides information, data, and interpretive material on public policies and La Raza activities through *Agenda*, a monthly newsletter and quarterly magazine.

Its program operations in Phoenix include economic development and housing development components. In economic development, the Council has been the major force in the formation of La Raza Investment Corporation (LRIC), a minority enterprise small business investment corporation organized to leverage financial assistance for minority entrepreneurs. In housing, the Council has formed La Raza Housing Development Corporation (LRHDC) which is involved in housing projects and in the training of housing management specialists.

The Council is also preparing to implement a La Raza Educational Development Center (LREDC) to conduct research, develop materials, and provide well-informed advocacy for Chicano educational interests.

The unique combination of a national council working with a network of autonomous, decentralized barrio organizations provides for flexible programmatic approaches on local levels and strong, responsible advocacy of La Raza interests on the national level.

The conditions of alienation and social neglect suffered by the Mexican-American minority in the United States are no longer confined to the border states. They now involve Chicano communities as distant from the United States—Mexico border as Seattle, Chicago, and Detroit.

Over the past fifty years, Mexican-Americans have moved into practically every state of the Union and have formed sizable communities in many of them, particularly in the Midwest. Today, while the bulk of this minority—the nation's second largest—is still anchored in the Southwest, millions of Americans of Mexican descent have spread through the Northwest, Midwest, Northeast, and the South.

Mexican-Americans are now an inextricable part of the total national scene and their organizations are breaking out of traditionally isolated environments to interact with the total national environment.

The Chicano movement's break-out may prove to be its most enduring contribution. National agendas require national organizations. Mexican-American national organizations already are responding.

Mexican-Americans already are opening the next era of their historic struggle for social justice and full equality—the development of national organizations.

NOTES

1. J. Patrick McHenry, *A Short History of Mexico* (Garden City, N.Y.: Doubleday & Co., 1962), p. 77.

2. Joan W. Moore with Alfredo Cuéllar, *Mexican Americans—Ethnic Groups in American Life Series* (Englewood Cliffs, N.J.: Prentice-Hall, Inc., 1970), p. 11.

3. Paul S. Taylor, *An American-Mexican Frontier* (Chapel Hill: University of North Carolina Press, 1934), p. 294.

4. Moore and Cuéllar, *Mexican-Americans*, p. 14.

5. Ibid., p. 18.

6. Ibid., p. 16.

7. Nancie L. González, *The Spanish Americans of New Mexico: A Distinctive Heritage,*

Advance Report #9, Mexican American Study Project (Los Angeles: University of California Press, 1967), p. 57.

8. Moore and Cuéllar, *Mexican Americans*, p. 142.

9. Matt S. Meier and Feliciano Rivera, *The Chicanos: A History of Mexican Americans*, p. 143.

10. Ibid., p. 241.

11. Moore and Cuéllar, *Mexican Americans*, p. 143.

12. Ibid., p. 144. The letter appeared on March 8, 1929, in the *Hidalgo County Independent*, Edinburgh, Texas.

13. Meier and Rivera, *The Chicanos*, pp. 169–70.

14. Ibid., p. 177.

15. Ernesto Galarza, *Merchants of Labor: The Mexican Bracero Story* (Charlotte/Santa Barbara, Calif.: McNally & Loftin, 1964), p. 216.

16. Moore and Cuéllar, *Mexican Americans*, p. 149.

17. Meier and Rivera, *The Chicanos*, p. 277.

18. Linda Aquilar, "Unequal Opportunity and the Chicana," *Civil Rights Digest* (Spring 1973):31.

Index